Y0-CBF-279

SIMPLE, LOWFAT & VEGETARIAN

Unbelievably Easy Ways to Reduce the Fat in Your Meals!

BY SUZANNE HAVALA, M.S., R.D.

RECIPES BY MARY CLIFFORD, R.D.

JANUARY 1994

LAYOUT & DESIGN BY VONNIE CRIST

FOREWORD BY DEAN ORNISH, M.D.

FAT TAX BY JEROME I. MARCUS, M.D.

THE VEGETARIAN RESOURCE GROUP
BALTIMORE, MARYLAND

Suzanne Havala is a nutrition consultant and advisor to The Vegetarian Resource Group. She is primary author of The American Dietetic Association position paper on vegetarian diets and past president of Vegetarian Nutrition, a dietetic practice group of The American Dietetic Association.

Mary Clifford is a freelance writer and clinical dietitian in Roanoke, Virginia. She was associate food editor at *Country Living Magazine* and is a nutrition advisor to The Vegetarian Resource Group.

ACKNOWLEDGMENTS

The Vegetarian Resource Group is comprised of a network of members and supporters, many of whom contributed in significant ways to the development of this book. This project was the vision of a team of creative, committed people who all lent their expertise, whether in conceiving the format of the book, brainstorming ideas to present, contributing personal stories, reviewing, editing, or shaping the book in a host of ways.

Many thanks to the following people: Katherine Alaimo, Vonnie Crist, Melissa Faust, Gwinn Firing, R.D., Amy Greenebaum, Carole Hamlin, Mary Jamieson, Elizabeth Kaufmann, Reed Mangels, Ph.D., R.D., Jerome I. Marcus, M.D., Israel Mossman, Debra Nagy, Smita Parekh, M.S., R.D., Rex Roe, Brad Scott, Angu Singh, M.S., R.D., Charles Stahler, Janice Stixrud, R.D., Ziona Swigart, Carol and John Tracy, Ann Truelove, and Debra Wasserman. Special thanks to Dean Ornish, M.D. for so generously giving of his time and talent to write the foreword.

Thank you to *Country Living* magazine for their kind permission to alter and/or reproduce recipes Mary originally wrote for their vegetarian cooking column, "The Veggie Table." Thanks also to Community Hospital of Roanoke Valley.

Vonnie Crist's dedication and patience with all our changes and improvements is greatly appreciated.

Project Supervisor: Charles Stahler
Scientific Review: Reed Mangels, Ph.D., R.D.   Cover Design: Vonnie Crist

© Copyright 1994 The Vegetarian Resource Group, Baltimore, Maryland.

Library of Congress Cataloging-in-Publication Data
Simple, Lowfat & Vegetarian: Unbelievably Easy Ways to Reduce the Fat in Your Meals!/Suzanne Havala & Mary Clifford; Foreword by Dean Ornish.
Library of Congress Catalog Card Number: 93-60271

ISBN 0-931411-09-2 (Soft-Cover)

Printed in the United States of America
10 9 8 7 6 5 4 3 2 1

All rights reserved. No portion of this book may be reproduced by any means whatsoever except for brief quotations in reviews, without written permission from The Vegetarian Resource Group.

CONTENTS

Foreword

By Dean Ornish, M.D.

It is becoming clear that our lifestyle choices can have a profound effect not only on how *long* we live but also on how *well* we live. For many people, lifestyle changes - eating a lowfat, vegetarian diet, managing emotional stress effectively, and enjoying moderate exercise - can result in better health and a greater capacity to enjoy life.

You may be considering making some of these changes yourself, including choosing to eat a vegetarian diet. Even if you are already a vegetarian, you may want to reduce your fat intake. If so, then *Simple, Lowfat, and Vegetarian* can help you begin.

In some ways, we are rediscovering what we have known for ages. Research has shown for many years, for instance, that vegetarian lifestyles reduce our risk for chronic, degenerative diseases. But we tend to think of medical breakthroughs as being things like new surgical techniques or new drugs. In medicine, we have gotten to the point where it sounds *radical* to ask people to eat a healthful diet, to walk, to manage stress better, or to stop smoking. It is considered medically conservative to recommend procedures such as bypass surgery and to prescribe powerful cholesterol-lowering drugs. It may be hard to believe at first that simple, ancient, inexpensive approaches to lifestyle - like eating a vegetarian diet - can be so effective. But I am becoming convinced that they are.

Cardiovascular research that I have directed over the past 17 years is yielding scientific evidence demonstrating that lifestyle changes, including a lowfat, vegetarian diet, often can begin to reverse heart disease without the use of drugs or surgery - and the only side effects are desirable ones. The incidence of heart attacks has been declining over the past decade in the U.S., but more men and women still die from heart and blood vessel diseases each year than from all other causes of death combined, including cancer, AIDS, other infectious diseases, accidents, and homicides. Knowing what we do now, heart disease may be preventable, and even *reversible*, for the majority of people who are willing to make fundamental lifestyle changes.

If enough people put this knowledge into practice, there could be a tremendous impact on health care costs. Our current health care system is really a disease care system. If it could be shown that for every dollar spent on lifestyle changes, four or five dollars could be saved in health care costs, then we may be on our way to finding viable solutions to the health care crisis. In addition to having less heart disease, a large body of research also shows that vegetarian lifestyles are associated with lower rates of obesity, high blood pressure, stroke, osteoporosis, diabetes, gallstones, and cancers of the breast, colon, and prostate. What our health care system can provide may be less important and less effective in determining our health than the lifestyle choices we make as individuals on a daily basis.

But there is another benefit to these lifestyle changes besides better health and lower health care costs - one that is just as important. A lowfat, vegetarian diet may help you to feel more energetic, think more clearly, and improve your physical performance - to get more enjoyment out of life. I made the switch to a vegetarian diet in my second year of college and have been eating this way ever since. Eating a lowfat, vegetarian diet will probably help me live longer, but that is not my primary motivation for maintaining this lifestyle. What motivates me most is that I *feel* so much better. There is no reason to give up something I enjoy unless I get back something that is even better. I still like the taste of meat, but I like the way I feel when I *don't* eat it even better.

People sometimes tell me, "I know what changes I need to make in the way I eat, but it's so hard to begin. What can I do?" Our lifestyle choices, such as diet, are the product of years of habit. And all changes involve some stress at first. The status quo is familiar and comfortable, even when it is killing us. In *Simple, Lowfat, and Vegetarian*, Suzanne Havala will show you how to make the transition to a lowfat diet easier. Fat does taste good, and our high fat foods are very familiar to us. But as you decrease the amount of fat in your diet, your palate will begin to readjust. Eventually, you will find that the new foods taste delicious, even though they are low in fat. The foods that used to taste good to you may seem too oily or rich. The transition period may pose some challenges for you, but I think you will find it is worth the effort. You can have lots of fun, too, experimenting with the recipes that are included in this book.

Lowfat, vegetarian food is not a diet of deprivation, but it does require you to make choices. This way of eating may be entirely different for those raised on lots of red meat and rich desserts, or even for vegetarians who are in the habit of eating lots of cheese, other high fat dairy foods, and eggs. But you have a spectrum of choices - it's not all or nothing. The more you change, the better you'll feel.

How low in fat should your diet be? Research suggests that a vegetarian diet with not more than ten percent of its calories from fat can begin to reverse heart disease. Other people may find they see benefits from a diet that allows a little more fat - fifteen percent of calories. The typical American gets more than forty percent of calories from fat. Even so, groups such as the American Heart Association and the National Cholesterol Education Program are still recommending less stringent goals -so-called "moderate" changes in diet - out of the belief that if they told Americans to make more significant changes, that they would not be willing to do so. But research is showing that this may not be true, and that more people may be willing to change their lifestyles than many doctors and other health professionals may believe.

"Moderate" changes in diet, as most Americans define the term, may not result in significant health benefits for most people. But even small changes can be a good first step. Some people feel most comfortable making these changes gradually. *Simple, Lowfat, and Vegetarian* can help you make these changes at a rate that is comfortable for you.

On the other hand, some people find it easier to make big changes than small, gradual ones. This may not seem to make sense at first. But if you make a moderate change in your diet, you have the inconvenience of being on a diet as well as a sense of deprivation from not being able to eat the old, familiar foods - and you may not feel that much better. By making bigger, comprehensive changes, you'll feel better faster, which can motivate you to stick with the changes.

Everybody has a right to accurate, scientific information that they can use to make informed, intelligent decisions about how they will live their lives. Whether or not you wish to change your lifestyle, and to what degree, is up to you. But if your choice is to adopt a lowfat, vegetarian diet, then *Simple, Lowfat, and Vegetarian* can help you with practical advice to make the transition to this new lifestyle easier and more enjoyable.

Dean Ornish, M.D.
President & Director
Preventive Medicine Research Institute
Sausalito, California
Author, *Dr. Dean Ornish's Program for Reversing Heart Disease* and *Eat More, Weigh Less*

Preface

The nutrition education efforts of The Vegetarian Resource Group are consistently unique, because they target the most practical issues that face consumers today as they work to improve their health and the health of the planet through smart dietary choices. This book addresses a major issue for Americans - how to actually put current dietary recommendations into practice.

What was needed was a guide to the most practical concerns of diet-conscious consumers and tools for carrying out the task. What simple choices can I make when I eat out to cut back on my fat intake? What can I make for supper tonight? What can I pack in a bag lunch? What are some ideas for quick meals? How can I help myself stay on track? This book answers these questions and more in a simple, straightforward way.

Like most things in life, nutrition advice is not black or white - there is a lot of gray area. One of the goals of this book is to show people how simple changes in their food choices can make a sizable impact on their fat intake. Some people may feel that the decreases in fat content in the menu conversions are not big enough ... that even greater reductions in fat intake are necessary to produce significant health benefits. This may be true. However, the position taken in writing this book is that there are always benefits to be had, even in small changes.

Bigger changes will yield bigger results. The small changes may represent a first step for many people. Some people are more comfortable making gradual changes in their eating habits, allowing their diet to slowly evolve as they learn and gain confidence. Others are comfortable with more drastic changes - even an overnight switch. The advice in this book can be used, then, to make even bigger reductions in fat intake if you choose to do so.

Eating a lowfat, vegetarian diet doesn't mean eating no fat, and it doesn't have to mean never eating a high fat food. It *can* mean avoiding high fat foods and not adding fat to foods. But fat cannot be totally avoided; there is some fat naturally present in grains and vegetables. We need a certain amount of fat to survive. On the other hand, some people can probably tolerate more fat in their diet than others. They may opt to eat a high fat food now and then and balance it with lower fat choices the rest of the day.

So, the suggestions in this book can be adapted by individuals to suit their particular needs. This is true for anyone who prefers to follow a vegan or strictly vegetarian diet, too. Vegans eat no meat, fish, poultry, eggs, and dairy products. Many also avoid the use of other animal products such as leather and wool. There is a section of the book that addresses questions that vegans and strict vegetarians may have.

Whatever reasons a person may have for adopting a lowfat or vegetarian diet, there is surely a need for accurate, reliable information to help in making the transition to this new lifestyle. Even those who already follow a vegetarian diet may need help in taking the next step in improving their diet by reducing their fat intake.

Lifestyle changes can be tough to make. But the switch to a lowfat, vegetarian diet can also be surprisingly pleasant as you discover new foods, develop new skills, confidence, and a sense of accomplishment, and as you open yourself up to new experiences along the way. The variety in food is in the plant world. Fruits, vegetables, and grains come in an almost infinite range of colors, textures, and flavors. Vegetarian meals can be beautiful and creative. Before long, you'll find that old habits will be forgotten and that new traditions will have taken their place. My hope is that the guidance this book provides will help to make this whole process simple and enjoyable.

Suzanne Havala, M.S., R.D.
Charlotte, North Carolina

Please note that the information contained in this book is not intended to provide personal medical advice. Medical advice should be obtained from your physician or other qualified health professional.

Menu Magic

Menu Magic is a series of "meal makeovers" that demonstrate how easy it is to cut down on the fat in meals just by making a few, simple changes. A typical high fat meal is transformed into a lower fat meal. A look at the nutritional breakdowns given below each "Before" and "After" menu shows how even small changes can add up to substantial fat savings. In addition, lists of "Good Choices" and foods to "Limit" as well as the "Fat Content of Selected Items" follow many of the meal makeovers. They will help you become more aware of where the fat hides in many foods. Also, there are "Helpful Hints" to assist you in putting your new knowledge into practice.

One thing to note: The purpose of Menu Magic makeovers is to show how easily improvements can be made in any meal, even in seemingly impossible circumstances. The menus that result are always lower in fat than the original, although in most cases they could be even lower if more changes were made. The point is that these changes are a start - a first step in the right direction. Some people prefer to make dramatic, overnight changes in their diets. But for others, the most comfortable approach is more gradual. Starting out with a few easy changes, you will learn as you go and gain confidence along the way so that you can master permanent lifestyle change.

An Explanation of the Charts in This Book:

♦ **Menu Magic:** Examples of easy changes to reduce fat in meals - **blue outline.**

♦ **Good Choices:** Which foods to choose and which to limit - **blue interior.**

♦ **Fat Content:** The fat content of selected items - **white interior.**

♦ **Helpful Hints:** Easy tips to lower fat - **gray interior.**

Abbreviations Used in this Book:

T = tablespoon/tablespoons

tsp./tsps. = teaspoon/teaspoons

oz. = ounce/ounces

lb./lbs. = pound/pounds

mg = milligram/milligrams

Kcal = Kilocalorie/Kilocalories: unit used to denote amount of energy a food provides. A Kilocalorie is also known as a Calorie.

Pro = Protein

Carb = Carbohydrate

 # Part I

Staying On Track Away From Home -

Mealtime On The Road

Eating out isn't just for special occasions anymore. Today, it's common for families to catch a quick meal away from home weekly and even daily. For school children and people who work outside the home, at least one meal each day is eaten out. Business travelers have a particularly difficult time finding healthy meal options, frequently finding themselves in unfamiliar territory and having to entertain or be entertained at many different restaurants.

It's certainly more difficult to stick to a lowfat diet away from home than in the controlled environment of your own kitchen. But with some forethought and planning, eating well while eating out can become much easier and more enjoyable.

While reading the tips that follow, keep a few other ideas in mind. If you have some control over the choice of a restaurant, choose one that will be likely to offer you at least a few good food options. Some types of restaurants are better bets than others. Ask to see the menu first, before being seated. If considering cafeteria fare or a buffet, survey the food line first to see if there will be enough choices before starting through with your tray or plate. If eating at a familiar place, think ahead about what you might order to avoid impulsive mistakes. A little planning up front can ensure that mealtime away from home will be a nutritional success.

Salad Bars

Menu Magic

Is your idea of a trip to the salad bar something like this?

1/2 cup iceberg lettuce
1 slice tomato
3 black olives
1/2 cup coleslaw
1/2 cup macaroni salad
2 tablespoons shredded cheese
1/4 cup ranch dressing
2 tablespoons croutons

If so, you've eaten 408 calories, 34 grams of fat, and very little fiber. **By increasing the plain vegetables and decreasing the salad dressing and mayonnaise-based salads**, the colorful alternate menu that follows saves you 13 grams of fat and 136 calories, without too drastically changing the original salad. Another trick is to take spinach or romaine lettuce if they are offered, instead of iceberg lettuce. Dark greens boost the vitamin and mineral content of the salad substantially.

(Note: the simple changes made to reduce fat are in bold.)

1/2 cup iceberg lettuce
1/2 cup spinach
4 slices *tomato*
3 black olives
1/4 cup *coleslaw*
1/4 cup *macaroni salad*
2 tablespoons shredded cheese
3 green pepper rings
2 tablespoons *ranch dressing*
2 tablespoons croutons

Here are some more examples of easy menu changes that will improve the nutritional profile of your salad bar meals:

#1 Before:		After:	
1 cup lettuce		*1 cup spinach*	
1/4 cup shredded carrots		1/4 cup shredded carrots	
1/4 cup chopped green peppers		1/4 cup chopped green peppers	
1/4 cup chopped tomatoes		1/4 cup chopped tomatoes	
1/4 cup sliced mushrooms		1/4 cup sliced mushrooms	
1/4 cup croutons		1/4 cup croutons	
4 T blue cheese dressing		*4 T salsa*	
Calories (Kcal):	374	Calories (Kcal):	90
Fat (grams):	32	Fat (grams):	2
Protein (grams):	6	Protein (grams):	5
Carbohydrate (grams):	18	Carbohydrate (grams):	18
Calcium (mg):	74	Calcium (mg):	78
Iron (mg):	2	Iron (mg):	3
Dietary fiber (grams):	3	Dietary fiber (grams):	4

Salad Bar Examples:

#2   Before: **After:**

Before:	After:
1 cup lettuce	1 cup lettuce
1/2 cup coleslaw	*1/4 cup coleslaw*
1/2 cup macaroni salad	*1/4 cup macaroni salad*
1/4 cup chopped green peppers	1/4 cup chopped green peppers
4 cherry tomatoes	4 cherry tomatoes
1/4 cup shredded carrots	1/4 cup shredded carrots
4 T Italian dressing	*4 T reduced-calorie Italian dressing*

Before		After	
Calories (Kcal):	409	Calories (Kcal):	148
Fat (grams):	33	Fat (grams):	9
Protein (grams):	3	Protein (grams):	2
Carbohydrate (grams):	27	Carbohydrate (grams):	17
Calcium (mg):	59	Calcium (mg):	39
Iron (mg):	1	Iron (mg):	1
Dietary fiber (grams):	3	Dietary fiber (grams):	3

Salad Bar Examples:

#3   Before:

2 cups lettuce

1/4 cup chopped tomatoes
1/4 cup shredded carrots
Several cucumber slices
2 T sunflower seeds
1/4 cup chopped eggs
3 T French dressing

Calories (Kcal):	409
Fat (grams):	33
Protein (grams):	3
Carbohydrate (grams):	27
Calcium (mg):	59
Iron (mg):	1
Dietary fiber (grams):	3

After:

1 cup spinach
   and 1 cup lettuce

1/4 cup chopped tomatoes
1/4 cup shredded carrots
Several cucumber slices
1 T sunflower seeds
1/4 cup garbanzo beans
3 T reduced-calorie
   French dressing

Calories (Kcal):	148
Fat (grams):	9
Protein (grams):	2
Carbohydrate (grams):	17
Calcium (mg):	115
Iron (mg):	1
Dietary fiber (grams):	3

Salad Bar Examples:

#4 Before:

1-1/2 cups lettuce
1/4 cup shredded cheese
1/4 cup chopped egg
3 cherry tomatoes
1/4 cup sliced mushrooms
1/4 cup chopped green pepper

4 T Thousand Island dressing

Calories (Kcal):	451
Fat (grams):	37
Protein (grams):	15
Carbohydrate (grams):	16
Calcium (mg):	257
Iron (mg):	2
Dietary fiber (grams):	4

After:

1-1/2 cups lettuce
2 T shredded cheese
1/2 cup kidney beans
6 cherry tomatoes
1/4 cup sliced mushrooms
1/2 cup chopped green pepper

2 T Thousand Island dressing

Calories (Kcal):	347
Fat (grams):	17
Protein (grams):	14
Carbohydrate (grams):	38
Calcium (mg):	172
Iron (mg):	5
Dietary Fiber (grams):	11

Plan salad bar creations so that most of the ingredients are high in fiber and low in fat. Use fattier options sparingly or not at all.

Good Choices Include:	Limit:
Shredded carrots	Fatty salads such as
Green peppers	macaroni and coleslaw
Cauliflower	Cheeses
Broccoli	Chopped eggs
Spinach leaves (iceberg	Salad dressings
lettuce is low in fiber and	Greasy croutons
not nearly as nutritious)	Seeds
Cucumbers	Nuts
Mushrooms	
Tomatoes	
Beans (kidney, garbanzo)	
Green peas	
Sprouts	
Fresh fruit	
Sliced beets	

Salad bars have sprouted up all over - from fast food chains to cafeterias to finer restaurants. Just like regular menu fare, salad bars offer healthful lowfat ingredients as well as fatty options that are best limited. But it's as easy to avoid fat as it is to load up on it. Being aware of the salad bar pitfalls and how to build a great salad without them is the key.

Fat Content of Selected Items

Oil-based salad dressing, regular, 1 T .... 9 grams
Oil-based dressing, reduced-calorie, 1 T .... 3 grams
Mayonnaise-based dressing, regular, 1 T .... 6 grams
Mayonnaise-based dressing, reduced-calorie, 1 T .... 2 grams
Sunflower seeds, 1 T .... 5 grams
Olives, 10 small or 5 large .... 5 grams
Plain fruits and vegetables (such as carrots,
         green peppers, mushrooms, beets, grapes) .... 0 grams
Shredded cheddar cheese, 1/4 cup or 4 T .... 9 grams
Crackers, butter-type, 6 .... 5 grams
Melba toast, saltine crackers (4) .... trace
Macaroni salad, 1/2 cup .... 12 grams
Coleslaw, 1/2 cup .... 7 grams
Three-bean salad, 1/2 cup .... 3+ grams
Pasta salad, 1/2 cup .... 5+ grams
Chopped egg, 1 (about 3 T) .... 5 grams
Potato salad, 1/2 cup ....10 grams

Salad dressings may be the biggest pitfall of all. Oil has 5 grams of fat in *only one teaspoon*.

HELPFUL HINTS

• Skip the salad dressing. Flavor salads with vinegar (no oil), lemon juice, and/or pepper.

• Try reduced-fat or nonfat salad dressings.

• If you're going to use dressing, remember that oil-based dressings spread more easily over salad than mayonnaise-based dressings, so you don't need as much.

• Three-bean salad, coleslaw, pasta salad, and macaroni salad already have "dressing" on them. If you add any of these to your salad plate or bowl, you may not need any additional salad dressing.

• Carry fat-free dressing from home.

• Keep salad dressing "on the side" instead of pouring it over the whole salad. Dip forkfuls of salad into the dressing - you'll use less dressing this way.

• Try salsa on salads instead of salad dressings.

Sometimes salad is not the only option at full-scale salad bars. Increasingly popular are soup bars and "hot bars" which offer a variety of hot items that accompany the traditional salad bar. Some additional pointers are in order when encountering these:

HELPFUL HINTS

• Avoid greasy biscuits, rolls, and crackers. Choose crisp, crunchy crackers and bread sticks instead.

• Broth-type soups are usually lower in fat than cream soups, but the broth may be made from beef or chicken. Ask to be sure it's vegetarian.

• Hot bars can mean trouble. It can be difficult to determine how much fat has been added to items like cooked vegetables. Casseroles and macaroni and cheese are probably loaded with fat. Desserts such as cobblers and puddings are probably high in fat, too.

• Baked potatoes are a good option. Just resist the temptation to add butter, margarine, or sour cream. Pepper and salt-free herbal seasonings add plenty of flavor. Try topping a potato with veggies from the salad bar. Catsup or salsa also add zip to a baked potato.

Questions and Answers

Q: How do I know if muffins and rolls served with salads are high in fat?

A: Most commercial muffins, yeast breads, biscuits, and many crackers are high in fat. If in doubt, use the finger or napkin test: if it leaves a greasy film on fingers or an oily spot on a napkin, then it's probably high in fat.

Q: How do salad toppings such as croutons, sunflower seeds, and bacon-flavored bits stack up in terms of fat content?

A: Toppings such as these typically add fat to a salad, but not as much fat as most salad dressings. One cup of croutons contains about 3 grams of fat, although some croutons are greasier. Sunflower seeds have 5 grams of fat in a tablespoon. Bacon-flavored bits, which are a soy product in most cases, contain about 2 grams of fat in a tablespoon (although many vegetarians do not eat these). In the end, the fat contribution of these toppings depends upon how much is added to the salad. Remember: a little can go a long way.

Q: Is romaine or leaf lettuce better for me than iceberg lettuce?

A: Romaine and leaf lettuce are somewhat higher in some vitamins and minerals - potassium, calcium, vitamin A and folacin - compared to iceberg lettuce. However, if you want your salad to really be nutrient-charged, go for the spinach.

Q: I eat at salad bars often and get bored with the same old thing. What can I do to make my salads more interesting?

A: Have you ever tried leaving off the lettuce and, instead, taking a colorful mixture of other raw vegetables such as broccoli and cauliflower florets, shredded carrots, beets, mushrooms, etc.? Or what about making a salad primarily of chick peas and kidney beans, and maybe adding some cherry tomatoes, onions, and some oil-free vinaigrette dressing? Experiment with some different dressing choices - flavored vinegars are available at some restaurants - or try some salsa. If available, order a couple of slices of whole wheat toast or an English muffin to eat along with the salad.

 **Pizza**

Menu Magic

When you make pizza a meal, does it look something like this?

Large pie (you eat 4 slices) with:

> *cheese*   *green peppers*
> *mushrooms*   *onions*

> *....and a soft drink*

If so, did you know that you consumed 1,319 calories, 34 grams of fat, and very little fiber? By making some simple changes like **replacing the cheese with extra sauce and adding a salad in place of some of the pizza**, this lowfat meal results:

(Note: the simple changes made to reduce fat are in bold.)

*Large **cheeseless pie** (you eat **3 pieces**) with:*

> *green peppers*   *onions*
> *mushrooms*   ***extra sauce***
> *.... a soft drink **and a mixed green salad topped with an oil-free dressing or a dollop of your favorite salsa***

This meal saves you 535 calories, 30 grams of fat, and it gives you more fiber, vitamins, and minerals, too.

Here are some more pizza makeovers:

#1 Before: After:

4 slices Domino's cheese pizza	4 slices Domino's cheese pizza *made with half the cheese with green peppers and onions added*
Soft drink	Soft drink

Calories (Kcal):	903	Calories (Kcal):	757
Fat (grams):	20	Fat (grams):	13
Protein (grams):	44	Protein (grams):	30
Carbohydrate (grams):	151	Carbohydrate (grams):	149
Calcium (mg):	272	Calcium (mg):	136
Iron (mg):	4	Iron (mg):	4
Dietary fiber (grams):	0	Dietary fiber (grams):	1

Pizza Examples:

#2 <u>Before:</u>

2 slices cheese pizza with
 green peppers and mushrooms
Salad (lettuce, tomato,
 cucumber, and green peppers)
2 T Italian dressing
2 beers

Calories (Kcal):	669
Fat (grams):	20
Protein (grams):	16
Carbohydrate (grams):	66
Calcium (mg):	228
Iron (mg):	2
Dietary fiber (grams):	2

<u>After:</u>

3 slices cheeseless pizza with
green peppers and mushrooms
Salad (same as "Before")

2 T Italian dressing
1 beer

Calories (Kcal):	364
Fat (grams):	10
Protein (grams):	6
Carbohydrate (grams):	68
Calcium (mg):	28
Iron (mg):	2
Dietary fiber (grams):	2

Pizza Examples:

#3   Before:

4 slices of a large cheese pizza
  with green peppers
Soft drink
Slice chocolate cake

Calories (Kcal):	1058
Fat (grams):	23
Protein (grams):	39
Carbohydrate (grams):	176
Calcium (mg):	595
Iron (mg):	4
Dietary fiber (grams):	2

After:

4 slices of a small cheese
  pizza with green peppers
Soft drink
Half slice chocolate cake

Calories (Kcal):	719
Fat (grams):	14
Protein (grams):	26
Carbohydrate (grams):	123
Calcium (mg):	394
Iron (mg):	3
Dietary fiber (grams):	1

Pizza Examples:

# 4 Before:		After:	
4 slices cheese pizza		*4 slices cheeseless pizza with extra sauce, green peppers, onions, zucchini squash, and broccoli*	
1/2 cup coleslaw		1/2 cup coleslaw	
Soft drink		*8 oz. orange juice*	
Calories (Kcal):	1509	Calories (Kcal):	1322
Fat (grams):	49	Fat (grams):	25
Protein (grams):	59	Protein (grams):	40
Carbohydrate (grams):	172	Carbohydrate (grams):	200
Calcium (mg):	918	Calcium (mg):	378
Iron (mg):	8	Iron (mg):	9
Dietary fiber (grams):	2	Dietary fiber (grams):	3

Pizza qualifies as "eating out," even though it's "ordered in" as often as it's eaten at a pizzeria. The nice thing about pizza is that leftovers never go to waste. Cold pizza is great for a snack or for breakfast the next morning, or it can be reheated in a conventional or microwave oven. Pizza can be created to suit just about anybody's taste.

Pizza toppings can be traditional or adventurous. The following lists distinguish the best choices from those that contribute more fat:

Good Choices Include:	Limit:
Chopped green peppers or green pepper rings	Cheese
Sliced mushrooms	Olives
Chopped onions	
Tomato slices	
Pineapple chunks	
Strips or slices of zucchini or yellow squash	
Chopped broccoli and cauliflower	

Fat Content of Selected Items

Olives, 10 small or 5 large	5 grams
Part skim mozzarella cheese, 1 oz.	5 grams
Regular mozzarella cheese, 1 oz.	8 grams
Parmesan cheese, grated, 2 T	3 grams
Plain fruit and vegetable toppings	0 grams
Domino's Pizza, medium, cheese, one slice	3 grams
Domino's Pizza, large, cheese, one slice	4 grams
Average cheese pizza, 1/4 of 10-inch pie	10 grams
Cheeseless pizza, 1/4 of 10-inch pie	2 grams

HELPFUL HINTS

• When you eat cheese pizza, hold your share to one or two slices and round out the meal with a salad, vegetable, or some fresh fruit.

• Ask that the pizza be cut into smaller slices. For instance, cut a large pie into 8 or 12 slices rather than 6.

• Order the pizza without cheese. Most of the fat in a meatless pizza comes from the cheese. Add extra sauce and vegetable toppings. Another alternative: ask for half the usual amount of cheese.

• Crushed red pepper or black pepper are great on pizza. A small amount of grated Parmesan cheese is also okay.

Questions and Answers

Q: Are deep-dish pizzas higher or lower in fat than thin-crust pizzas?

A: The fat content of various styles of pizza varies, depending upon how much oil is added to the crust or pan. What makes the biggest difference is how much cheese is used and whether the cheese is part-skim or whole milk cheese. Incidentally, two slices of a medium cheese Pizza Hut Pan Pizza contain 18 grams of fat, as compared to 17 grams of fat in two slices of a medium cheese Pizza Hut Thin 'n Crispy Pizza.

Q: If I order a pizza with less cheese or no cheese at all, I'll get less calcium. Wouldn't it be better to get a little more fat than to get less calcium?

A: Dairy products such as cheese and whole milk can add a large amount of fat to your diet. They also contain no fiber and contribute to the overabundance of protein in the typical American diet. Recommendations for calcium intake in this country reflect the fact that Americans take in so much protein. Excessive amounts of protein in the diet cause us to lose calcium. To compensate for this, American recommendations for calcium intake are jacked up well above what would otherwise be necessary.

People who moderate their protein intake, like those who follow a lowfat vegetarian diet, need less calcium than the Recommended Dietary Allowances suggest. Studies show that vegetarians, for instance, absorb and retain more calcium than do non vegetarians. Intakes of calcium somewhat below the RDA do not appear to pose a problem for vegetarians.

It may be more appropriate for vegetarians to aim for the amount of dietary calcium recommended by the World Health Organization in the FAO/WHO* Recommended Dietary Intakes: about 400 - 500 milligrams of calcium per day for adults. This goal is easily achieved by most vegetarians eating a reasonably varied diet.

If you stick to a lowfat vegetarian diet and regularly eat a variety of vegetables, especially dark green and leafy varieties, fruits, legumes, and grains, you don't need dairy products to obtain adequate amounts of calcium.

* United Nations' Food & Agriculture Organization and World Health Organization

 # Italian

Menu Magic

Some people don't realize how much fat can be contained in a typical Italian meal like this one:

> *1 cup tossed salad with*
> *   3 tablespoons Italian dressing*
> *3 slices garlic bread*
> *8 oz. cheese manicotti*
> *1 cup coffee with 2 teaspoons cream*
> *1 cannoli*

This meal is laden with fat, primarily from the cheeses which play a big role in many traditional Italian dishes. Even a few easy changes such as **replacing a cheesy dessert with some sweet, refreshing fruit and cutting back a little on the amount of fat added to foods such as salad and coffee**, can make a big dent in the fat content of the meal. Instead of the meal above, which contains at least 60 grams of fat and 1,000 calories, try this alternative:

(Note: the simple changes made to reduce fat are in bold.)

> *1 cup tossed salad with **1 tablespoon** Italian dressing*
> *3 slices garlic bread*
> *8 oz. cheese manicotti*
> *1 cup coffee with **1 teaspoon** cream*
> ***Bowl of fresh strawberries with powdered sugar***

This slightly-altered version of the first meal contains about 34 grams of fat and 802 calories.

Simple changes, such as substituting extra sauce for some of the cheese, increasing the vegetables, or cutting back on added butter and dressings are all it takes to make these menus better:

#1 Before:

Baked ziti with marinara sauce (melted mozzarella on top)

3 pieces Italian bread with butter

Tossed salad with
 4 T Italian dressing
6 oz. red wine

Calories (Kcal):	1376
Fat (grams):	61
Protein (grams):	40
Carbohydrate (grams):	136
Calcium (mg):	525
Iron (mg):	8
Dietary fiber (grams):	9

After:

Baked ziti **with extra marinara sauce (no cheese on top)**

3 pieces Italian bread **(no butter, dipped in tomato sauce)**

Tossed salad with
 4 T Italian dressing
6 oz. red wine

Calories (Kcal):	1046
Fat (grams):	30
Protein (grams):	24
Carbohydrate (grams):	139
Calcium (mg):	83
Iron (mg):	7
Dietary fiber (grams):	9

Italian Examples:

#2   Before: **After:**

Tossed salad with 4 T Italian   Tossed salad *with fresh*
  dressing   *lemon wedges*
Fettucine Alfredo   *Half order Fettucine Alfredo*
                                           Bowl of minestrone soup
6 oz. red wine   6 oz. red wine

Calories (Kcal):	852		Calories (Kcal):	719
Fat (grams):	57		Fat (grams):	45
Protein (grams):	13		Protein (grams):	11
Carbohydrate (grams):	39		Carbohydrate (grams):	35
Calcium (mg):	16		Calcium (mg):	50
Iron (mg):	1		Iron (mg):	2
Dietary fiber (grams):	1		Dietary fiber (grams):	2

Italian Examples:

#3 Before:	After:
Bowl of lentil soup	Bowl of lentil soup
2 pieces of Italian bread with butter	2 pieces Italian bread *(no butter)*
4 stuffed shells with marinara sauce	*2 stuffed shells with extra marinara sauce*
	3/4 cup cooked green beans, tomatoes, and potatoes (with no oil)
Water	Water

Calories (Kcal):	601	Calories (Kcal):	396
Fat (grams):	20	Fat (grams):	3
Protein (grams):	28	Protein (grams):	18
Carbohydrate (grams):	75	Carbohydrate (grams):	73
Calcium (mg):	54	Calcium (mg):	82
Iron (mg):	4	Iron (mg):	5
Dietary fiber (grams):	2	Dietary fiber (grams):	3

Italian Examples:

#4 Before:	After:
Fried mozzarella cheese with tomato sauce (appetizer)	*Bowl minestrone soup*
2 cups spaghetti with tomato sauce	2 cups spaghetti with tomato sauce
Tossed salad with 4 T Italian dressing	Tossed salad *with 2 T Italian dressing*
2 pieces Italian bread with butter	2 pieces Italian bread with butter
6 oz. red wine	6 oz. red wine
1 cannoli	*1 cup cappuccino*

Calories (Kcal):	1958	Calories (Kcal):	1328
Fat (grams):	103	Fat (grams):	46
Protein (grams):	53	Protein (grams):	37
Carbohydrate (grams):	180	Carbohydrate (grams):	162
Calcium (mg):	701	Calcium (mg):	325
Iron (mg):	10	Iron (mg):	9
Dietary fiber (grams):	12	Dietary fiber (grams):	12

Good Choices Include:

Lentil soup
Minestrone soup
Pasta e fagioli (pasta and beans)
Green salads
Fresh vegetable appetizers
Pasta primavera
Pasta with marinara sauce
Plain Italian bread
Cooked vegetables
Fresh fruit

Limit:

Olives
Cheese
Salad dressings
Fried foods
Buttery garlic bread
Added butter, excess
added oil
Rich desserts such
as cannoli and
cakes

Fat Content of Selected Items

Lentil soup, 1 cup	3 grams
Minestrone soup, 1 cup	3 grams
Green salad, no dressing	0 grams
Italian dressing, 1 T	7 grams
Fresh vegetables, plain	0 grams
Italian bread, 1 chunk	0 grams
Butter, 1 tsp	5 grams
Plain pasta, 1 cup	1 gram
Olive oil, 1 tsp	5 grams
Marinara sauce, 1/2 cup	4 grams
Mozzarella cheese, 1 oz.	8 grams
Ricotta cheese, 1/4 cup	8 grams
Parmesan cheese, 2 T	3 grams
Cannoli, one	16+ grams
Fresh fruit	0 grams

There are many vegetarian options available at Italian restaurants. To keep those options low in fat, watch out for cheese, the culprit in many Italian dishes. High fat cheeses may include whole milk mozzarella, Parmesan, and ricotta cheeses, plus others. Cheeses are used as fillings in stuffed shells, lasagna, cannelloni and manicotti, or mixed into and melted on top of other pasta dishes, including baked ziti and pizza. Fettucine Alfredo sports its trademark creamy cheese sauce. Antipasto platters contain chunks of cheese, and slabs of hot cheese covered with tomato sauce are a popular appetizer.

Other hazards are Italian bread slathered with oil or butter, large amounts of oil added to some pasta dishes, and rich desserts. These can all be avoided, however, and there are lots of great lowfat choices that are available.

HELPFUL HINTS

• Plain pasta - linguine, fettucine, spaghetti, angel hair - tastes great with marinara (meatless) sauce. Top with a sprinkling of grated Parmesan cheese if you're so inclined, and add mushrooms sautéed in wine for a real treat.

• Try minestrone soup, lentil soup, or the traditional bean and pasta dish, pasta e fagioli, which is often also served as a soup. (These are usually vegetarian, but check with your waiter to be sure.)

• Home-style Italian restaurants may serve vegetable side dishes made with boiled potatoes, string beans, tomatoes, and mushrooms. Ask if fat is added and request that yours be prepared without, if possible.

HELPFUL HINTS

- Ask that salad dressings be served on the side, or omit them altogether.

- Plain Italian bread is low in fat. Garlic bread usually has been brushed with oil.

- Avoid the temptation to butter your bread. Dip it in tomato sauce instead.

Questions and Answers:

Q: How do pasta primavera and pesto pasta rate in their fat content?

A: The fat content of these dishes varies, depending upon how much oil is added by the cook. Pasta primavera is usually made with fettucine mixed with a variety of steamed vegetables and tossed with olive oil or a high-fat cream sauce. This dish is delicious and can be a good choice if the oil is used sparingly (or not at all). Ask your waiter if the cook will oblige. Likewise, pesto pasta is a delicious, aromatic dish of pasta mixed with an oil, Parmesan cheese, and basil sauce, with pine nuts added. You might ask for the pesto sauce and pine nuts to be served on the side, so you can add only the amount you want. If the sauce and nuts can be controlled, this can also be a good choice. Otherwise, the dish can be high in fat and portions should be kept small.

Q: What are some acceptable dessert choices at an Italian restaurant?

A: As an alternative to rich desserts, ask for a bowl of fresh fruit. Some dessert carts feature beautiful bowls of seasonal berries, for instance. Ask that the whipped cream be left off, or ask for just a dollop. Another idea: order a cup of cappuccino - a hot espresso mixed with steamed milk, sometimes topped with a sprinkling of cinnamon or unsweetened cocoa (decaffeinated cappuccino is available in some restaurants).

Q: A glass of wine just seems to go with an Italian meal. How does alcohol stack up within the total diet? If I cook with wine, how does this affect my diet?

A: Whereas fat provides 9 calories per gram, alcohol provides 7 calories per gram. So, alcohol is a concentrated source of calories, just like fat. Although it's not encouraged, a glass of wine once in a while is probably okay for most people. The current Dietary Guidelines for Americans recommend that Americans consume alcohol "in moderation," **if at all**. Moderation is defined as not more than one drink a day for women and two drinks a day for men. What counts as one drink? One drink is 12 ounces of regular beer, 5 ounces of wine, or 1-1/2 ounces of distilled spirits (80 proof). As far as cooking with alcohol is concerned: the amount used in cooking is usually minimal - just enough to impart a certain flavor. The alcohol usually evaporates during cooking and doesn't significantly affect the nutritional value of the food.

Fast Food

Menu Magic

Is your idea of a quick and filling breakfast something like this?

1 egg and cheese biscuit
6 oz. orange juice
1 cup coffee with cream

If so, you've started out the day with over 45 grams of fat, 590 calories, and a hefty dose of cholesterol, too. It's possible to do much better without giving up all of your favorite foods. Look at these two options:

(Note: the simple changes made to reduce fat are in bold.)

Option A
1 plain biscuit with jelly
6 oz. orange juice
1 cup coffee with cream

Option B
2 fat-free muffins *(available at some restaurants)*
6 oz. orange juice
1 cup coffee with cream

Option A adds up to about 23 grams of fat and 429 calories; Option B comes in at about 10 grams of fat and about 245 calories.

How about lunch? Instead of this....

> *Tossed salad with 3 T Thousand Island dressing*
> *Large order of French fries with catsup*
> *Medium shake*

.... which totals at least 55 grams of fat and 1,040 calories - **use a "diet" dressing and have 2 fat-free muffins in place of the greasy French fries:**

> <u>Option A</u>
> *Tossed salad with **"diet" dressing***
> ***2 fat-free muffins***
> *Medium shake*

....or cut out some fat by **switching from a shake to orange juice and swapping a few of the fries for a meatless burger** (that is, the bun and lowfat toppings without the "burger"):

> <u>Option B</u>
> *Tossed salad with Thousand Island dressing **(2 T)***
> ***Regular order** of fries*
> ***1 meatless burger (extra tomatoes;***
> ***   hold the cheese and mayo)***
> ***6 oz. orange juice***

Option A yields about 25 grams of fat and 686 calories, and Option B totals 31 grams of fat and only 584 calories.

Here are some more examples of easy changes that can be made to make these fast food meals leaner:

#1   **Before:**   **After:**

2 pancakes with syrup and   2 pancakes with syrup
  1 T whipped butter   *(skip the butter)*
6 oz. orange juice   6 oz. orange juice
1 cup coffee with 1 tsp. of cream   1 cup coffee, *black or with sugar*

	Before		After
Calories (Kcal):	605	Calories (Kcal):	515
Fat (grams):	13	Fat (grams):	3
Protein (grams):	9	Protein (grams):	9
Carbohydrate (grams):	113	Carbohydrate (grams):	113
Calcium (mg):	113	Calcium (mg):	113
Iron (mg):	2	Iron (mg):	2
Dietary fiber (grams):	0	Dietary fiber (grams):	0

#2   **Before:**   **After:**

2 bean burritos   2 bean burritos *without cheese*
Medium soft drink   Medium soft drink

	Before		After
Calories (Kcal):	846	Calories (Kcal):	634
Fat (grams):	24	Fat (grams):	6
Protein (grams):	22	Protein (grams):	10
Carbohydrate (grams):	134	Carbohydrate (grams):	133
Calcium (mg):	208	Calcium (mg):	80
Iron (mg):	6	Iron (mg):	6
Dietary fiber (grams):	7	Dietary fiber (grams):	7

Fast Food Examples:

#3   Before:

Meatless burger with cheese, lettuce, tomato, mayonnaise, catsup, and mustard

Large order of fries
Medium milkshake

Calories (Kcal):	914
Fat (grams):	35
Protein (grams):	26
Carbohydrate (grams):	127
Calcium (mg):	703
Iron (mg):	3
Dietary fiber (grams):	4

After:

Meatless burger with cheese, lettuce, *extra tomato*, catsup, and mustard *(hold the mayonnaise)*

Large order of fries
6 oz. orange juice

Calories (Kcal):	600
Fat (grams):	21
Protein (grams):	16
Carbohydrate (grams):	90
Calcium (mg):	264
Iron (mg):	4
Dietary fiber (grams):	5

Fast Food Examples:

#4 Before:

Tossed salad with lettuce, tomatoes,
  cucumbers, red cabbage,
  and 3 T French dressing
Large baked potato with chopped
  broccoli and 1/3 cup cheese sauce

Medium soft drink

Calories (Kcal):	1042
Fat (grams):	54
Protein (grams):	37
Carbohydrate (grams):	104
Calcium (mg):	828
Iron (mg):	4
Dietary fiber (grams):	9

After:

Tossed salad (as "Before")
  with 2 T dressing on the side

Large baked potato with
  chopped broccoli, *salt,
  pepper, and 2 T cheese
  sauce*
Medium soft drink

Calories (Kcal):	628
Fat (grams):	19
Protein (grams):	13
Carbohydrate (grams):	100
Calcium (mg):	206
Iron (mg):	4
Dietary fiber (grams):	9

Good Choices Include:	Limit:
Some salads	Fried foods such as
Fruit juice	pies and French fries
Some lowfat muffins	Mayonnaise
Meatless burgers without	Cheese
mayonnaise	Guacamole and sour
Bean burritos without cheese	cream
Bean tacos or tostados without cheese	Whole milk
Some lowfat frozen desserts	Most frozen desserts
Pancakes, plain	and shakes
English muffins, unbuttered	Snack chips
Fresh vegetable sticks	Breakfast pastries
Lowfat yogurt	Biscuits
	Eggs
	Pancakes with butter

Fat Content of Selected Items:

Egg and cheese biscuit	39 grams
Scrambled eggs, 2	14 grams
Pancakes, unbuttered, two 4-inch	4 grams
Orange juice, 6 oz.	0 grams
English muffin, unbuttered	0 grams
Fried apple turnover	14 grams
Taco salad with dressing	65 grams
Bean burrito with cheese	14 grams
Bean burrito without cheese	6 grams
Meatless burger (no patty), no cheese or mayonnaise	0 grams
Whole milk, 1 cup	8 grams
French fries, 10	15 grams

Fast food restaurants have responded to consumers' demands for lower fat menu choices, but the number of truly lowfat options is still greatly limited. The many faces of fast food include the usual burger-and-fries establishments as well as pizza and ethnic food options. Choices tend to be much more limited, however, than in full-scale restaurants. Overall, fast food restaurants are a nutritional minefield and are best avoided by those who want to keep their fat intake in control. If that's not possible, then keep the following tips in mind:

HELPFUL HINTS

• Baked potato and salad bars are found in many fast food restaurants. See Salad Bar section. Avoid adding cheese sauce to baked potatoes.

• Ask for a meatless burger. A bun with lettuce, tomato, pickles, mustard, and catsup is low in fat and better than nothing. Order two. Skip the mayonnaise. Ask for extra tomato. A slice of cheese adds several grams of fat. (Note: some buns contain lard; vegetarians can check with the manager.)

• At Mexican-style fast food restaurants, take a bean burrito. If you order it without cheese, you'll save several grams of fat. Another option: bean tacos with hard or soft shells. Tostados can be made with beans and no meat. Watch out for guacamole, cheese, and sour cream.

• Pizza is sold as fast food - see Pizza section.

• Avoid fried snack chips, French fries, fried pies, and onion rings.

HELPFUL HINTS

• Be wary of items billed as "lowfat" or "lower fat." Ask to see nutrition information on the product to check how many grams of fat it contains.

• Many frozen desserts and shakes are high in fat. See if nutrition information is available and check.

Questions and Answers:

Q: Are the prepackaged salads good choices at fast food places?

A: Although most of the packaged salads available are not much more than chopped iceberg lettuce, which has little nutritional value, the fat content can be low if salad dressing is avoided or limited. On the other hand, salads on some menus, like taco salads, can be very high in fat with all of the cheese and other toppings they contain. Packages of fresh vegetables such as carrot and celery sticks may be available at some restaurants.

Q: What can I order for breakfast?

A: The best breakfast items are orange juice, unbuttered English muffins with jelly, other fat-free muffins, and pancakes without added butter (although these are still moderately high in fat). Biscuits and egg dishes, especially those containing cheese, and breakfast pastries, are all very high in fat. Yogurt is available in some places. Check to see that it is lowfat.

 # Mexican

Menu Magic

A typical Mexican meal such as this one contains 54 grams of fat and 1,096 calories:

>*10 tortilla chips with salsa*
>*Combination platter with a cheese enchilada, a bean
> burrito with 1 tablespoon sour cream, and a chalupa
> (contains about 1/3 cup guacamole)*
>*Water (a beer or mixed drink adds another 150-250
> calories!)*

By simply **replacing the fatty cheese enchilada with a green salad topped with salsa, and by reducing the amount of guacamole on the chalupa**, this delicious meal results:

(Note: the simple changes made to reduce fat are in bold.)

>*10 tortilla chips with salsa*
>***Green salad with fresh vegetables, topped with salsa***
>*Bean burrito with sour cream and a chalupa (**2 T**
> guacamole)*
>*Water*

Now the meal has 30 grams of fat and 714 calories - a big improvement - without totally giving up treats such as sour cream and chips.

Note how easy it is to make simple changes. By substituting salsa for salad dressing, ordering a vegetable side dish instead of a larger entree, and reducing the amount of cheese in a dish, you will lower the fat content of the following menus:

#1   Before:

20 tortilla chips with salsa
Combination platter with one
  cheese enchilada, one bean burrito,
  and one cheese quesadilla
1/2 cup fried rice
One margarita

Calories (Kcal):	1610
Fat (grams):	76
Protein (grams):	44
Carbohydrate (grams):	166
Calcium (mg):	1023
Iron (mg):	8
Dietary fiber (grams):	5

After:

20 tortilla chips with salsa
One cheese enchilada and
 one bean burrito (no cheese)
Side salad with salsa dressing
1/2 cup fried rice
One margarita

Calories (Kcal):	1201
Fat (grams):	44
Protein (grams):	29
Carbohydrate (grams):	147
Calcium (mg):	527
Iron (mg):	8
Dietary fiber (grams):	5

Mexican Examples:

#2 Before:	After:
10 nachos (tortilla chips, beans, cheese, chilies, black olives) with salsa	10 nachos (as "Before") with salsa
Taco salad (greens, tomatoes, cucumbers, mushrooms, beans, grated cheese, guacamole, sour cream, and salad dressing in a fried tortilla shell)	Taco salad (greens, tomatoes, cucumbers, mushrooms, beans, *1 T guacamole, skip the sour cream and salad dressing, add several T salsa, and 1 T grated cheese on top; eat 1/4 of the shell)*
Water	Water

Before		After	
Calories (Kcal):	1283	Calories (Kcal):	760
Fat (grams):	90	Fat (grams):	39
Protein (grams):	37	Protein (grams):	30
Carbohydrate (grams):	93	Carbohydrate (grams):	86
Calcium (mg):	681	Calcium (mg):	482
Iron (mg):	7	Iron (mg):	7
Dietary fiber (grams):	7	Dietary fiber (grams):	7

Mexican Examples:

#3 <u>Before:</u>

10 tortilla chips with salsa
Green salad with vinaigrette
  dressing
Bean and spinach burrito

1/2 cup rice
1/2 cup steamed vegetables
One beer
Mexican fried ice cream

Calories (Kcal):	1553
Fat (grams):	76
Protein (grams):	46
Carbohydrate (grams):	165
Calcium (mg):	819
Iron (mg):	11
Dietary fiber (grams):	12

<u>After:</u>

10 tortilla chips with salsa
Green salad *with salsa
  dressing*
Bean and spinach burrito
  (no cheese)

1/2 cup rice
1/2 cup steamed vegetables
One beer
Mexican fried ice cream
  (split dessert with a friend)

Calories (Kcal):	981
Fat (grams):	26
Protein (grams):	32
Carbohydrate (grams):	147
Calcium (mg):	473
Iron (mg):	11
Dietary fiber (grams):	10

Mexican Examples:

#4 Before:	After:
10 tortilla chips with salsa	10 tortilla chips with salsa
1 chile relleno and 1 cheese enchilada	*1 chile relleno,*
1/2 cup refried beans	*rice, and refried beans*
1/2 cup rice	*1 cup gazpacho*
1 beer	1 beer

Calories (Kcal):	1249	Calories (Kcal):	834
Fat (grams):	52	Fat (grams):	26
Protein (grams):	48	Protein (grams):	38
Carbohydrate (grams):	130	Carbohydrate (grams):	93
Calcium (mg):	1044	Calcium (mg):	580
Iron (mg):	8	Iron (mg):	7
Dietary fiber (grams):	7	Dietary fiber (grams):	5

Good Choices Include: Limit:

Bean fillings   Fried tortilla chips
Lettuce, tomato, onion toppings   Guacamole
Salsa   Sour cream
Gazpacho (cold, spicy,   Salad dressings
    tomato-based soup)   Deep fried foods,
Green salad, no dressing   including desserts
Steamed vegetables   such as fried ice cream
Seasoned rice, (not fried)   or sopapillas
Bean enchilada   Cheese
Flour and corn tortillas, (steamed not fried)
Bean and spinach burrito
Bean taco or tostada
Chalupa
Fresh fruit

Fat Content of Selected Items

Refried beans, 1/2 cup .... 1+ grams
Salsa, 1/4 cup .... 0 grams
Sour cream, 2 T .... 5 grams
Guacamole, 1/4 cup .... 8 grams
Flour tortilla, one .... 2 grams
Corn tortilla, one .... 1 grams
Taco Bell bean burrito, one .... 14 grams
Bean burrito (no cheese), one .... 4 grams
Cheese enchilada, one .... 19 grams
Fried tortilla chips, 10 .... 7 grams

Mexican-style food is very popular in the U.S. It runs the gamut from fast food varieties to mom-and-pop and chain restaurant fare. There are even some fancier Mexican restaurants. So, there can be big variations in the number of lowfat options available at one restaurant versus another. This may depend, in part, upon how much flexibility there is in altering some menu items and whether or not animal fat has been added to that staple of vegetarian Mexican dining - the beans. As always, if you do not understand the content of some of the menu items, ask your waiter. Even if you are familiar with Mexican cuisine, it doesn't hurt to clarify with your waiter how a particular item is prepared - there can be variations from one place to another.

HELPFUL HINTS

• Take it easy on the guacamole, often added to items such as chalupas and nachos. Avocado, which is the base of guacamole, is nearly all fat.

• Restaurants frequently put a big dollop of sour cream on the top of many menu items. This is fat. Ask them to leave it off.

• Rice served with meals is usually fried and is frequently fried in animal fat. Ask your waiter how the rice is prepared. Some restaurants will substitute extra beans or a vegetable for fried rice.

• Flour or corn tortillas are low in fat.

HELPFUL HINTS

• Avoid items that are fried, such as chimichangas. Chile rellenos are bell peppers which are usually filled with cheese, then breaded and fried. When in doubt, remember to ask questions.

• Taco salads usually contain ground beef and grated cheddar cheese. With the salad dressing, these "salads" can contain over 65 grams of fat. Instead, ask for a salad made with greens, mushrooms, tomatoes, onions, and green pepper. Salsa makes a zippy dressing.

Questions and Answers

Q: I fill up on tortilla chips before my meal even gets to the table. How can I handle the tortilla chip dilemma?

A: Resist the temptation to load up on fried tortilla chips before the meal is served. These are often brought to the table as a complimentary appetizer, with salsa. Either ask that the chips be removed from the table and don't eat them, or limit how many you eat. Don't accept a second basket of chips after the first is gone. The salsa is fine - it's fat free.

Q: So many Mexican entrees are high in fat. Where does all of this fat hide?

A: Cheese is one of the biggest culprits. It's added to most of the menu items. Cheese is melted onto nachos and inside burritos and enchiladas. It may be grated on top of salads, tostadas, tacos, and chalupas. Either ask that cheese not be added to your food, or ask that the amount be reduced. Guacamole and sour cream are typical "add-ons" that also "add on" lots of fat in Mexican restaurants.

Q: Refried beans usually have some sort of fat added to them. Isn't this a problem?

A: It's true that refried beans usually have fat added - either animal fat or oil. Unless you are a vegetarian and lard has been added to the beans, even *with* the fat added to the beans, refried beans are still the best filling choice for enchiladas, burritos, tacos, etc. Some restaurants may also offer a spinach filling. Other toppings such as chopped tomato, onion, and lettuce can also be added.

 # Indian

Menu Magic

Does your idea of an Indian meal look something like this?

Poori (2 pieces of bread), spread with ghee
Plate of 2 samosas with 2 vegetable pakoras
1/3 cup basmati rice with ghee
1 cup cooked vegetables with ghee
Hot tea

Fat from cooking oils and ghee (clarified butter) adds up quickly. The meal above contains at least 80 grams of fat and 1,400 calories. Try this delicious lower fat alternative:

(Note: the simple changes made to reduce fat are in bold.)

*1 cup dal **(no ghee added)***
1 cup green salad with chutney
*1/3 cup basmati rice **(no added oil or ghee)***
1 cup cooked vegetables, cooked with fresh spices
    (no added oil or ghee)
*1 piece chappatti **(no ghee)***
Hot tea
Fresh fruit

This satisfying meal contains less than 10 grams of fat and only about 465 calories - a fragrant and colorful alternative to higher fat options.

See how easily the following menus are improved* by making simple changes, such as avoiding deep-fried foods and decreasing added fats such as ghee:

* Note: Nutritional breakdowns are not given for the menus in the Indian section, however all of the modified menus are significantly lower in fat than the "before" versions. Preparation methods (especially the amount of fat added) and serving sizes (such as breads) vary considerably from one restaurant to another. Those who would like to try their hand at Indian cooking at home may be interested in Fatima Lakhani's book, *Indian Recipes for a Healthy Heart.* This book, while not specifically vegetarian, includes 140 lowfat Indian recipes, with nutrition information. Softcover; 1992, 286 pages; $14.95; available from the Center for Science in the Public Interest, Suite 300, 1875 Connecticut Ave., NW, Washington, DC 20009.

#1 Before:	After:
2 vegetable samosas (deep-fried turnovers stuffed with potatoes and peas) with chutney	2 *dhoklas* (steamed rice and bean cakes; order as an appetizer)
Chappatti (thin, unleavened bread) with ghee	Chappatti *(no ghee added)*
Palak panir (spinach and cheese)	*Kachumbar salad* (cucumber, tomatoes, and spices)
Tarka dahl (lentils with butter)	Tarka dahl *(no extra butter added)*
Basmati rice	Basmati rice
Water	Water

Indian Examples:

#2   Before: **After:**

2 vegetable pakoras   *1* vegetable pakora *(split order with a*
(vegetables deep-fried   *friend)* and *papadum (crisp, lentil*
in chickpea batter)   *wafers; ask for them roasted, not*
Onion nan (unleavened bread   *deep-fried; split order with friend)*
stuffed with onions and spices) Onion nan (roasted or baked)
Navratan curry (vegetables   Navratan curry *(split with a friend)*
in a nuts and cream sauce)
Basmati rice   *Extra* basmati rice
                                Raita (yogurt mixed with vegetables
                                    and spices; split with a friend)
Water   Water

#3   Before: **After:**

Alu paratha (pan fried bread   *Khasta roti (roasted bread, not fried)*
stuffed with potatoes)   *Idli with chutney (steamed*
                                    rice and bean cake appetizer)
Mattar panir (garden peas   Mattar panir *(ask that*
with cheese)   *extra fat not be added)*
Basmati rice   Basmati rice
Masala tea   Masala tea

Indian Examples:

#4 **Before:**	**After:**
	Vegetarian plate consisting of:
Mattar panir	Mattar panir, chana masala, and tarka dahl
Chana masala	*- ask that less fat be used and that*
Tarka dahl	*extra butter or ghee not be added*
Raita	Raita
Poori	*Alu nan (in place of poori;*
	ask that no ghee be added)
Rice	Rice
Gulab jamun	*Ras gulla or chum chum*
	in place of fried gulab jamun
Tea	Tea

Indian cuisine is quickly gaining popularity, especially in larger cities. Restaurants specializing in Northern Indian cuisine are the most common in the U.S., but in large metropolitan areas, foods from other regions of India may be offered.

For the uninitiated, an Indian menu can look a bit mysterious. Ask your waiter for help, and be ready to experiment with the flavors and fragrances of new Indian dishes. Traditional Indian food includes many lowfat vegetarian choices as well as some that are high in fat. If you are eating out with friends, consider sharing your orders with each other to gain exposure to as many new items as possible.

Good Choices Include:

Dal (without added ghee)
Vegetable curries
Rice (without ghee)
Chappatti
Salad, no dressing
Chutneys
Raitas (yogurt dishes)
Fresh exotic fruit
Hot tea
Mazza mango drink
Idli or dhokla (steamed bean
  and rice cakes)
Papadum (ask for roasted instead
  of deep-fried)
Menu listings for breads with the
  words "roti" or "nan" are usually
  baked or roasted (i.e. khasta roti
  or rogini nan)
Kachumbar (raw vegetables)
Dosa (thin pancake stuffed with potatoes
  or plain)
Chum chum (lower fat dessert)
Gajar kahalwa (carrot pudding with
  raisins and almonds - a lower fat dessert)

Limit:

Ghee
Poori and paratha
(deep fried breads)
Samosas
Gulab jamun (deep-
fried dessert)
Kofta (deep-fried)
Pakoras
Other fried foods
Vegetables fixed with
rich, creamy
sauces

Fat Content of Selected Items:

Rice, 1/2 cup .... 0 grams
Ghee, 1 tsp .... 5 grams
Fresh fruit .... 0 grams
Chutney, most varieties .... 0 grams
Dal, or lentil soup, 1 cup .... 3 grams
Chappatti, 1 piece .... 0 grams
Kachumbar salad, 1/2 cup .... 0 grams
Raita, 1/2 cup .... 4 grams
Samosa, one .... 10+ grams
Pakora, one .... 10+ grams

HELPFUL HINTS

• Ask that ghee (melted, clarified butter) not be spread on breads or added to vegetable dishes and dahl after they are heated.

• Vegetables are often available cooked with fresh ginger and other spices. Ask that they be prepared without ghee and with limited amounts of oil.

• Chutneys are a good lowfat condiment.

• Spicy yogurt sauces are also acceptable. Cooling raitas - yogurt preparations that may be mixed with vegetables or fruits help to balance hot, spicy curry dishes.

• Avoid deep-fried foods such as some Indian breads. Papadum, a crisp lentil wafer, can be roasted rather than deep-fried.

HELPFUL HINTS

• Try fragrant basmati rice, steamed. Dal, a traditional lentil soup, is also a good choice. A plate of rice, some dal, a piece of chappatti (Indian bread), a green salad, and some chutney makes a simple and delicious meal.

• Steer clear of rich desserts. Instead, try some exotic, fresh fruit or a cup of hot tea.

• Samosas and pakoras are always deep-fried, although it may not state so on the menu.

Questions and Answers:

Q: Which are the best beverages to choose at an Indian restaurant?

A: There are some unique Indian beverages that you may want to try, although some are higher in fat than others. For instance, masala tea is nonfat, unless you add milk to it. Mazzo mango drink is only about 10% fruit juice, but it is fat-free. Lassi is a yogurt drink that can be ordered sweet or salted. Usually it's made with whole milk yogurt, so 8 ounces will contain about 8 grams of fat. With the exception of milkshakes, beverages offered on an Indian menu are probably all low in fat.

Q: Samosas and pakoras are common Indian appetizers, but they are deep-fried. What lower fat appetizers would you suggest I try instead?

A: Not only are samosas and pakoras deep-fried, but extra fat is even added to the dough of samosas. See if the restaurant offers idli or dhokla instead. These are steamed rice and bean cakes that may be served as a main dish or appetizer in some restaurants. Idli is sometimes served with lentil soup if it is listed as an entree. Dhokla is typically served with chutney.

Q: There are so many Indian bread choices. Which are the lowest in fat, and which ones should I avoid?

A: Indian breads are delicious. Typically, small pieces of the bread are torn off of the whole piece and are used to "pinch" or scoop some food (vegetables, rice) off the plate. Paratha is always fried like a pancake, and poori is always deep-fried, so limit these. Chappatti is commonly served at every meal in India, especially lunch and dinner, and it is nonfat if ghee is not spread onto it. Bread items on the menu that end in "roti" or "nan" are lowfat if they are roasted or baked. Examples include khasta roti, rogini nan, alu nan, onion nan, and garlic nan.

Q: I expected choices in the vegetables section of the Indian menu to be low in fat, but they all seem to be prepared with high fat ingredients. What do you suggest I order from this section?

A: You are right - most of the menu listings in the vegetables section at Indian restaurants *are* high in fat. Most have butter or creamy sauces added. If you are dining with a group, you might consider ordering a few vegetable dishes and sharing them. Ask that extra fat not be added to the food. Sometimes ghee is added while the food is being heated. For instance, if you order dahl, ask that ghee not be added to it. Avoid the vegetable dishes that are fixed with cream sauces. Ask for lots of basmati rice with the vegetable dishes you do order. Also, kachumbar salad - raw, chopped vegetables - is a good choice for a side dish. Raita, a yogurt and vegetable blend, is also okay as a side dish. If you order an appetizer and bread that are not fried, and get rice with the meal, then combining a vegetable dish with all of this can still result in a meal that is fairly low in fat overall.

Q: I love the smell and taste of Indian food, but my stomach usually rebels. Can the spices be altered somewhat when I order my food so that I can tolerate it better?

A: Many people who are not used to Indian cooking find the food to be very spicy. Most Indian restaurants can adjust the level of spiciness to suit individual preferences. Just ask your waiter to make the food more mild for you.

Q: If I decide to order dessert, what is the best choice?

A: You can always go with a cup of hot tea and an order of some type of exotic fruit, if available. Otherwise, the standard dessert selections tend to be high in fat, although some are better choices than others. Gulab jamun is a common Indian dessert. It's something like a deep-fried donut hole served in a little cup of syrup. It's very high in fat. Ras gulla would be lower in fat. Ras gulla is a panir (cheeselike food) rolled into round balls and cooked in syrup. Chum chum is similar - like panir in a sugar syrup. Gajar kahalwa is a carrot pudding with raisins and almonds. This or badami kheer, a rice pudding blended with almonds and raisins, would be lower in fat than most other desserts.

 # Chinese

<u>Menu Magic</u>

Does this look like a typical vegetarian meal for you at a Chinese restaurant?

2 egg rolls with mustard and plum sauce
1 cup of vegetable soup
3/4 cup Chinese fried noodles
Bean curd (6 ounces) family-style with vegetables
3/4 cup steamed rice
Hot tea and 1 fortune cookie

The meal above contains 35 grams of fat and 1,295 calories. But with a few simple changes, a lower fat menu results. **Replace the greasy egg rolls with steamed dumplings, pass on the fried noodles, ask for a smaller portion of bean curd, and a serving of steamed or stir-fried Chinese greens.**

(Note: the simple changes made to reduce fat are in bold.)

2 steamed dumplings with soy sauce
*1 cup vegetable soup **(skip the fried noodles)***
***3 ounces** bean curd family-style with vegetables*
***1 cup** steamed rice*
Hot tea and 1 fortune cookie

Now the meal is not only more interesting, it also contains 20 fewer grams of fat and 830 fewer calories. And it contains more fiber, vitamins, and minerals, too.

These menus also show how simple changes can cut way back on the fat content of a single meal:

#1 **Before:**		**After:**	
1 cup vegetable soup		1 cup vegetable soup	
1/2 cup fried noodles		*(pass on the fried noodles)*	
6 ounces fried gluten with		*3 ounces* fried gluten with	
sweet and sour sauce and		sweet and sour sauce and	
1/2 cup mixed Chinese vegetables		*1 cup* mixed Chinese vegetables	
1/2 cup steamed rice		*1 cup* steamed rice	
Hot tea		Hot tea	
Fortune cookie		Fortune cookie	
Calories (Kcal):	568	Calories (Kcal):	481
Fat (grams):	21	Fat (grams):	8
Protein (grams):	22	Protein (grams):	16
Carbohydrate (grams):	75	Carbohydrate (grams):	83
Calcium (mg):	369	Calcium (mg):	243
Iron (mg):	6	Iron (mg):	6
Dietary fiber (grams):	8	Dietary fiber (grams):	9

Chinese Examples:

#2   Before: **After:**

1 cup hot and sour soup   1 cup hot and sour soup
12 ounces seasoned rice   *Half order* (share with friend)
  with raisins, cashews   seasoned rice with raisins,
  and peanut sauce   cashews, and *2 T peanut*
                                  sauce, on the side
                                1/2 cup steamed greens
Chilled fruit salad   Chilled fruit salad
Hot tea   Hot tea

Calories (Kcal):   700   Calories (Kcal):   407
Fat (grams):   26   Fat (grams):   14
Protein (grams):   23   Protein (grams):   17
Carbohydrate (grams):   98   Carbohydrate (grams):   57
Calcium (mg):   70   Calcium (mg):   166
Iron (mg):   5   Iron (mg):   6
Dietary fiber (grams):   9   Dietary fiber (grams):   8

Chinese Examples:

#3

Before:	After:
Small green salad with spicy hot vinaigrette dressing	Small green salad with spicy hot vinaigrette dressing
2 vegetarian egg rolls with mustard and plum sauce	*1 vegetarian egg roll* with mustard and plum sauce
10 ounces vegetable fried rice	*Half order vegetable fried rice (share with a friend)*
	Half order mixed Chinese vegetables (share with a friend)
	1/2 cup steamed rice
Hot tea	Hot tea
Fortune cookie	Fortune cookie

	Before		After
Calories (Kcal):	1034	Calories (Kcal):	753
Fat (grams):	33	Fat (grams):	24
Protein (grams):	27	Protein (grams):	19
Carbohydrate (grams):	139	Carbohydrate (grams):	108
Calcium (mg):	55	Calcium (mg):	124
Iron (mg):	4	Iron (mg):	5
Dietary fiber (grams):	5	Dietary fiber (grams):	7

Chinese Examples:

#4   Before:

2 vegetarian egg rolls with
  mustard and plum sauce
Szechuan bean curd
  (6 ounces) with vegetables

Broccoli with garlic sauce
1 cup steamed rice
Hot tea
Fortune cookie

Calories (Kcal):	1088
Fat (grams):	27
Protein (grams):	45
Carbohydrate (grams):	163
Calcium (mg):	559
Iron (mg):	9
Dietary fiber (grams):	11

After:

1 cup vegetable soup
2 vegetable pot stickers
Szechuan bean curd *(ask for*
  half the usual amount of
  bean curd) with mixed
  vegetables
Broccoli with garlic sauce
1-1/2 cups steamed rice
Hot tea
Fortune cookie

Calories (Kcal):	914
Fat (grams):	14
Protein (grams):	33
Carbohydrate (grams):	155
Calcium (mg):	444
Iron (mg):	9
Dietary fiber (grams):	14

SIMPLE, LOWFAT & VEGETARIAN

Good Choices Include:	Limit:
Vegetable soups	Egg rolls
Spring rolls (lower in fat than	Bean curd
regular egg rolls)	Peanut sauce
Pot stickers (steamed vegetable dumplings)	Egg foo yung
Chinese salads	(egg dishes)
Mixed Chinese vegetables	Americanized
Sautéed broccoli	menu items
Broccoli with garlic sauce	Fried noodles
Sautéed snow peas	Nuts (in Kung Pao
Steamed greens	dishes with peanuts
Steamed rice	or sweet and
Vegetable lo mein (soft noodles)	sour walnuts)
Mustard	Fried rice
Soy sauce	American desserts
Plum sauce	such as ice cream
Fresh fruit	Deep fried items

Fat Content of Selected Items

Vegetables (broccoli, snow peas,
  water chestnuts, carrots, bok choy) .... 0 grams
Soft noodles (lo mein) 1 cup .... 2 grams
Steamed rice 1/2 cup .... 0 grams
Bean curd, 4 ounces .... 5 grams
Egg roll, one .... 5+ grams
Fried noodles, 1 cup .... 11 grams

HELPFUL HINTS

• Watch out for deep-fried items such as Chinese noodles (which may be served with soups), or greasy egg rolls.

• Bean curd is moderately high in fat. Order bean curd dishes mixed with Chinese vegetables, where the bean curd is a minor ingredient. You can also request less or smaller pieces of bean curd in dishes.

• Egg foo yung might be described as a "Chinese-style omelet." Although vegetarian, this dish is moderately high in fat and is high in cholesterol.

• Request that foods be steamed or cooked with only a little oil, if any.

• Eggplant dishes are usually oily. Like other high fat choices, it may be better to share this one; make a lower fat dish the largest part of the meal.

Chinese-style restaurants almost never disappoint when it comes to offering lowfat menu options. In fact, the trouble can be in deciding which of the many good choices to order. Many dishes can also be altered slightly to suit individual tastes. Some people request that the flavor-enhancing additive, monosodium glutamate (MSG) be omitted from their dish. Traditional Chinese food is usually healthful, because it focuses on vegetables and rice, includes no dairy, and if meat is added, it is added in tiny amounts, as a condiment or a minor ingredient. The result is high fiber, lowfat cuisine. Note the "words of wisdom" in this chapter, and you won't go wrong when you go Chinese.

Questions and Answers:

Q: Which Chinese entrees are the highest in fat?

A: The higher fat menu choices are actually apt to be the "Americanized" foods - learn to recognize them. Most of these dishes are meat-based, such as pepper steak, sweet-and-sour shrimp, and other foods that focus on meat and seafood (especially fried). These are not good choices. If some items are unfamiliar to you, ask your waiter to describe them. You are looking for mixtures of vegetables that are usually served with steamed rice.

Q: Are Chinese soups low in fat?

A: Chinese restaurants offer a wide variety of soups made with Chinese vegetables and a clear broth. These are often served family-style in large bowls, or are offered in large single-serving bowls. They are typically low in fat, delicious, and filling. Ask that eggs be left out. Also, since chicken broth is frequently used in soups, be sure to explain to the waiter that you want only vegetable broth. Wonton soup, higher in fat, is also made with a clear broth. However, the wontons - Chinese-style dumplings - are usually filled with meat.

Q: What can you tell me about other Oriental restaurants, such as Thai and Vietnamese?

A: Like Chinese restaurants, Thai and Vietnamese restaurants also offer some good menu choices. Again, be aware of high fat ingredients or cooking methods which may be used in some dishes. Limit peanut sauce, and ask that eggs be left out. Coconut milk, which is high in fat, is used as a base in many Southeast Asian curries and Thai soups. Vegetable-based dishes, with a minimum of fat added, are the best bet and are delicious.

Q: So many of the menu items are new to me. Do you have any suggestions for newcomers?

A: A great way to experiment with Chinese food is to eat out with a group. Order several dishes and share, family-style. Not only is it fun to try different dishes, but sharing can take some of the risk out of ordering something new, like a spicy Szechuan-style dish. Also, if a higher fat item is ordered, such as fried gluten or bean curd, everyone can have a little without making it the entire meal. Instead, lower fat vegetable dishes can make up most of the meal. If it's just you or you and a friend eating out, remember this: experimenting with anything new entails some risk, but if it opens up new horizons or introduces you to a new favorite food, it will be worth it. Along the way, you'll find some duds, but you'll find some gems, too - it's all part of the experience!

 # Cafeterias

Menu Magic

After a walk through the cafeteria line, does your tray look like this?

> *Tossed salad with ranch dressing*
> *8 ounces vegetable lasagna*
> *1/2 cup broccoli with cheese sauce*
> *1 cloverleaf roll with 1 pat margarine*
> *1 slice apple pie*
> *Coffee with cream*

This meal totals 66 grams of fat and 1,127 calories. In reality, your tray may actually contain more food than that. Impulse decisions are a hazard at cafeterias, and most people feel compelled to eat everything they take, even if it means overeating. Instead, plan what you will take before walking through the line. If you do, your tray can look like this:

> *Tossed salad with **2 T of ranch dressing, on the side***
> ***Vegetable plate:** 1/2 cup pinto beans, 1/2 cup*
> *   broccoli **(no cheese)**, 1/2 cup parslied new potatoes*
> *1 cloverleaf roll **(skip the butter)***
> ***Fresh fruit salad***
> *Coffee with cream*

A meal like this one, while not totally free of added fats, still saves you at least 37 grams of fat and 368 calories. Can't resist dessert? Split one with a friend.

Once again, employing some "cafeteria strategies" and making some simple changes makes these menus healthier:

#1 Before:	**After:**
Tossed salad with 4 T Thousand Island dressing	Tossed salad *with 2 T Thousand Island dressing*
1 slice spinach-cheese quiche	*1/2 cup pinto beans*
1/2 cup parslied potatoes cooked in butter	1/2 cup parslied potatoes cooked in butter
1/2 cup broccoli with cheese sauce	1/2 cup broccoli *(ask for pieces without sauce)*
1 roll with butter	1 roll *(no butter)*
	1/2 cup mixed melon salad
1 cup coffee with cream and sugar	1 cup coffee with cream and sugar

Before		After	
Calories (Kcal):	1443	Calories (Kcal):	508
Fat (grams):	86	Fat (grams):	19
Protein (grams):	46	Protein (grams):	11
Carbohydrate (grams):	122	Carbohydrate (grams):	77
Calcium (mg):	422	Calcium (mg):	203
Iron (mg):	6	Iron (mg):	4
Dietary fiber (grams):	7	Dietary fiber (grams):	9

Cafeteria Examples:

#2   **Before:**

Mixed fruit salad
Vegetable lasagna

1/2 cup steamed green beans
1/2 cup home-fried potatoes

1 roll with a pat of butter
1 slice Boston cream pie

Water

Calories (Kcal):	1088
Fat (grams):	52
Protein (grams):	26
Carbohydrate (grams):	133
Calcium (mg):	112
Iron (mg):	4
Dietary fiber (grams):	9

After:

Mixed fruit salad
Vegetable lasagna *(split
     with a companion)*

1/2 cup steamed green beans
1/2 of a large baked potato
1/2 cup cooked carrots
1 roll *(no butter)*
1 slice Boston cream pie
     (split with a companion)

Water

Calories (Kcal):	798
Fat (grams):	22
Protein (grams):	17
Carbohydrate (grams):	105
Calcium (mg):	108
Iron (mg):	4
Dietary fiber (grams):	9

Cafeteria Examples:

#3 Before:	After:
Tossed salad with 4 T Italian dressing	Tossed salad *topped with marinated tomato/cucumber salad*
Vegetable plate with: 1/2 cup broccoli with cheese sauce, 1/2 cup seasoned pinto beans, 1/2 cup macaroni and cheese, and half of a twice-baked potato	Vegetable plate with: 1/2 cup broccoli with cheese sauce and 1/2 cup pinto beans *1/2 cup mashed potatoes* *Fresh strawberries and bananas*
1 bran muffin with a pat of margarine	1 bran muffin *(no butter)*
Water	Water

Before		After	
Calories (Kcal):	990	Calories (Kcal):	721
Fat (grams):	62	Fat (grams):	27
Protein (grams):	29	Protein (grams):	16
Carbohydrate (grams):	79	Carbohydrate (grams):	76
Calcium (mg):	695	Calcium (mg):	360
Iron (mg):	4	Iron (mg):	5
Dietary fiber (grams):	9	Dietary fiber (grams):	11

Cafeteria Examples:

#4 <u>Before:</u>

Mixed green salad with
  2 T French dressing
1-1/2 cups spaghetti with
  tomato sauce
1 T grated Parmesan cheese
3 broccoli spears with 1 tsp butter

2 slices buttered garlic bread
1 slice chocolate cake
Water

Calories (Kcal):	1015
Fat (grams):	37
Protein (grams):	24
Carbohydrate (grams):	148
Calcium (mg):	272
Iron (mg):	7
Dietary fiber (grams):	11

<u>After:</u>

Mixed green salad *with*
  2 T "diet" dressing
1-1/2 cups spaghetti
  with tomato sauce
1 T grated Parmesan cheese
3 broccoli spears *with*
  lemon juice (no butter)
1 large hard roll (no butter)
1 slice chocolate cake
Water

Calories (Kcal):	793
Fat (grams):	17
Protein (grams):	23
Carbohydrate (grams):	141
Calcium (mg):	281
Iron (mg):	7
Dietary fiber (grams):	10

25

Good Choices Include:

Fresh vegetable salads
Fresh fruits and fruit salads
Fruit juices
Steamed rice
Boiled or baked potatoes
Noodles
Steamed vegetables
Lowfat breads, crackers, or
bread sticks
Lemon juice and vinegar for salads
and vegetables

Limit:

Mayonnaise-laden salads
Fried potatoes or
cheese-laden potatoes
Macaroni and cheese
Cheese sauces
Greasy breads
Margarine, butter pats
Regular salad dressings
Most casseroles, cheese-
topped pasta dishes
Rich desserts

Fat Content of Selected Items:

Yeast roll .... 3 grams
Macaroni and cheese, 6 ounces .... 19 grams
Cheese sauce, 2 Tablespoons .... 2 grams
Apple pie, 1 slice .... 14 grams
Chocolate cream pie, 1 slice .... 15 grams
Chocolate cake, 1 slice .... 10 grams
Margarine pat, one .... 5 grams
Boiled potatoes, 1/2 cup .... 0 grams
Steamed vegetables, plain .... 0 grams
Fruit salad .... 0 grams

SIMPLE, LOWFAT & VEGETARIAN

Some unique strategies need to be applied when dining in cafeterias. Due to their design, cafeteria (or buffet) lines offer more opportunity for impulse choices than any other type of restaurant. Good cafeteria managers know this. Desserts and other "extras" are often placed at the front of the line, where hungry diners are likely to pick them up before deciding on an entree. By the time a person passes the dessert and salads sections, their tray is not likely to be empty. The entrees are usually situated next, and a variety of vegetables and other hot side dishes such as rice, noodles, and potatoes follow. Breads and beverages usually bring up the rear and by this time a tray can be loaded with more than the diner could ever eat. Needless to say, this type of environment can encourage overeating, and many of the food items are likely to be high in fat.

HELPFUL HINTS

• Split an entree with a companion and have a salad or vegetable along with it.

• If desserts are irresistible, share one.

• Apply the "grease test" to breads. If muffins, biscuits, rolls or other breads leave shiny, oily-looking spots on doilies, trays, or napkins, they are probably high in fat.

• Margarine and butter pats are often sold individually near the bread section of the line. Leave them off the tray entirely, or limit yourself to one.

• Limit the amount of salad dressing you take. Some people carry fat-free dressings from home.

HELPFUL HINTS

• Some people also like to carry butter substitutes from home, such as Molly McButter or other brands.

• Fresh fruit may be found with the salads and is a good choice for dessert.

• Remember to resist the temptation to take too much. If in doubt, leave it. Hunger can make people choose impulsively!

Questions and Answers

Q: I usually have good intentions when I visit the cafeteria, but my tray always seems to end up loaded down with more than I need to eat. What can I do to gain a little control?

A: Planning ahead helps out a lot at cafeterias. It's always a good idea to survey the cafeteria line first, before you walk through with your tray. Since almost everything may look good (especially if you are hungry), decide ahead of time what you will actually take, then go ahead and walk through.

Q: Many times I just order a vegetable plate at the cafeteria. Is that a good choice?

A: Some cafeterias offer the option of a vegetable plate, even if it's not actually posted as a menu choice. A vegetable plate, which may consist of three or four different vegetables or other side dishes, can be low or high in fat - it all depends upon which items you choose. For instance, cheese sauce on broccoli, fried vegetables, or "twice-baked" and other cheese-laden potatoes are all high in fat. Macaroni and cheese is often counted as a "vegetable" and is very high in fat. On the other hand, steamed rice and baked potatoes are good choices. As far as the other vegetables go, some may be cooked in oil or margarine, but the amount of fat is likely to be much less than an entree would contain.

Q: It seems as though most of the cafeteria entrees are high in fat - either meat-based or made with lots of cheese or rich sauces. What can I eat if I am tired of asking for vegetable plates?

A: It's true that many cafeteria entrees are high in fat. Meat and cheese are the usual culprits. Some types of grain-and-vegetable casseroles or bean-containing soups or chili may be available in some places, but this is unusual in standard cafeterias. Many cafeterias offer a variety of fresh salads - fruit salads and different kinds of vegetable salads. If some of them look good (and aren't swimming in mayonnaise), consider taking two or three and some bread, and make that your meal. Likewise, a few side dishes may be enough. No rule says you must take an entree.

Amusement Parks

Menu Magic

Here's what a typical day's "nourishment" at an amusement park probably looks like for most people (without dinner):

> *1 ice cream bar*
> *12 ounces of cola drink*
> *1 slice cheese pizza*
> *1 order of French fries (about 15 fries)*
> *12 ounces of lemonade*
> *Bag of snack chips*
> *Another 12 ounces of cola drink*

The example above totals about 36 grams of fat, 1,127 calories, and little else besides simple sugar. With some planning and shopping around, however, the picture might look like this instead:

(Note: the simple changes made to reduce fat are in bold.)

> ***1 apple (brought from home)***
> ***3 cups (small bag) popcorn (no extra butter added)***
> ***Water***
> *1 slice cheese pizza **(if available cheeseless, have 2-3 pieces)***

Frozen fruit bar
6 ounces fruit juice
Another bag of popcorn
12 ounces of cola (better yet, have fruit juice)

With about 10 grams of fat and 611 calories, this example of amusement park dining is a realistic alternative. It may be possible to do better if more food is carried from home or if the park is large enough to offer more lowfat options. On the other hand, impulse choices and lack of planning could result in fat intakes that are much higher.

By making simple substitutions, or by increasing the lowfat foods and decreasing the high fat foods, the fat content of these amusement park snacks can be substantially lowered:

#1 Before:		After:	
Milkshake		**Large soft drink or juice**	
French fries		French fries	
Calories (Kcal):	608	Calories (Kcal):	491
Fat (grams):	18	Fat (grams):	10
Protein (grams):	13	Protein (grams):	4
Carbohydrate (grams):	102	Carbohydrate (grams):	96
Calcium (mg):	405	Calcium (mg):	27
Iron (mg):	2	Iron (mg):	2
Dietary fiber (grams):	5	Dietary fiber (grams):	4

Amusement Park Examples:

#2   Before: After:

Milkshake   Milkshake
French fries   *Soft pretzel with mustard*

	Before		After
Calories (Kcal):	608	Calories (Kcal):	536
Fat (grams):	18	Fat (grams):	12
Protein (grams):	13	Protein (grams):	13
Carbohydrate (grams):	102	Carbohydrate (grams):	94
Calcium (mg):	405	Calcium (mg):	446
Iron (mg):	2	Iron (mg):	3
Dietary fiber (grams):	5	Dietary fiber (grams):	3

#3   Before: After:

2 slices cheese pizza   2 slices cheese pizza
Nacho chips with cheese sauce & chilies *Candy apple*
Soft drink   Soft drink

	Before		After
Calories (Kcal):	866	Calories (Kcal):	711
Fat (grams):	28	Fat (grams):	10
Protein (grams):	29	Protein (grams):	22
Carbohydrate (grams):	129	Carbohydrate (grams):	141
Calcium (mg):	288	Calcium (mg):	136
Iron (mg):	3	Iron (mg):	2
Dietary fiber (grams):	2	Dietary fiber (grams):	3

Amusement Park Examples:

#4   Before:

1 slice cheese pizza
Bag of potato chips
Ice cream cone (one scoop)
Soft drink

Calories (Kcal):	592
Fat (grams):	24
Protein (grams):	10
Carbohydrate (grams):	85
Calcium (mg):	185
Iron (mg):	1
Dietary fiber (grams):	0

After:

1 slice cheese pizza
Bag of potato chips
Frozen fruit bar
Soft drink

Calories (Kcal):	473
Fat (grams):	13
Protein (grams):	8
Carbohydrate (grams):	83
Calcium (mg):	116
Iron (mg):	1
Dietary fiber (grams):	0

Good Choices Include:	Limit:
Unbuttered popcorn	Fried foods such as
Corn-on-the-cob	French fries
Cold drinks	Deep fried foods such
Frozen fruit bars	as funnel cakes
Fruit-flavored slushes	Ice cream
Take-alongs: fresh fruit,	Snack chips
boxes of raisins, graham	Nuts
crackers, and other lowfat,	Rich sweets such as
portable snacks from home	pies and candy bars
The best of the worst: candy	Caramel apples
apples, cotton candy, sno-cones	Nachos

Fat Content of Selected Items:

Buttered popcorn, 3 cups .... 6 grams
Unbuttered popcorn, 3 cups .... 0 grams
Frozen fruit bar .... 0 grams
Ice cream, 1/2 cup .... 12 grams
Peanuts, 1/4 cup .... 18 grams
Potato chips, 1 ounce (about 15 - 20 chips)...................... 10 grams
French fries, 10 .... 15 grams
Caramel apple .... 6 grams
Candy apple .... 0 grams
Cotton candy, one bag .... 0 grams

Amusement parks. Enter the world of corn dogs and cotton candy. At least the latter is fat-free. In the broadest sense, amusement parks can take many forms, from the neighborhood traveling carnival or county fair to the huge, permanent state-of-the-art theme parks across the country, such as Disney World or Six Flags. The smaller, old-time carnivals may offer little in the way of food besides the traditional snacks: candy apples, corn dogs, and popcorn, for instance. The larger establishments offer not only the expected fare, but a variety of ethnic spin-offs and other snacks, as well as full-service cafeterias and restaurants of all types. In fact, some of the restaurant offerings at Disney's Epcot Center in Orlando, Florida rival that of many cities for their diversity, authenticity, and quality.

So, amusement park dining experiences can vary a great deal. In some of the larger places that have cafeterias and restaurants, advice given in previous sections for ethnic and American restaurants and cafeterias may apply. For the others, and for some advice about amusement parks in general, try some of the following suggestions:

HELPFUL HINTS

• Carry along some fresh fruit from home, small boxes of raisins, or a few graham crackers or other lowfat, portable snacks for a mid-morning pick-me-up or a bite for later on.

• Lemonade, soft drinks, and other non-alcoholic beverages may be worthwhile if fruit juices and water are not available or convenient. Fluids are particularly important on hot days, and most are fat-free.

• Frozen fruit bars may be available in some places. A vendor selling cold chunks of fresh pineapple was spotted at Disney World in Orlando, Florida.... and MGM Studios has vendor carts selling fresh fruit!

• Disney World offers the option of a clump of grapes in lieu of the French fries that usually accompany some sandwich selections.

Questions and Answers

Q: My kids want to start snacking as soon as we get to the park, and there are so few healthy choices. What do you suggest I do?

A: If you are making the amusement park a day trip, start out by eating a good breakfast - not one that is high in fat, but one that is nutritious and will get you off on the right foot. Encourage kids to eat a good breakfast, too, and they may not be hungry for junky snacks as quickly. Whole grain cereals, toast or English muffins, and fresh fruits and juices are good breakfast choices. Then, take some fresh or dried fruit along from home for snacks, or other portable, nonperishable lowfat snacks like graham crackers or bagels. Even oatmeal cookies (made at home with less fat) may be a better snack than some amusement park fare.

Q: Some of the bigger parks offer a fair variety of food choices now. However, I have trouble deciding what to eat when I am at the smaller, carnival-type parks. What should I do when the choices are extremely limited?

A: At smaller amusement parks or carnivals, the best of the worst of the choices may be some of the sweets that are lowest in fat, such as cotton candy, sno-cones and slushes, and candy apples (not caramel). Popcorn is also a good choice; try to get it unbuttered. Avoid snack chips and French fries, and deep-fried foods like funnel cakes.

All-American

Menu Magic

The scene is lunch hour, mid-week, at a neighborhood restaurant. Your order looks something like this:

> *Tossed salad with Thousand Island dressing*
> *Grilled cheese sandwich on rye*
> *French fries with catsup*
> *Soft drink*

It's a quick "all-American" lunch during a busy work week at any of a number of typical American restaurants. What's also typical is that it's loaded with fat - about 55 grams - and contains about 1,000 calories.

By making simple changes, like **selecting a lowfat or fat-free salad dressing, choosing a toasted cheese sandwich instead of grilled cheese (hold the mayonnaise), and either leaving off half of the fries or replacing them with a baked potato with catsup**, this lower fat meal results:

(Note: the simple changes made to reduce fat are in bold.)

Tossed salad with **vinegar and oil (ask for dressing on the side so you can control the amount of oil)**
Toasted cheese, lettuce, and tomato sandwich on rye, with mustard
Baked potato with catsup
Soft drink

This version contains less than 30 grams of fat and about 800 calories.

Notice in the menus below how just a few simple changes can substantially lower the fat content of these meals, while still allowing favorite foods to have a place on the plate:

#1 **Before:**		**After:**	
Belgian waffle with whipped cream, sliced strawberries, and maple syrup		Belgian waffle *(omit the whipped cream)* **with extra strawberries** and maple syrup	
Large orange juice		Large orange juice	
Coffee (2 cups) with cream and sugar		Coffee (2 cups) *with skim milk* and sugar	
Calories (Kcal):	1022	Calories (Kcal):	853
Fat (grams):	45	Fat (grams):	26
Protein (grams):	18	Protein (grams):	17
Carbohydrate (grams):	138	Carbohydrate (grams):	140
Calcium (mg):	420	Calcium (mg):	398
Iron (mg):	6	Iron (mg):	6
Dietary fiber (grams):	5	Dietary fiber (grams):	6

All-American Examples:

#2 Before:

Three-cheese hoagie with onions, lettuce, tomatoes, vinegar, oil, and crushed red pepper

1/2 cup coleslaw
Handful of potato chips
Soft drink

Calories (Kcal):	1192
Fat (grams):	54
Protein (grams):	34
Carbohydrate (grams):	141
Calcium (mg):	773
Iron (mg):	4
Dietary fiber (grams):	1

After:

Three-cheese hoagie *(cut the amount of cheese in half)* with onions, lettuce, tomatoes, vinegar *(skip the oil)*, and crushed red pepper
1/2 cup coleslaw
Dill pickle spear
Soft drink

Calories (Kcal):	769
Fat (grams):	18
Protein (grams):	24
Carbohydrate (grams):	126
Calcium (mg):	445
Iron (mg):	4
Dietary fiber (grams):	1

All-American Examples:

#3a Before: **After:**

Small orange juice   Small orange juice
Cheese omelet   *1 scrambled egg on toast*
2/3 cup hash browns   2/3 cup hash browns
2 slices toast with butter and jelly 1 slice toast with jelly
                                        (no butter)

Coffee (2 cups) with   Coffee (2 cups) *with*
  cream and sugar   *skim milk* and sugar

Calories (Kcal):	1084	Calories (Kcal):	572
Fat (grams):	64	Fat (grams):	19
Protein (grams):	39	Protein (grams):	15
Carbohydrate (grams):	91	Carbohydrate (grams):	88
Calcium (mg):	559	Calcium (mg):	152
Iron (mg):	5	Iron (mg):	4
Dietary fiber (grams):	3	Dietary fiber (grams):	2

All-American Examples:

#3b **Before:**   **After:**

Small orange juice   Small orange juice
Cheese omelet   Cheese omelet *(made with*
2/3 cup hash browns   *egg substitute, available at*
                                   many restaurants now) split
                                   with a companion

2 slices toast with butter   2 slices toast with jelly *(skip*
  and jelly   *the butter)*
                                Sliced fresh melon (instead
                                   of hash browns)

Coffee (2 cups) with cream   Coffee (2 cups) with cream
  and sugar   and sugar

Calories (Kcal) :	1084		Calories :	610
Fat (grams) :	64		Fat (grams) :	20
Protein (grams) :	39		Protein (grams) :	24
Carbohydrate (grams) :	91		Carbohydrate (grams) :	87
Calcium (mg) :	559		Calcium (mg) :	656
Iron (mg) :	5		Iron (mg) :	4
Dietary fiber (grams) :	3		Dietary fiber (grams) :	3

All-American Examples:

#4 Before:

Meatless Reuben sandwich
(grilled Swiss cheese,
sauerkraut, and Thousand
Island dressing on rye)

French fries
Coleslaw
Iced tea

Calories (Kcal):	849
Fat (grams):	48
Protein (grams):	26
Carbohydrate (grams):	81
Calcium (mg):	656
Iron (mg):	5
Dietary fiber (grams):	8

After:

Toasted meatless Reuben
sandwich (sauerkraut and
Thousand Island dressing on
rye, but *ask for half of the
usual amount of cheese*)
Baked potato with catsup
Coleslaw
Iced tea

Calories (Kcal):	593
Fat (grams):	23
Protein (grams):	17
Carbohydrate (grams):	83
Calcium (mg):	386
Iron (mg):	4
Dietary fiber (grams):	8

Good Choices Include:	Limit:
Cooked and dry cereals	Fried foods
Plain breads, including pita	Mayonnaise
pockets, whole wheat, rye,	Regular salad dressings
bagels, hoagie rolls, and	Margarine, butter
English muffins	Cream cheese
Fresh fruits and vegetables	Sour cream
Fruit juices	Cream soups
Vegetable sandwiches	Grilled sandwiches
Vegetable plates	French fries, chips
Baked potatoes	Fried hash browns
Rice, steamed	Cream sauces
Noodles	Cheese
Salads (without fatty ingredients)	Creamy coleslaw or
Mustard	potato salad
Fat-Free salad dressings	Egg salad
Salsa	Biscuits
	Rich desserts

Fat Content of Selected Items:

Grilled cheese sandwich	31 grams
Egg salad sandwich	15+ grams
Potato salad, 1/2 cup	15+ grams
French fries, approx. 10	15 grams
Potato chips, 1 ounce	10 grams
Cream of tomato soup, 8 ounces	6 grams
Vegetable soup, 8 ounces	0 grams
Baked potato, plain	0 grams
English muffin, plain	0 grams

Neighborhood "greasy spoons," diners, many chain or family restaurants, and your favorite breakfast place probably all fall into the category of "All-American." These eating establishments have one thing in common: they serve traditional American fare. The scope of the menu probably does not include much in the way of ethnic food choices; instead burgers and fries are the mainstay.

It may take some skill to avoid the pitfalls in restaurants such as these, where almost every order may be accompanied by a heap of French fries or a handful of chips. Some places may be more limited than others in menu options. Ask to see a menu before you are seated, and scan it to see if there are some acceptable items or some choices that may be able to be modified for you. Be creative.

HELPFUL HINTS

• Good breakfast choices include English muffins, bagels, and toast. Order a double serving of one or an assortment of all, if you want a larger meal. Avoid or limit margarine or cream cheese and use more jelly instead.

• For breakfast, splurge on fresh-squeezed fruit juice and fresh fruit. Cooked and dry cereals are good choices. If you do not use milk, try apple or orange juice on your cereal.

• Split an entree with a friend. With soup, salad, or a baked potato, you may find the portion size is just right.

• Try a veggie pita pocket sandwich, and add a little diet Italian dressing. If pita bread is unavailable, ask for a hoagie roll. Limit or avoid cheese and avocado.

HELPFUL HINTS

• Restaurants always have lettuce and tomatoes. Ask for a lettuce and tomato sandwich on whole wheat toast or a Kaiser roll. Add mustard or salsa, if available, instead of mayonnaise.

• Fruit or a hot drink can be a good dessert choice instead of high fat sweets like pie and cake.

• Avoid fried foods - hash browns, grilled sandwiches, and deep fried items such as zucchini sticks, French fries, and onion rings.

• Choose fresh foods like baked potatoes and fresh fruits and vegetables. If chips come with a meal, ask for a fresh fruit replacement or just ask that they be left off your plate.

Questions and Answers

Q: Are there some simple ways that I can cut back on the fat in some of my favorite sandwiches?

A: Sure - some traditional sandwiches (and even salads) can be improved in the fat department by cutting back on cheese and added fats such as mayonnaise and dressings. For instance, swap half of the cheese in a grilled cheese sandwich for tomato slices, or try the sandwich toasted instead of grilled. Order a meatless Reuben sandwich, but ask for less cheese and extra sauerkraut. Order the dressing on the side, too, and add it to the sandwich yourself with a light hand.

Q: What are some other ways that I can get creative with the menu at an "All-American" style restaurant?

A: Vegetable plates can be delicious. If cooked or raw vegetables are on the menu as side dishes or as a part of a meal, ask for a variety of whatever is available. Avoid items that are mixed with mayonnaise, like most coleslaws, or those that have significant amounts of other fatty ingredients, like au gratin potatoes. However, even if a little margarine has been added to some cooked vegetables, the fat content of the vegetable plate will probably still be far less than other entrees.

Another idea: there are three items that can almost always be found at a typical American restaurant - soup, baked potatoes, and salads. Any combination of these can be a meal in itself. In fact, at restaurants that serve salad or soup with meals, many people find that after eating these, they don't have as much room as they thought they would for the entree still to come. (See sections on salad and potato bars.) Cream soups are usually high in fat, so broth-based soups are a better bet (vegetarians need to check, though, to see if chicken or beef broth has been used). If you are eating in a group, ask for the salad to be served first and the soup or potato to be served when the others receive their entrees.

Vegetarian & Natural Food

Menu Magic

Lunch at the neighborhood natural foods store could look like this:

> *Veggie burger on a bun with cheese, mayonnaise,*
> *sprouts, lettuce, tomato, and avocado*
> *1/2 cup pasta salad*
> *10 tortilla chips with salsa*
> *Hot tea*

The lunch above contains at least 50 grams of fat and 975 calories. By making simple changes like **"hold the cheese, mayo, and avocado"** and asking for **extra sprouts and tomatoes, and by choosing a lowfat vegetarian soup in place of an oily pasta salad,** this lowfat meal would result:

(Note: the simple changes made to reduce fat are in bold.)

> 1 cup gazpacho (in place of pasta salad)
> Veggie burger on a bun **with sprouts, lettuce, and
>   tomato (skip the cheese and avocado; add catsup
>   and mustard)**
> 10 tortilla chips with salsa
> Hot tea

Now the meal has less than 25 grams of fat and about 680 calories.

The menus below have been altered slightly, by making simple changes, to result in meals that are lower in fat but every bit as delicious:

#1 **Before:**		**After:**	
1 cup meatless chili with grated cheddar cheese and chopped scallions on top		1 cup meatless chili with chopped scallions *(skip the cheese)*	
1/2 cup steamed brown rice		1/2 cup steamed brown rice	
1 cup mixed green salad with 3 T ranch-style dressing		1 cup mixed green salad with *3 T salsa*	
1 corn muffin with butter		1 corn muffin *(skip the butter)*	
Hot tea		Hot tea	
Calories (Kcal):	821	Calories (Kcal):	509
Fat (grams):	36	Fat (grams):	6
Protein (grams):	30	Protein (grams):	22
Carbohydrate (grams):	97	Carbohydrate (grams):	95
Calcium (mg):	352	Calcium (mg):	148
Iron (mg):	7	Iron (mg):	7
Dietary fiber (grams):	16	Dietary fiber (grams):	16

Vegetarian and Natural Food Examples:

#2   Before:

Three cheese sandwich with
   grated carrots, sprouts, lettuce,
   and tomato on Kaiser roll with
   mayonnaise and mustard
Handful tortilla chips with salsa
Cup of black bean soup
   garnished with grated cheese
   and chopped onions
Soft drink

Calories (Kcal):	1274
Fat (grams):	47
Protein (grams):	47
Carbohydrate (grams):	166
Calcium (mg):	932
Iron (mg):	7
Dietary fiber (grams):	3

After:

Sandwich as "Before" but with
*one slice of cheese, skip
the mayo, add extra tomato*

Handful tortilla chips with salsa
Cup of black bean soup
   with chopped onions
   (skip the cheese)
Soft drink

Calories (Kcal):	954
Fat (grams):	21
Protein (grams):	29
Carbohydrate (grams):	163
Calcium (mg):	385
Iron (mg):	7
Dietary fiber (grams):	3

Vegetarian and Natural Food Examples:

#3   Before:

8 ounces vegetable lasagna
  with fresh fruit garnish

1/2 cup marinated vegetable salad
1/2 cup sour cream potato salad

Small loaf multigrain bread
  with butter

Iced tea

Calories (Kcal):	928
Fat (grams):	49
Protein (grams):	25
Carbohydrate (grams):	92
Calcium (mg):	72
Iron (mg):	3
Dietary fiber (grams):	6

After:

Half portion vegetable
  lasagna *(share with a
  companion)* with fresh
  fruit garnish
1/2 cup marinated vegetable
  salad
1/2 cup sour cream potato
  salad
Small loaf multigrain bread
  (skip the butter)
Extra fresh fruit (melon
  and strawberries)
Iced tea

Calories (Kcal):	693
Fat (grams):	29
Protein (grams):	19
Carbohydrate (grams):	87
Calcium (mg):	83
Iron (mg):	3
Dietary fiber (grams):	8

Vegetarian and Natural Food Examples:

#4   Before: **After:**

Mixed green salad with 3 T   Mixed green salad *with 2 T*
  honey-mustard dressing   *honey-mustard dressing,*
Tofu dog on a bun with   *on the side*
  chili and onions   Tofu dog on a bun with chili
                                           and onions
                                         1 cup vegetable soup
Carob and peanut butter   *1 chocolate-mint patty*
  brownie   *(to appease the sweet tooth)*
Hot herbal tea   Hot herbal tea

Calories (Kcal):	604		Calories (Kcal):	576
Fat (grams):	35		Fat (grams):	24
Protein (grams):	19		Protein (grams):	21
Carbohydrate (grams):	56		Carbohydrate (grams):	63
Calcium (mg):	160		Calcium (mg):	187
Iron (mg):	5		Iron (mg):	6
Dietary fiber (grams):	6		Dietary fiber (grams):	6

"Vegetarian" and "natural" don't necessarily translate into "lowfat." In fact, vegetarian, natural food or health food stores and restaurants offer many food items that are high in fat. This is due, in many cases, to liberal amounts of added fats such as oil or tahini, and to the addition of high fat dairy products such as cheese or cream. In other cases, the food items themselves are simply high in fat, such as seeds, nuts, tofu, and avocados. Many convenience items - tofu hot dogs, snack bars, and soy cheeses, for example - are also fatty.

Good Choices Include:

Rice dishes
Pasta dishes without cheese
and with minimal oil added
Lentil soup
Vegetable soup
Meatless chili
Fat free condiments
Fresh vegetable dishes with
minimal fat added
Fresh fruit
Whole grain breads without
added butter or margarine
Fresh salads (fat free)

Limit:

Avocado
Nut butters, tahini
Oil, margarine, butter
Fried foods
Cheese, eggs
Quiche
Cheesy casseroles
Creamy or cheese sauces
Salad dressings, mayonnaise
Sour cream
Cream cheese
Rich desserts
Snack chips
Tofu
Processed soy products

Fat Content of Selected Items:

Avocado, half .... 15 grams
Tahini, 1 tablespoon .... 8 grams
Peanut butter, 1 tablespoon .... 8 grams
Tofu, 2-1/2 by 2-3/4 by 1-inch slice .... 5 grams
Cheddar cheese, 1 ounce (2 tablespoons, 1 slice) .... 8 grams
Cream cheese, 1 ounce (2 tablespoons) .... 10 grams
Quiche, 1/8 of an 8-inch diameter quiche .... 40+ grams
Hummus, 1/4 cup .... 15+ grams

HELPFUL HINTS

- Limit dishes that use cheese as a major ingredient, such as many casseroles and pasta dishes.

- Avoid rich cheese sauces and other creamy sauces (like peanut sauces), unless you know the ingredients are nonfat.

- Some foods, like pasta primavera or some vegetable stir-fries, may have lots of oil added. Ask the cook to go "light on the oil."

- Avoid fried foods.

- On sandwiches, stick with lowfat condiments such as mustard, chutney, or salsa.

- Avocado, popular in salads and on sandwiches, is almost all fat. Eat it sparingly or ask that it not be included at all.

- Margarine, butter, salad dressings, cream, sour cream, and mayonnaise all spell FAT. Since small amounts add up quickly, learn to leave these off your food.

- Flavor foods with mustard, pepper, salt, herbs, vinegar, chutney, salsa, lemon juice, and catsup, for starters.

- Go easy on nut butters, such as peanut and almond butters, and tahini.

HELPFUL HINTS

- Stay away from grilled sandwiches. Ask for sandwiches on hard rolls or toast instead.

- Cream soups are usually high in fat. Stick with vegetable broth soups such as minestrone or lentil.

Questions and Answers

Q: It's difficult for me to guess the fat content of some of the entrees I order at vegetarian restaurants, especially the combination dishes, such as some casseroles, and even some of the sandwiches, such as the veggie burgers. I'm afraid I may be underestimating the amount of fat I'm eating. Do you have any suggestions?

A: Ask the manager if recipes are available for the dishes in question. A quick peek at a recipe may reveal high fat ingredients you might not have known were in there, or you might learn there is considerably more of a high fat ingredient, such as oil, than you might have guessed. Some vegetarian restaurants may actually use recipes out of familiar vegetarian cookbooks, some of which include a nutritional analysis of recipes.

Other menu items may be made with ingredients that come with nutrition labeling on the package. For instance, the restaurant may use ready-made frozen veggie burger patties which may come in a box that lists their fat content.

Movie Theaters

Menu Magic

Is a typical at-the-movies snack for you a large box of buttered popcorn and a soft drink? If so, you may be downing as much as 20 grams of fat, when a simple change - like **taking a smaller box of buttered popcorn and a larger drink** - could cut your fat intake in half. Or simply **ask for unbuttered popcorn**, if it's available, and your snack could be essentially fat-free.

As any weight-watcher will attest, movie theaters are notorious for being cues that trigger the urge to snack. For some, a movie is just not a movie without a barrel of popcorn and a drink. If that sounds like you, then it may be worth giving some consideration to the food choices that confront movie-goers and how to deal with them.

Simple changes in the movie snacks below (even *without* bringing anything from home) result in substantial fat savings:

(Note: the simple changes made to reduce fat are in bold.)

Movie Theater Examples:

#1   Before:

6 cups buttered popcorn
Medium soft drink

Calories (Kcal):	400
Fat (grams):	12
Protein (grams):	6
Carbohydrate (grams):	68
Calcium (mg):	18
Iron (mg):	1
Dietary fiber (grams):	2

After:

6 cups *unbuttered* popcorn
Medium soft drink

Calories (Kcal):	310
Fat (grams):	0
Protein (grams):	6
Carbohydrate (grams):	68
Calcium (mg):	18
Iron (mg):	1
Dietary fiber (grams):	2

#2   Before:

10-cup tub buttered popcorn
Medium soft drink

Calories (Kcal):	560
Fat (grams):	20
Protein (grams):	10
Carbohydrate (grams):	88
Calcium (mg):	22
Iron (mg):	2
Dietary fiber (grams):	4

After:

5-cup bag buttered popcorn
Large soft drink

Calories (Kcal):	439
Fat (grams):	10
Protein (grams):	5
Carbohydrate (grams):	83
Calcium (mg):	23
Iron (mg):	1
Dietary fiber (grams):	2

Movie Theater Examples:

#3   Before: **After:**

2 ounce Butterfinger candy bar   *Hard candies*
Small soft drink   Small soft drink

Calories (Kcal):	390
Fat (grams):	12
Protein (grams):	4
Carbohydrate (grams):	71
Calcium (mg):	not available
Iron (mg):	not available
Dietary fiber (grams):	0

Calories (Kcal):	216
Fat (grams):	0
Protein (grams):	0
Carbohydrate (grams):	54
Calcium (mg):	14
Iron (mg):	1
Dietary fiber (grams):	0

#4   Before: **After:**

1 oz. Peter Paul Mounds bar   *Medium box unbuttered popcorn*

Medium soft drink   Medium soft drink

Calories (Kcal):	309
Fat (grams):	7
Protein (grams):	1
Carbohydrate (grams):	61
Calcium (mg):	not available
Iron (mg):	not available
Dietary fiber (grams):	0

Calories (Kcal):	256
Fat (grams):	0
Protein (grams):	6
Carbohydrate (grams):	56
Calcium (mg):	14
Iron (mg):	1
Dietary fiber (grams):	2

Good Choices Include:

Fresh fruit such as grapes
and cherries (from home)
Dried fruit such as raisins
Graham cookies
Gingersnaps
Unbuttered popcorn
The best of the worst:
        hard candy
        soft drinks
        licorice
        other non-chocolate candies

Limit:

Buttered popcorn
Chocolate and
chocolate-covered
candies
Snack chips

Fat Content of Selected Items:

Raisins	0 grams
Unbuttered popcorn	0 grams
Grapes	0 grams
Licorice	0 grams
Soft drinks	0 grams
Hard candy	0 grams
Reese's peanut butter cups, 1.8 oz	17 grams
Hershey's bar, 1.55 oz	14 grams
Kit Kat bar, 1.6 oz	13 grams
Junior Mints, 1 oz	3 grams
LifeSavers, one roll	0 grams

From a behavioral point of view, snacking at the movies may be simply a conditioned response for some and worthy of intervention from that angle. But for those who do intend to grab a snack at the movies, some choices are better than others. Try some of these ideas:

HELPFUL HINTS

• Carry a snack from home - something convenient to eat in the theater. A bag of cherries or grapes, a box of raisins, or a handful of gingersnaps or "graham animals" are good choices.

• Buy a box or bag of popcorn, but make sure it is unbuttered. If unbuttered popcorn is not available, take a small bag of what is available, but don't add extra butter.

• Bring a butter substitute along and sprinkle it on the unbuttered popcorn.

• Just have a beverage and skip the food.

• Avoid chocolate and chocolate-covered candies.

• Hard candy, licorice, or non-chocolate candies are the best candy choices. Consider carrying a roll or small bag of hard candy from home.

Questions and Answers

Q: I have a hard time resisting the concession counter at the movies, and try as I might, I usually end up taking something that I later wish I hadn't eaten. How can I break the habit of eating at the movies?

A: For many people, eating popcorn or candy at the movies is a tradition that has, over time, become a conditioned response. Just as we associate birthday cake with birthday celebrations, or even a certain time of day with a particular meal, some people have conditioned themselves to expect a snack when they go to the movies.

Reconditioning this behavior might be accomplished a couple of ways. One idea is to eat a meal or snack before leaving home. For instance, have dinner immediately before heading out to the movies, or have a piece of fruit or a bagel (a light snack) before you go. Then, when you arrive at the theater, walk directly to your seat without stopping at the candy counter. Over time, you may begin to disassociate the theater and candy or popcorn.

Another way of dealing with the problem may be to take a roll of hard candy along to the theater and, instead of stopping at the concession stand, avoid it entirely and just eat the hard candy during the movie. Likewise, planning and bringing any lowfat snack from home will give you more control than impulsively choosing something from the concession stand.

School Lunch

Menu Magic

A common sight on school lunch trays is this one:

> *1 slice of pizza (cheese, for vegetarians)*
> *1 serving of Tator Tots*
> *Tossed salad with Thousand Island dressing (some*
> *schools offer reduced-calorie dressings)*
> *1/2 pint of lowfat milk*
> *Slice of chocolate cake*

Not all of the above may be eaten, and it's a good possibility that a candy bar and/or soft drink from the school canteen may replace part of it. However, the meal above contains at least 45 grams of fat and 800 calories.

Or take a look at this real-life example: these two fat-laden menus (with a still-fatty alternate meal available for each) are examples of lunches actually served at a private school in North Carolina.

The Suggested Menu:	**Another Option Offered:**
Sausage Dog with Sautéed Onions	Corn Dog
Steamed Cabbage	Bean Soup
Applesauce	French Fries
Calories (Kcal): 474	Calories (Kcal): 1227
Fat (grams): 30	Fat (grams): 72
% Calories from fat: 57	% Calories from fat: 52

The Suggested Menu:	**Another Option Offered:**
Chicken Nuggets	Fish Sandwich
Green Beans	Onion Rings
Wheat Roll	Cream of Spinach Soup
Calories (Kcal): 903	Calories (Kcal): 1548
Fat (grams): 47	Fat (grams): 93
% Calories from fat: 47	% Calories from fat: 54

Kids can learn to choose wisely at lunchtime. Review weekly school lunch menus at home with your children and plan which meals will be eaten at school and which will be brought from home. An improvement on the earlier pizza meal might look like this:

(Note: the simple changes made to reduce fat are in bold.)

> *1 slice of cheese pizza*
> *1 serving of Tator Tots*
> *Tossed salad with **reduced-calorie dressing***
> ***Flavored seltzer water brought from home***
> *Fresh seasonal fruit brought from home*

The fat content of the meal has been reduced to about 18 grams with 410 calories; the overall nutritional quality of the meal has also been improved, too!

Let's look at some more examples of school lunch makeovers. One note, however, before you read on: You may gasp when you see how high in fat the "modified" menus remain. Remember the promise of this book was to show what an impact just a few simple changes can make in high fat meals - - and you'll see this when you compare the "Befores" with the "Afters." The modified menus that follow are still high in fat by any standards. The problem of fatty school lunches is not an easy one to solve. This issue is addressed again further on in this section.

#1 Before:

Vegetable lasagna
1/2 cup steamed broccoli
  with a pat of margarine
Handful of French fries
  with catsup
1/2 pint whole milk
Ice cream sandwich

Calories (Kcal):	970
Fat (grams):	50
Protein (grams):	30
Carbohydrate (grams):	103
Calcium (mg):	488
Iron (mg):	2
Dietary fiber (grams):	4

After:

Vegetable lasagna
1/2 cup steamed broccoli
  (no margarine)
Handful of French fries
  with catsup
1/2 pint *skim milk*
Apple (from home)

Calories (Kcal):	805
Fat (grams):	31
Protein (grams):	29
Carbohydrate (grams):	109
Calcium (mg):	421
Iron (mg):	3
Dietary fiber (grams):	7

School Lunch Examples:

2   Before:

Grilled cheese sandwich
1/2 cup green beans with
  1 pat of margarine
2/3 cup home fries with catsup
Tossed salad with 2 T
  French dressing
Slice of Devil's food cake

1/2 pint whole milk

Calories (Kcal):	1192
Fat (grams):	71
Protein (grams):	31
Carbohydrate (grams):	113
Calcium (mg):	774
Iron (mg):	5
Dietary fiber (grams):	6

After:

Grilled cheese sandwich
1/2 cup green beans
  with salt and pepper
2/3 cup home fries with catsup
Tossed salad *with 2 T*
  reduced-calorie dressing
Handful of gingersnaps
  (from home)
1/2 pint *skim milk*

Calories (Kcal):	905
Fat (grams):	47
Protein (grams):	30
Carbohydrate (grams):	94
Calcium (mg):	753
Iron (mg):	4
Dietary fiber (grams):	6

School Lunch Examples:

#3 Before:	After:

Before:

Salad bar: lettuce, tomatoes, green pepper slices, cucumber slices, grated carrot, 4 T grated cheddar cheese, 2 T chopped egg, croutons, and 4 T blue cheese dressing

6 saltine crackers
12 oz. cola

Calories (Kcal):	766
Fat (grams):	46
Protein (grams):	17
Carbohydrate (grams):	71
Calcium (mg):	314
Iron (mg):	3
Dietary fiber (grams):	4

After:

Salad bar: lettuce, tomatoes, green pepper slices, cucumber slices, grated carrot, *1/2 cup garbanzo beans (omit the cheese, egg, and croutons)*, and 4 T *reduced-calorie dressing*
Peach (from home)
6 saltine crackers
12 oz. cola

Calories (Kcal):	579
Fat (grams):	12
Protein (grams):	14
Carbohydrate (grams):	109
Calcium (mg):	140
Iron (mg):	5
Dietary fiber (grams):	13

School Lunch Examples:

#4   **Before:**   **After:**

8 oz. macaroni and cheese   *4 oz.* macaroni and cheese
                                         (ask for half portion)

1/2 cup mixed vegetables   *1 cup* mixed vegetables
with 1 pat of margarine   *(ask for double portion)*
Tossed salad with 2 T   *with salt and pepper*
  Italian dressing   *instead of margarine*
Roll   Roll
2 large chocolate chip cookies   2 large chocolate chip cookies
1/2 pint whole milk   *1/2 pint skim milk*

Calories (Kcal):	1092		Calories (Kcal):	831
Fat (grams):	60		Fat (grams):	38
Protein (grams):	32		Protein (grams):	26
Carbohydrate (grams):	109		Carbohydrate (grams):	102
Calcium (mg):	711		Calcium (mg):	562
Iron (mg):	4		Iron (mg):	4
Dietary fiber (grams):	6		Dietary fiber (grams):	7

Good Choices Include:	Limit:
Fresh fruit	Cream cheese
Bagels	Mayonnaise
Fruit juice	Salad dressings
Steamed vegetables	Margarine
Baked potato	Sour cream
Vegetable-broth based soups	Cheese
Pizza with vegetable toppings	French fries
Veggie sandwiches on whole grain	Rich desserts
bread or in pita pockets	Snack chips
Some ethnic options like bean	Ice cream
burritos or stir-fried vegetables	Cheese and egg-rich
over steamed rice	entrees such as
Veggie burger on a bun with extra	macaroni and cheese
lettuce and tomato	or lasagna
Skim milk	Grilled sandwiches
	Fried or deep-fried items
	2% milk and whole milk

School food service personnel have a tough job. Sometimes it seems as if the goals of cost containment, serving nutritious meals, and serving meals that students will like and actually eat are incompatible. So many factors are involved in the difficulty of planning school lunch programs that changes and improvements come about very slowly. While it is acknowledged that everyone has the best interests of the students and school staff at heart, the fact remains that, currently, most school lunches are too high in fat.

Fat Content of Selected Items:

French fries, 10 .... 10 grams
Tortilla chips, 10 .... 10 grams
Bagel, 2 halves .... 0 grams
Cheese pizza, 1 slice .... 5 grams
Macaroni and cheese, 6 ounces .... 19 grams
Bean burrito without cheese .... 2 grams
Bean burrito with cheese .... 10 grams
Grilled cheese sandwich .... 31 grams
Skim milk, 1/2 pint .... 0 grams
2% milk, 1/2 pint .... 5 grams
Whole milk, 1/2 pint .... 8 grams

Obesity is a major public health problem for school age children in this country. Children, parents, and teachers alike worry about getting meals at school that are palatable, yet health-supporting. Dealing with what is available is a big hurdle to overcome. Just as schools vary in size, they vary in the number of food choices available to students and staff. Some school districts have made more progress than others in improving the fat content of meals. Therefore, the tips that follow may be easier to apply in some schools than in others.

HELPFUL HINTS

• Review school lunch menus with children at the beginning of each week, or even daily. Discuss which choices on that day's menu are best.

• On days when no appropriate choice is available, a bag lunch may be an alternative (see Bag Lunches section).

• A school meal can be supplemented by something brought from home. For instance, a slice of pizza might be purchased at school, and an apple and whole grain muffin might be brought from home.

• Salad bar is an option at some schools. See the Salad Bars section for advice about building a lowfat salad.

__An Inside Peek:__ Debra Nagy, a first grade teacher at a private school in North Carolina, offers these comments ----

"The hot meals offered at our school do tend to be very high in fat. However, the school also offers some really healthful alternatives. Everyday, the kids can get fresh fruit cups, bagels (usually served with cream cheese, however), and bottles of mineral water and 100% fruit juices. There is a sandwich bar with some lowfat choices and a pretty salad bar with a good selection of fresh vegetables and other ingredients. Our school uses reduced-fat mayonnaise and serves reduced-fat salad dressings at the salad bar. There is also a basket of assorted breads, and pieces of fresh fruit are available every day. But guess what the typical middle school student eats for lunch? Two orders of fries, a Coke, and a donut. It's really tough to get kids to eat right. And this is at a private school where there are probably more lunch options than kids get in public schools."

Questions and Answers

Q: What can I do to get more lowfat meal options on the menu at my child's school?

A: First, contact the school's food service manager. Express your concern and ask what plans, if any, are in the works for addressing the problem. Is there some way you could be of assistance?

Find out if other students or parents are also interested in this problem and get them involved as well. Request lowfat, meatless entrees, more fresh fruits and vegetables, and more whole grain choices. The Vegetarian Resource Group has quantity lowfat vegetarian recipes available for institutional use (see Resources list at end of book).

Q: Some people say it doesn't do any good to serve more healthful, lowfat foods in the schools, because the kids won't eat them. Pizza, cheeseburgers, and hot dogs are what sells. How can we motivate our kids to choose healthful food if it is offered?

A: All kids don't necessarily reject "healthy" food options. School food service personnel at many schools report that when they serve attractive, thoughtfully-prepared "healthy" food items, these foods are well-received by kids. The manner in which food is presented and the attitude with which it is served can make all the difference in acceptance levels by kids and adults alike.

The task of educating kids about good nutrition has to be shared by the school, the family, and other community educators. Schools can provide support by having good food choices available for those who want them.

Ultimately, motivating kids to eat well will require educating them about the benefits of choosing a health-supporting lifestyle and instilling healthful lifestyle choices as a value (adults can set an example by their own food choices). And just as with many adults, what may be the most motivating for kids about changing their eating habits are improvements in the way they feel - be it in improved athletic performance, better weight control, more energy, etc.

Q: In the meal conversion example using the grilled cheese sandwich, the total fat content of the meal drops from 71 grams of fat to 47 grams of fat. That still seems pretty high. How do you rationalize a child's meal that contains 47 grams of fat?

A: This is a good example of how meatless foods may not always be lower in fat than nonvegetarian fare. Short of toasting the sandwich instead of grilling it, or using only one piece of cheese instead of two, it's difficult to make a lowfat grilled cheese sandwich. This menu is certainly not ideal. However, realistically, if the child has to take the grilled cheese sandwich as prepared, this example shows how other modifications in the meal (like omitting the margarine on the vegetables) can help to bring the total fat content of the meal down. The purpose of this and many other similar examples is not to show an ideal meal, but rather to show how some simple changes can make a big dent in the fat content of meals.

Q: What about kids who need to gain weight - kids that are too skinny or are growing rapidly and need more calories. Is it okay for them to get more fat?

A: Most health professionals agree that very young

children - those two years of age and under - need more fat in their diets than do adults. Children over the age of two, however, can eat the same lowfat diet as their parents. Children and adults alike who need more calories should eat "more of the good stuff." They may need to eat second helpings, and they may need to snack between meals. But eating habits developed in childhood carry over into adulthood. Children should be encouraged to adopt healthy eating habits from an early age.

Growth rates differ for individuals, and a child who appears "skinny" in comparison to his peers may be growing at a normal rate for that child. Check with your physician or a registered dietitian if you are concerned. There are many factors that may need to be considered in assessing the situation.

 # Bag Lunches

Menu Magic

Some bag lunches pack loads of fat, like this one:

> *Cheese (2 ounces), lettuce, and tomato sandwich with*
> *   1 tablespoon mayonnaise*
> *Bag of snack chips*
> *Apple*
> *4 chocolate chip cookies*

The lunch above is typical. It contains about 44 grams of fat and 833 calories. The alternative below is just as satisfying but packs more nutrition and less fat for the calories:

(Note: the simple changes made to reduce fat are in bold.)

> *Cheese **(1 ounce)**, lettuce, and tomato sandwich **in a***
> ***   pita pocket with grated carrots, chopped green***
> ***   peppers, and mushrooms with 1 tablespoon oil-***
> ***   free vinaigrette dressing***
> ***1 homemade lowfat muffin***
> *Apple*
> *4 chocolate chip cookies*

By reducing the fatty cheese to only 1 ounce, adding more vegetables to the sandwich for extra color and flavor, replacing greasy mayonnaise with an oil-free alternative, and swapping high fat snack chips for a wholesome lowfat muffin, the fat content of this meal is trimmed significantly. This lunch contains about 24 grams of fat and 647 calories.

Take a look at some more examples of simple changes that easily lower the fat content of the following meals:

#1   **Before:**   **After:**

Peanut butter sandwich (3 T   Peanut butter sandwich
  peanut butter) on whole wheat   *(1-1/2 T peanut butter)*
  bread with strawberry jam   on whole wheat bread *with*
                                       thinly sliced apples
Bag of potato chips   *Green pepper and carrot*
                                       sticks with salsa dip

Banana   Banana
Brownie   Brownie

Calories (Kcal):	764		Calories (Kcal):	566
Fat (grams):	42		Fat (grams):	23
Protein (grams):	23		Protein (grams):	16
Carbohydrate (grams):	86		Carbohydrate (grams):	86
Calcium (mg):	76		Calcium (mg):	96
Iron (mg):	4		Iron (mg):	5
Dietary fiber (grams):	12		Dietary fiber (grams):	14

Bag Lunch Examples:

#2   <u>**Before:**</u>   <u>**After:**</u>

Egg salad sandwich   *Tofu salad* sandwich on rye
  on rye bread   bread, *made with reduced-*
                                        fat mayonnaise

Bag of corn chips   *Carrot sticks*
Package of 2 chocolate   *3 oatmeal raisin cookies*
  cupcakes   *(homemade)*
Fresh pear   Fresh pear

Calories (Kcal):	776	Calories (Kcal):	498
Fat (grams):	32	Fat (grams):	17
Protein (grams):	17	Protein (grams):	9
Carbohydrate (grams):	112	Carbohydrate (grams):	93
Calcium (mg):	217	Calcium (mg):	117
Iron (mg):	4	Iron (mg):	3
Dietary fiber (grams):	9	Dietary fiber (grams):	13

An Inside Peek at Sue Havala's Lunch Bag -----

"I grab whatever is left over from the day before, and I try to add a couple of pieces of fresh fruit. If all else fails, I can always make a peanut butter and banana sandwich on whole grain bread, or pack a couple of rolls or muffins. Like a proper dietitian, I also make my lunch colorful - sometimes I take green pepper and carrot sticks. They're pretty and super nutritious, and I always feel good about myself if I think I'm eating well."

Bag Lunch Examples:

#3 Before:		After:	
Cheese and crackers (6 one-inch cubes cheddar with 12 saltines)		*Poppyseed bagel*	
8 oz. bean chili in a thermos		8 oz. bean chili in a thermos	
Green pepper slices		Green pepper slices	
Piece of apple cake		Piece of apple cake	
Calories (Kcal):	1110	Calories (Kcal):	707
Fat (grams):	50	Fat (grams):	14
Protein (grams):	52	Protein (grams):	26
Carbohydrate (grams):	118	Carbohydrate (grams):	124
Calcium (mg):	900	Calcium (mg):	173
Iron (mg):	9	Iron (mg):	8
Dietary fiber (grams):	16	Dietary fiber (grams):	17

An Inside Peek at Brad Scott's Lunch Bag --

"On weekends, I'll make a large pot of soup: black bean, split pea, lentil, tomato, or chili and freeze it in single-serving containers. During the week, I grab a container of soup, add some fruit, fresh bread, carrot sticks or rice cakes, and leftover rice or microwaved potatoes for a quick and easy lunch. In the summer, I'll make fresh vinegar-based coleslaw, tabouli, vinegar-based potato salad, or a fruit salad to enjoy throughout the week. Leftovers, such as spaghetti or couscous, also make an easy lunch. While minimizing my preparation time during the week when I'm so busy, I can still enjoy delicious, minimally-processed, lowfat lunches."

Bag Lunch Examples:

#4   Before:

2 slices leftover cheese pizza

Bag of snack chips
Apple

Calories (Kcal):	454
Fat (grams):	15
Protein (grams):	14
Carbohydrate (grams):	70
Calcium (mg):	227
Iron (mg):	2
Dietary fiber (grams):	5

After:

1 slice leftover cheese pizza
*8 oz. vegetable soup in a
thermos or a microwave-
safe container*
6 whole grain crackers
Apple

Calories (Kcal):	340
Fat (grams):	5
Protein (grams):	10
Carbohydrate (grams):	59
Calcium (mg):	122
Iron (mg):	2
Dietary fiber (grams):	7

An Inside Peek at Mary Clifford's Lunch Bag ----

"I deal with lunch the same way I cook dinner - in batches, ahead of time. When I'm making dinner for the week, I freeze some in lunch-size containers. Since I don't have the time (or inclination) to pack a lunch each morning, I grab a piece of fruit and a container from the freezer. By lunch, it's thawed and ready for reheating. By having it portioned out ahead of time, there's no excuse not to pack my own lunch, and I'm not tempted to buy the mostly high fat foods from the cafeteria. Often I'll make and freeze sandwiches, too. My favorites that freeze well are a lowfat hummus and what used to be called a `hobo' sandwich: mashed baked beans and mustard on whole grain bread."

Good Choices Include:	**Limit:**
Fresh fruit and fruit salads	Mayonnaise
Fresh vegetables	Eggs
Three bean salad	Cheese
Tomato and cucumber salad	Snack chips
Beet salad	Candy
Mixed green salads	Snack cakes
Homemade whole grain muffins	Most commercial
Bagels	cookies and other
Tofu salad sandwich	desserts
Grated veggie pita pocket sandwich	Cheese
Hummus sandwich	Peanut butter and
Herbed tofu sandwich	other nut butters
Bean soup	
Gazpacho	
Bean chili	
Vegetable soup	
Leftovers	
Zucchini bread (homemade)	
Banana bread (homemade)	
Oatmeal raisin cookies (homemade)	
Graham crackers	
Nonfat yogurt	
Whole grain bread with apple butter, pumpkin butter, or apricot butter	

People have a tendency to fall into the same trap packing a bag lunch as they do when planning a meal at home - that there has to be a "main course." A sandwich is the focal point of many bag lunches, but there are many other options for a good lunch, too. Be creative. The possibilities are endless.

Fat Content of Selected Items:

Veggie pocket sandwich, no-oil dressing .... 0 grams
Homemade apple spice muffin .... 2 grams
Bagel .... 0 grams
Gazpacho, 1 cup .... 0 grams
Tofu salad sandwich, 2 tsp. soy mayo .... 8 grams
Fruit salad .... 0 grams
Bean chili, 1 cup .... 2 grams
Peanut butter, 1 T .... 8 grams
Oatmeal raisin cookies, 2 .... 5 grams
Graham crackers, 2-1/2 inch squares, 2 .... 1 gram

Sometimes a bag lunch is the most practical way to have a meal away from home. Advantages include having more control over the food choices and fat content of the meal, as well as being able to eat just about anywhere, anytime. The disadvantages include some limitation on what can be packed, depending upon whether or not the food has to be kept cold or has to be heated before eating.

HELPFUL HINTS

• Pack leftovers from yesterday's dinner for lunch the next day.

• Use mustard, chutney, no-oil dressings, or salsa in place of mayonnaise on sandwiches.

• Nonfat yogurt is portable and is an option if refrigeration is available.

HELPFUL HINTS

• Soups can stay warm if carried in a thermos, or they can be heated in a microwave oven if one is available. Some soups are good cold, such as gazpacho, and others may be fine at room temperature.

• Messy sandwich fillings work well served in pita pockets. For instance, chopped or grated vegetable fillings, topped with a no-oil vinaigrette dressing, can be spooned into a pita pocket.

• Vary the breads used to make sandwiches. Try rye, multi-grain, sourdough, pumpernickel, herb breads, and Italian or French bread. Use Kaiser rolls or onion rolls, yeast rolls, and bagels.

• Use round slices of green pepper in sandwiches instead of lettuce to separate tomato slices from the bread and prevent sogginess.

• Muffins can be a good portable snack. Homemade muffins can be made low in fat and the variety can be endless. Try pumpkin muffins, apple-spice muffins, carrot or zucchini muffins, banana muffins, oatmeal, or any number of mixed grain varieties.

• Fresh fruit is always appropriate for bag lunches. A variation is fresh fruit salad carried in a reusable container. Good mixtures include cantaloupe chunks and blueberries, sliced peaches and blueberries, mixed melon chunks, sliced apples and pears mixed with cinnamon and chopped figs, or grapefruit and orange sections.

HELPFUL HINTS

• Cans of fruit juice can be frozen overnight and packed with a bag lunch the next morning. The frozen juice will help keep the contents of the bag cool, and by lunchtime it should be melted enough to drink.

• Fresh vegetables, like carrots and green pepper slices, and salads pack well. Also try some vegetable mixtures, such as tomatoes and cucumbers with no-oil vinaigrette, or a marinated mixture of broccoli and cauliflower florets with onions, mushrooms, and carrots.

Questions and Answers

Q: Some children will balk at bringing food to school that is too "different" from what the other kids bring. Also, some of the ideas you are suggesting will be new to my kids - I'm concerned about whether they will like them and will actually eat them.

A: There are many healthful bag lunch ideas that are very familiar to kids. For instance, cookies can be made at home using whole grains and less fat than traditional recipes, thus improving the nutritional profile while retaining the familiarity and flavor. Using tofu instead of egg in making egg salad sandwiches, as another example, would probably go unnoticed.

On the other hand, just taking soup or chili in a thermos may be outside the lunchroom norm in some schools and might be enough to mark a child as "different." Kids differ in their sensitivity to these situations. Parents can discuss specific issues with their kids and help to boost their confidence about their lunch box choices. Sitting down with your child and composing a list of favorite lunch box ideas, and getting the child involved in planning and fixing lunches will also improve the chances that the lunch will be enjoyed and that it won't end up in the garbage can.

Q: What kinds of leftovers are practical to pack in bag lunches?

A: Almost any leftover food can be packed for lunches, but if the food contains egg or dairy products such as cheese or milk, it should be refrigerated until lunchtime. Dishes such as pasta-and-vegetables or rice-and-vegetable mixtures can be kept at room temperature for several hours, as can most vegetable soups or bean chili. Pack leftovers in reusable plastic containers. If a microwave oven is available, leftovers can be reheated. If not, some leftovers can be eaten cold or at room temperature. For example, some people like to eat cold pizza, and some casseroles are just as good at room temperature as hot.

Q: Most of my favorite sandwich fillings, like peanut butter, egg salad, and cheese are high in fat. How can I still have these occasionally but make them lower in fat?

A: It's true that many of the old stand-bys are high in fat, and some of those need to be refrigerated. A few simple changes can make them lower in fat and easier to keep at room temperature, too. Peanut butter sandwiches can be made with just a thin layer of peanut butter on whole grain bread, adding slices of fruit such as apples or bananas. On other sandwiches, use mayonnaise sparingly. Soy mayonnaise is lower in cholesterol than regular mayonnaise, or use reduced-fat varieties. Tofu is better than egg in traditional egg salad recipes, since it's cholesterol-free. In cheese sandwiches, use only one piece of cheese and load up on shredded vegetables and tomato slices. Try using a slice of barbecued tofu or seitan instead of cheese. Again, tofu is moderately high in fat, but it's cholesterol-free and still lower in fat than many cheeses.

Q: I'm bored with my usual sandwich fillings. What are some other sandwich ideas?

A: Use your imagination. Lowfat cottage cheese mixed with chopped apples, pears, dates, raisins, and a little cinnamon is good. A thin layer of hummus topped with grated carrots and cucumber slices on whole grain bread is also good. Or try this: mashed tofu seasoned with herbs and mixed with chopped celery, green pepper, and minced onion. This can be spread on bread and topped with tomato slices and alfalfa sprouts. Another idea is leftover baked beans on whole grain bread. Or how about tomato slices on rye bread with a pesto spread?

An Inside Peek At Reed Mangels' Lunch Bag ----

"In my brown-bag days, I ate at my desk so I could take leftovers from the night before's lowfat dinner. I also liked to take a potato or an ear or two of corn and cook them in the microwave. Tossed salads with lots of vegetables and a handful of chickpeas are also good for lunch.

My husband usually eats his lunch in the car, so he prefers sandwiches which he can eat with one hand. I've found that almost any leftover cooked grain (rice, millet, couscous, even grits) can be mixed with cooked, chopped vegetables, seasoned with a little soy sauce and spices, shaped into patties (chilling helps them hold together) and baked on a lightly oiled cookie sheet. Mashed beans, flour or cornmeal, or a little water can be added to achieve a burger that will hold together. These patties are good with lettuce, tomato, and catsup. Bean spreads are also an easy lowfat sandwich filling. They're made by mashing cooked beans, adding catsup, tomato sauce or soy sauce, and spices. Spread on bread and garnish with sprouts. A variation on this theme is mashed chickpeas and grated carrots, with lemon juice and cumin - a lowfat hummus!

To go with the sandwich, we usually take a piece or two of fresh fruit. Dessert possibilities include homemade lowfat muffins or cookies, a bagel and jelly, or a cinnamon raisin bagel."

Planes, Trains, and Cruise Ships

Dietary goals for business travelers may be different from dietary goals of people traveling for pleasure. Since travel is a way of life for some people, sticking to a good, lowfat diet while away from home can be very important. On the other hand, someone who is on vacation or on a special trip may feel like they want to indulge in foods they would ordinarily limit at home. So, there are some times that it might be appropriate to be looser about dietary habits than at other times. The suggestions below assume that the goal is to keep the fat content of the diet low while traveling for those who wish to do so.

There are many modes of travel, each with its own unique form of meal service. Meal service on a plane, for instance, is very different from what you might expect on a cruise ship. Tips for handling meals on three forms of travel are included in this section. Some of these suggestions may be applicable to other travel situations not covered in this section, too. Also, other sections may contain suggestions appropriate for modes of travel not covered here. For instance, sections on bag lunches and restaurant dining might be helpful for bus travelers.

 # Planes

Menu Magic

You're 30,000 feet over the Mississippi River, and it's dinner time aboard your 737. Here comes the flight attendant with your "special" meal. You've requested a vegetarian dinner. Let's see what you got:

> *Tossed salad with a packet of French dressing*
> *Pasta primavera*
> *Hard roll with a pat of margarine*
> *1 whole grain cookie*
> *An apple*

Not bad. This meal, as is, contains 733 calories and 30 grams of fat.

To reduce the fat content of the meal even further, you could **forgo the salad dressing and margarine:**

(Note: the simple changes made to reduce fat are in bold.)

> *Tossed salad with **pepper instead of French dressing***
> *Pasta primavera*
> *Hard roll **(skip the margarine)***
> *1 whole grain cookie*
> *An apple*

Now the meal contains only 496 calories and 6 grams of fat. Take a look at some more airline meal makeovers:

Plane Examples:

#1 **Before:**		**After:**	
1/3 cup trail mix		*2 tablespoons of raisins (skip the rest of the trail mix)*	
2 crackers		2 crackers	
2 oz. block of cheese		*1 oz. cheese (just eat 1/2 of the block of cheese)*	
1/2 cup applesauce		1/2 cup applesauce	
A banana		A banana	
Calories (Kcal):	783	Calories (Kcal):	373
Fat (grams):	44	Fat (grams):	9
Protein (grams):	30	Protein (grams):	11
Carbohydrate (grams):	77	Carbohydrate (grams):	67
Calcium (mg):	620	Calcium (mg):	300
Iron (mg):	2	Iron (mg):	1
Dietary fiber (grams):	9	Dietary fiber (grams):	5

Plane Examples:

#2 Before: After:

Before:	After:
Mixed green salad with packet (3 T) of Italian dressing	Mixed green salad *with pepper*
Stuffed bell pepper (filled with vegetarian chili)	Stuffed bell pepper (filled with vegetarian chili)
1/2 cup rice with 1 pat of margarine	1/2 cup rice *(skip the margarine)*
Slice of bread with 1 pat of margarine	Slice of bread *(skip the margarine)*
1/2 cup mandarin orange slices	1/2 cup mandarin orange slices

Before		After	
Calories (Kcal):	669	Calories (Kcal):	391
Fat (grams):	32	Fat (grams):	2
Protein (grams):	15	Protein (grams):	15
Carbohydrate (grams):	86	Carbohydrate (grams):	81
Calcium (mg):	132	Calcium (mg):	126
Iron (mg):	6	Iron (mg):	6
Dietary fiber (grams):	16	Dietary fiber (grams):	15

Plane Examples:

#3 <u>**Before:**</u>   <u>**After:**</u>

6 oz. orange juice
2 pancakes with maple syrup
  and 1 T whipped butter
Cantaloupe and honeydew
  melon slices
Coffee with cream and sugar

Calories (Kcal):	786
Fat (grams):	13
Protein (grams):	9
Carbohydrate (grams):	182
Calcium (mg):	193
Iron (mg):	5
Dietary fiber (grams):	3

6 oz. orange juice
2 pancakes with maple syrup
  (skip the butter)
Cantaloupe and honeydew
  melon slices
Coffee with sugar or black
  (skip the cream)

Calories (Kcal):	708
Fat (grams):	5
Protein (grams):	9
Carbohydrate (grams):	182
Calcium (mg):	180
Iron (mg):	5
Dietary fiber (grams):	3

Plane Examples:

#4 **Before:**		**After:**	
Curried vegetables with rice		Curried vegetables with rice	
1/2 cup cooked lentils		1/2 cup cooked lentils	
1/2 cup cooked broccoli		1/2 cup cooked broccoli	
with 1 pat of margarine		*(skip the margarine)*	
Dinner roll with 1 pat		Dinner roll *(skip*	
of margarine		*the margarine)*	
1/2 cup mixed fruit pieces		1/2 cup mixed fruit pieces	
Calories (Kcal):	463	Calories (Kcal):	391
Fat (grams):	10	Fat (grams):	2
Protein (grams):	18	Protein (grams):	18
Carbohydrate (grams):	78	Carbohydrate (grams):	78
Calcium (mg):	129	Calcium (mg):	126
Iron (mg):	5	Iron (mg):	5
Dietary fiber (grams):	13	Dietary fiber (grams):	13

Have you ever wondered who fixes the meals you eat on the plane? Airlines contract with caterers that produce meals according to airline specifications. Some of the food production is taken care of on-site at the airports by the caterer; the food is prepared, the meal trays are assembled, the trays are loaded onto carts, then the carts are loaded onto the planes. Some airlines also purchase some of their meals ready-made and frozen; the meals are loaded onto the plane and reheated at mealtime.

Along with the standard meal offerings on any airline, airlines usually also accommodate special requests. For instance, if a traveler is diabetic or on a cholesterol-lowering diet, he or she can request a diabetic meal or a lowfat, low cholesterol meal. In fact, a long list of special meal offerings is available on most major carriers.

One large airline catering organization is Sky Chefs. Sky Chefs' Miami facility services American Airlines as well as Mexicana. According to Tom Prior, Production Manager at Sky Chefs' Miami facility, of the approximately 10,000 meals produced at his facility each day, about 1% of those are vegetarian meals that have been requested by passengers. In other words, his facility prepares about 100 vegetarian meals per day, including breakfast, lunch, dinner, and snacks.

Surprisingly, more vegetarian meals are ordered than lowfat, low cholesterol meals (which make up only about 1/2% of the total special meals ordered). "Probably the most frequently ordered special meals are the vegetarian meal, the seafood plate, and the fruit bowl," explained Prior. Most people don't realize that all of these options are available, and the airlines don't necessarily go out of their way to advertise it, since the special meals are costlier to produce. However, many frequent flyers take advantage of the special meal options.

About a year ago, the facility began making all of their vegetarian meals dairy-free and egg-free, or vegan, unless a passenger requests otherwise. Stated Prior, "We've been consolidating some of our diets, and it made more sense to do it that way. Also, most of the people who request vegetarian meals want the vegan option."

Throughout most of the airline industry, the designation VGML is used to denote a standard, animal-product-free vegetarian meal. Those who request a vegetarian meal that includes dairy or egg may see the designation, "DVEG" on their tray when it arrives at their seat. Fruit bowls are also a popular request for vegetarians, especially at breakfast.

Airlines differ in what they serve for vegetarian meals. Some airlines offer only one vegetarian menu, so frequent travelers may notice that every time they fly a certain airline, they get the same dinner meal - pasta primavera, for instance. Other airlines may offer a few menus, sometimes on a rotating basis and sometimes not. American Airlines, for example, uses four different vegetarian meals. So, passengers are likely to see any of these four on any given flight; they may get the same meal two or three times in a row, or they might get a different meal on each of four flights.

The meals may vary by region, as well, especially on international flights or flights that are frequented by certain cultural groups. For instance, vegetarian meals on flights from the U.S. to London, or elsewhere in Europe, are likely to be "Asian-vegetarian" - a curried lentil and rice dish, for instance - which would be more familiar to some vegetarian international travelers. On the other hand, vegetarian meals served on flights in the domestic market are more likely to be Western-style vegetarian meals - pasta primavera or chili-stuffed peppers.

Mike Agius is Executive Chef for the Sky Chefs' Miami facility. According to Agius, it isn't feasible or practical for travelers to get much information ahead of time about what specifically is going to be on the menu for special meals on any given flight. The reservation clerks don't have this information readily available to them, and in some cases, such as when a caterer is being supplied with frozen meals from another source, even *they* don't know precisely what is being delivered for any given day. Mike suggests, "If you aren't sure that you'll like the meal being served on a certain flight, vegetarians can always order a fruit plate." Especially on international flights, when a non-Western-style vegetarian meal is more likely to be served, a fruit plate can be a "sure bet" for some people. It can also be light and refreshing. On the other hand, the non-Western-style vegetarian meals can be delicious, too - maybe even better than the Western-style fare!

Here are the plane travel "how-to's":

At least 24 hours in advance of the flight, or at the time you make your reservation, call the airline reservations desk and check to see if a snack or meal is being served on your flight(s). If so, tell the clerk that you would like to request a special meal. Airlines offer a variety of special meal options. Depending upon the airline, there may be several meal options that are low in fat, vegetarian and nonvegetarian. Ask about what options are available on that specific airline. Frequently, they will be able to read you a sample menu. The following information was what was available from some of the major airlines at the time of writing:

AIRLINE: CONTINENTAL

Vegetarian Options: Strict vegetarian; Vegetarian with eggs

Samples: *Strict vegetarian* **breakfast** - fruit, tomato, hash browns, roll

Vegetarian **breakfast** - broiled tomato, egg dish, broiled peach or pear, pancake or French toast

Vegetarian **lunch** - salad with dressing, macaroni and cheese, 2 vegetables, dinner roll, and dessert

Vegetarian **snack** - egg salad sandwich or fresh fruit

AIRLINE: NORTHWEST

Vegetarian Options: Vegetarian with dairy; Vegetarian without dairy

Samples: *Vegetarian with dairy* **breakfast** - fresh fruit, cottage omelet, hash browns, broiled tomato, croissant and jam

Vegetarian with dairy **lunch** - (January - April) peach and cottage cheese salad; (May - August) vegetarian stuffed pepper; (September - December) vegetarian shepherds pie; each entree comes with a dinner roll, margarine, and fresh fruit.

Vegetarian with dairy **dinner** - (January - April) millet and vegetables; (May - August) curried vegetables with coconut; (September - December) sweet and sour stuffed cabbage; each entree comes with a dinner roll, margarine, and fresh fruit.

Vegetarian with dairy **snack** - orange juice, Danish or croissant, and margarine

Vegetarian without dairy **breakfast** - orange juice, brown rice and fruit mixture, buckwheat and groats, croissant*, and margarine*

Vegetarian without dairy **lunch** - tossed greens with garden vegetables, salad dressing, vegetarian stuffed pepper, dinner roll, margarine*, and fresh fruit

*Vegans note: Although Northwest labels dairy free, margarine and croissants may contain dairy ingredients.

NORTHWEST continued...

***Vegetarian without dairy* dinner** - tossed salad greens, millet and vegetables, roasted peanuts, carrots and tomato sauce, dinner roll, margarine*, and fresh fruit

***Vegetarian without dairy* snack** - orange juice, Danish or croissant*, and margarine*

*Vegans note: Although Northwest labels dairy free, margarine and croissants may contain dairy ingredients.

AIRLINE: USAir

Vegetarian Options: Vegetarian (meal items containing milk products are packaged separately so that those wishing to avoid dairy can do so; egg may be present, however, in any food item); Fruit plate is available in First Class but not in Coach

Samples: ***Vegetarian* Breakfast/Brunch/Snack** - fruit chunks, oatmeal crepe, fruit and nut dish

Vegetarian **Snack** - yogurt, applesauce, banana, and biscuit

Vegetarian **Lunch/Dinner/Snack** - salad with a melon and orange plate and a biscuit

Vegetarian **Lunch/Dinner** - California salad with dressing, whole grain biscuit, dinner roll with butter, and a fancy fruit plate

AIRLINE: DELTA

Vegetarian Options: Lacto-ovo vegetarian; Strict vegetarian

Samples: *Lacto-ovo vegetarian* **breakfast/brunch** - scrambled eggs, broiled tomato, diced potato, whole wheat toast, orange slices, and orange juice

Lacto-ovo vegetarian **lunch/dinner (hot)** - macaroni and cheese, broccoli, tomato and chive salad, pineapple and kiwi, and raisins

Lacto-ovo vegetarian **lunch/dinner/snack (cold)** - pineapple and strawberry salad, cottage cheese, whole wheat bread, and raisins

Strict vegetarian **breakfast/brunch** - vegetarian French toast, orange slices, raisins, and orange juice

Strict vegetarian **lunch/dinner (hot)** - vegetarian chili with brown rice, spinach salad, whole wheat

Strict vegetarian **lunch/dinner/snack (cold)** - tomato and cucumber on whole wheat bread, coleslaw, raisins, pineapple and kiwi salad

AIRLINE: AMERICAN

Vegetarian Options: Vegetarian (special meals can be requested up to 6 hours before the flight)

Samples: not available

AIRLINE: UNITED

Vegetarian Options: Vegetarian

Samples: *Vegetarian* - meals contain no meat, fish or fowl but may include egg or milk. Meals include whole grains, vegetables, dried beans or peas, bread products or starches, coffee, tea, soft drinks, fruit and vegetable drinks

In general ....

Throughout the airline industry, the vegetarian meal (or, in airline lingo, the VGML) is likely to be vegan, free of dairy and egg. But vegans might still want to specify "no dairy, no eggs" when they place their request, just to make sure. Vegans are also advised to read food labels on packets of salad dressing and cookie wrappers, for instance, just to be sure they don't contain animal products. Those who prefer to have some dairy or egg with their meal may be able to specify a lacto-ovo-vegetarian meal (or DVEG).

A fruit bowl or fruit plate is often available upon request. This is typically made with fresh, sliced fruit and can be a refreshing, light meal. Frequently, this option is fat-free. Sometimes, however, a fruit bowl includes a scoop of cottage cheese. Vegans may need to request "no dairy," just to be sure.

For non vegetarians, a regular lowfat or low cholesterol menu is usually available, too.

HELPFUL HINTS

• With any snacks or meals, there may be items on the tray that are high in fat; the traveler has the option of eating them or not. For instance, in a vegetarian snack kit a wedge of cheese spread may be given with a few crackers, or a bag of trail mix may be included. These items are high in fat. If everything else on the tray is fat-free, then the amount of fat in one of these items may not be a concern to some people.

• Especially at breakfast, it may be wise to order a fruit bowl or vegan meal to increase the probability that the meal will be low in fat. Otherwise, a regular vegetarian meal might include high fat items such as eggs, a cheese omelet, or French toast.

• If a snack or meal is offered on a plane trip and you are not hungry or have eaten very recently, leave your seat tray up and pass on the meal. Accept a beverage, instead, if you want something. Otherwise, anticipate that you'll eat on the plane and work that meal into your schedule beforehand. That way, you won't find yourself eating the same meal twice.

• There are many good beverage options available on plane flights. The best choices include mineral waters and fruit or vegetable juices. Bags of nuts that may accompany beverage service are high in fat.

• When meals are being handed out to passengers, the flight attendant may need to be alerted that you have ordered a special meal. Give your name and tell the flight attendant that you have ordered a special meal (or a vegetarian meal, fruit plate, etc.).

Questions and Answers

Q: You suggest requesting a fruit plate while traveling by plane. How do you rationalize eating only fruit for a meal - this isn't very balanced?

A: Every meal you eat does not have to include a variety of foods. Overall, however, it is wise to aim for diversity in your food choices. In the case of air travel, a fruit plate can be a refreshing, lowfat meal option. An added advantage is that, for many people, fresh fruits and vegetables fall by the wayside when they are traveling. Any opportunity then, that a traveler has to eat fresh fruit or vegetables is a good idea. Also, some people eat more high fat meals while they are traveling, and they may overeat, in general. A fruit plate is fat-free and high in fiber, which may help to offset some of those higher fat meals.

 **Trains**

Menu Magic

Have you ever traveled across country by rail? If so, then you've probably also had the unique experience of eating your meals on a train. Maybe the following lunch menu looks familiar:

Tossed green salad with ranch dressing
Vegetarian lasagna
Dinner roll with margarine
Brownie
Coffee or tea

Eaten "as is," this typical meal contains 40 grams of fat and about 800 calories.

How could you cut back on the fat? Easy. **Skip the salad dressing**, for starters. Ask for a few fresh lemon wedges, and **squeeze lemon juice on your salad instead** (add some pepper, too). **Do you really want all of the lasagna? If they serve a huge piece, share part of it with a companion or leave a portion on your plate. Eat the roll without the margarine.**

*Tossed green salad **with lemon juice and pepper***
*Vegetarian lasagna **(half portion)***
*Dinner roll **(skip the margarine)***
Brownie
Coffee or tea (or water!)

All of this saves you 24 grams of fat and 220 calories - and that's *including* the brownie.

Here are some more menu makeovers. (Note: the simple changes made to reduce fat are in bold.)

Train Examples:

#1   Before:

6 oz. tomato juice
3-egg omelet

Croissant with butter
  and preserves

Coffee or tea

Calories (Kcal):	481
Fat (grams):	29
Protein (grams):	20
Carbohydrate (grams):	35
Calcium (mg):	110
Iron (mg):	5
Dietary fiber (grams):	2

After:

6 oz. tomato juice
1 scrambled egg (request
  egg substitute product)
2 slices whole wheat toast
  with preserves (skip
  the butter)
Coffee or tea (optional)

Calories (Kcal):	307
Fat (grams):	9
Protein (grams):	12
Carbohydrate (grams):	48
Calcium (mg):	85
Iron (mg):	4
Dietary fiber (grams):	9

Train Examples:

#2   <u>**Before:**</u>

6 oz. orange juice
Dry cereal with 1/2 pint
 whole milk
Sliced fruit
Bagel with cream cheese

Mini Danish and preserves

Coffee or tea

Calories (Kcal):	894
Fat (grams):	28
Protein (grams):	26
Carbohydrate (grams):	145
Calcium (mg):	418
Iron (mg):	9
Dietary fiber (grams):	9

<u>**After:**</u>

6 oz. orange juice
Dry cereal with *1/2 pint*
 skim milk
Sliced fruit
Bagel with preserves *(skip the*
 cream cheese and the
 Danish; have an extra bagel
 if still hungry - it's fat-free)
Coffee or tea

Calories (Kcal):	824
Fat (grams):	5
Protein (grams):	28
Carbohydrate (grams):	175
Calcium (mg):	399
Iron (mg):	10
Dietary fiber (grams):	10

Train Examples:

#3 Before:

7-inch pizza prepared on board
 with tomato sauce, mozzarella
 cheese, and assorted vegetable
 toppings
Garden salad with creamy
 poppyseed dressing
Coffee or tea

Calories (Kcal):	456
Fat (grams):	26
Protein (grams):	16
Carbohydrate (grams):	43
Calcium (mg):	230
Iron (mg):	2
Dietary fiber (grams):	4

After:

7-inch pizza with tomato sauce
 and assorted vegetable
 toppings *(skip the cheese -
 just try it!)*
Garden salad with *vinegar or
 lemon juice and pepper*
Coffee or tea *(or try
 mineral water instead)*

Calories (Kcal):	332
Fat (grams):	trace
Protein (grams):	14
Carbohydrate (grams):	68
Calcium (mg):	80
Iron (mg):	4
Dietary fiber (grams):	8

Train Examples:

#4 **Before:**		**After:**	
Tossed salad with Italian dressing		Tossed salad with *reduced calorie Italian dressing on the side*	
Pasta primavera		Pasta primavera *(ask that it be made with minimal oil)*	
Dinner roll with margarine		Dinner roll *(skip the margarine)*	
Baked potato with margarine and sour cream		Baked potato *(skip the margarine and sour cream; use catsup instead)*	
Apple pie		*Fresh fruit (ask for this in place of the pie)*	
Coffee or tea		Coffee or tea	
Calories (Kcal):	1177	Calories (Kcal):	677
Fat (grams):	57	Fat (grams):	13
Protein (grams):	19	Protein (grams):	16
Carbohydrate (grams):	152	Carbohydrate (grams):	130
Calcium (mg):	172	Calcium (mg):	154
Iron (mg):	6	Iron (mg):	5
Dietary fiber (grams):	16	Dietary fiber (grams):	17

Not all trains offer meal service. Whether or not meals are served, as well as the kind of meal service offered, varies from one train line to the next. It depends upon factors like the length of the route, which class of service you have booked, even which region you happen to be traveling through (if traveling abroad).

Meal service can vary from none at all (especially on the shorter, commuter trains) to elegant restaurant-style meals on long-haul trains in full-service dining cars. In between, some train lines have canteens or lounges that serve snacks or there may be tray service for many meals. Some train lines even serve buffet meals.

The degree of service available also varies between train lines and even within the same line. In other words, you may have more success in having special requests or instructions honored on some trains than on others. If you have questions or concerns about your meals - especially on longer trips, call the train line's customer service representative before you book your reservation and ask about your options.

Here are the train travel "how-to's":

Again, since the specifics about meal service can vary so widely from train to train, check with a customer services represent-ative before you book your reservation to find out what your options are. The information from the following train lines was available at the time of writing:

TRAIN LINE: AMTRAK

Vegetarian Options: Vegetarian entrees are offered on all long-haul dining cars, and on some other services. These are regular menu selections and no special service request is needed. All vegetarian entrees, however, contain dairy or egg products. At the time of writing, *Nile Spice* brand soups - all free of animal products - were being added to menus on all trains.

Samples: **Breakfast** - 2 eggs or cholesterol-free egg substitute with hash brown potatoes or grits, white or wheat toast, butter and jelly, juice, coffee, tea or milk

Breakfast - railroad French toast with syrup or fruit sauce, juice, coffee, tea or milk

Lunch - Gourmet pizza, prepared on board, with tomato sauce, mozzarella cheese, primavera (with broccoli florets, sliced onion, green peppers, olives) served with garden salad or soup, coffee, tea or milk

Dinner - Vegetarian pasta (varies - examples include lasagna, shells Florentine, manicotti, and cheese-stuffed shells), tossed salad with dressing, dinner breads, vegetable, rice or potato du jour, dessert (apple pie and/or vanilla ice cream, cheesecake or layer cake), coffee, tea or milk

For more information: For more help with specific questions, travelers can call 1-800-USA-RAIL or 202/906-3672

TRAIN LINE: VIA RAIL CANADA

Vegetarian Options: Available with 48 hours' advance notice. Meal service varies depending upon the length of trip and class of service. Most shorter trips offer tray service snacks; overnight trips offer meals cooked to order in the dining car. However, in both cases, travelers are advised to call ahead and make special arrangements, since vegetarian options are not routinely offered on these trains.

Samples: Not available. On trips that include meals prepared on board, some vegetarians may be able to make do with items that the dining car has on hand for regular menus. Otherwise, call ahead to make special arrangements for vegetarian meals.

For more information: For more help with specific questions, travelers can call 1-800-561-3949 or write Via Rail Canada, Customer Relations, PO Box 8116, Station A, Montreal, Quebec, H3C 3N3

TRAIN LINE: EURORAIL

Vegetarian Options: Vegetarian meals are available upon request. Arrangements for special meals must be made ahead of time. Menus vary from country to country and depend upon which line you are traveling on.

For more information: Call 1-800-848-7245

In general ....

Meal service on trains may resemble that found in full-service restaurants, or it may be more limited. If you are ordering from a menu, look for the best lowfat choices. Focus on any fresh fruits and vegetables that might be available. Some menu items may be altered to make them more acceptable. For instance, a sandwich may be made with less cheese and more tomato, and the mayonnaise can be omitted. Another example might be a pasta dish offered with an Alfredo sauce which could be altered to make a pasta primavera - pasta tossed with steamed vegetables and a small amount of olive oil - giving you less fat. As always, if you are unsure about what will be available on your trip, inquire about meals at the time you make the reservations.

Some trains offer no meal service of any kind, especially on the short haul, commuter trains. On trips that will take less than a day, it may be necessary to carry lowfat snacks from home. The "Bag Lunches" section described earlier in the book can help you with ideas for take-along meals.

 # Cruise Ships

Menu Magic

No doubt you've heard stories about the extravagant meal service aboard cruise ships. John and Carol Tracy of Charlotte, North Carolina had this to say about a cruise they recently enjoyed:

Cruising with John and Carol Tracy ----

"Going on a cruise? Don't worry about getting enough to eat on a vegetarian diet. At least one cruise line, Royal Caribbean, even has vegetarian menus. The food is wonderful and the staff will compete with each other to try to please you the most. You can ask for lower fat options, but most of the food is intentionally rich."

"Breakfast can include any type of hot or cold cereal, fruit, juice and a selection of breads and rolls. There is more butter than margarine. Lunch and dinner are up to seven courses, depending on how long you last! Entrees such as vegetable strudel and pasta \ dishes follow inventive soups (chilled strawberry bisque and vichyssoise) and salads. After the entrees, you may choose cheese and fruit and/or dessert."

"For those who can stay up, the midnight buffet is actually the best meal. There is too much to even describe. On the last night, the chefs had a food competition which took 300 man hours to create. We were allowed to photograph prior to digging in. Bon voyage!"

Depending upon *"how long you last,"* a typical meal aboard a cruise ship could look like this:

> *Melon cocktail*
> *Cream of broccoli soup*
> *Fettucini Alfredo*
> *Eggplant Parisienne*
> *Apple custard pie*
> *Herb tea*

This is a real sample taken from one cruise line's luncheon menu. As it stands, this meal contains 56 grams of fat and 988 calories. It could have been even fattier, depending upon the menu choices made. But it could also be much lower in fat, as you will see in this menu makeover:

Melon cocktail
**Chiffonade of iceberg lettuce mimosa (in place of
cream soup; use lemon juice for dressing)**
**Carpaccio of fresh vegetables (this is a fancy
vegetable plate identified on the menu as a "lowfat
choice")**
**Raspberry sherbet (this is also identified as a
"lowfat choice")**
Herb tea

By **opting for the choices on the menu that were identified as
being low in fat, and skipping the usual fatty salad dressing,**
this menu contains only 3 grams of fat and 393 calories.

Of course, not everyone will choose to stick so closely to a
lowfat diet when they are on vacation or on a special trip. They
might decide to take the Fettucini Alfredo and enjoy it - even if
it *is* high in fat. On the other hand, there is so much available
on most cruise ships today, that it makes sticking to a healthy
diet much easier and enjoyable. Even the lowfat menu options
are beautifully prepared and delicious.

Here are some other realistic cruise ship meals and their
alternatives. On these menus, substitutions have been made for
more menu items than were made in Menu Magic in previous
sections. The reason? ...... There are *so many* good food options
to be had on cruise ships that it's easy to replace high fat
choices with wonderful lowfat alternatives. Just see for yourself!

Cruise Ship Examples:

#1 Before:

Apricot nectar
Tossed salad with blue
  cheese dressing
Poached egg sardou (artichoke
  hearts, spinach, and Hollandaise
  sauce served with French fries)
Tangerine layer cake
Coffee

Calories (Kcal):	1190
Fat (grams):	80
Protein (grams):	23
Carbohydrate (grams):	105
Calcium (mg):	265
Iron (mg):	7
Dietary fiber (grams):	9

After:

Apricot nectar
Tossed salad with a *lo-cal*
  dressing on the side
Chilled green pepper soup
Tropical fruit platter
Cherry streusel pie
  (lowfat version)
Coffee

Calories (Kcal):	672
Fat (grams):	10
Protein (grams):	9
Carbohydrate (grams):	153
Calcium (mg):	172
Iron (mg):	7
Dietary fiber (grams):	11

Cruise Ship Examples:

#2 <u>**Before:**</u>   <u>**After:**</u>

Grapefruit juice   Grapefruit juice
Bean salad with lemon   Bean salad with *low*
  cream dressing   *calorie dressing*
Vegetarian quesadilla served   Vegetarian quesadilla *(skip*
  with guacamole and pico de   *the guacamole; ask for*
  gallo sauce   *tomato slices and*
                                      less cheese)

Sautéed crookneck squash   Sautéed crookneck squash
Mocha eclair   *Blueberry frozen yogurt*
                                      (lowfat)

Coffee or tea   Coffee or tea *(or water)*

Calories (Kcal):	986	Calories (Kcal):	642
Fat (grams):	55	Fat (grams):	26
Protein (grams):	36	Protein (grams):	24
Carbohydrate (grams):	90	Carbohydrate (grams):	81
Calcium (mg):	765	Calcium (mg):	589
Iron (mg):	4	Iron (mg):	4
Dietary fiber (grams):	2	Dietary fiber (grams):	2

Cruise Ship Examples:

#3 Before:

Cranberry - apple juice
Chilled watercress soup
Heart of lettuce salad with
  carrot curls and Italian dressing
Stuffed baked potato with
  cheddar cheese
Tomato with broccoli florets
  in Hollandaise sauce
Buttered fan zucchini and
  yellow squash
Black Forest cake
Coffee or tea

Calories (Kcal):	1376
Fat (grams):	84
Protein (grams):	25
Carbohydrate (grams):	143
Calcium (mg):	411
Iron (mg):	6
Dietary fiber (grams):	13

After:

Cranberry - apple juice
Chilled watercress soup
Heart of lettuce salad with
  carrot curls *and fresh*
  lemon juice
Spaghetti with julienne of
  fresh vegetables and
  mushrooms
Grilled plum tomatoes
Steamed broccoli
Lemon sherbet
Coffee or tea *(or water)*

Calories (Kcal):	550
Fat (grams):	6
Protein (grams):	6
Carbohydrate (grams):	119
Calcium (mg):	218
Iron (mg):	6
Dietary fiber (grams):	10

Cruise Ship Examples:

#4 Before:

Celery stuffed with blue cheese
Clear vegetable soup with ginger
Mixed Island salad (tossed salad
    with pineapple and guava slices)
    with house dressing
Gourmet toast jardiniere
    (creamed mushrooms with diced
    vegetables on a toasted muffin
    topped with cheese, then baked)
Buttered penne pasta
Buttered baby carrots
Pineapple upside down cake
Herb tea

Calories (Kcal):	1400
Fat (grams):	80
Protein (grams):	38
Carbohydrate (grams):	136
Calcium (mg):	858
Iron (mg):	6
Dietary fiber (grams):	10

After:

Mango nectar
Clear vegetable soup
    with ginger
Mixed Island salad *with fresh
    lemon juice and pepper*
Gourmet toast jardiniere
    (skip the cheese)
Penne pasta *(no
    butter added)*
Baby carrots *(no
    butter added)*
Lime sherbet
Herb tea

Calories (Kcal):	777
Fat (grams):	21
Protein (grams):	18
Carbohydrate (grams):	133
Calcium (mg):	369
Iron (mg):	5
Dietary fiber (grams):	7

Cruise ships vary in the extent to which their menus accommodate travelers on lowfat diets. Some have menus which clearly differentiate the lowfat choices from all of the others. Some ships have separate vegetarian menus from which to order.

But even those ships that do not obviously cater to people on restricted diets can usually accommodate special requests. Since most of the food is prepared to order, and since there is *so much* food on hand, it's not much of a problem for most people to get a menu item altered to suit their individual needs or to find an acceptable substitute.

Also, cruise ships frequently serve meals buffet style, which in some ways can make it easier for many passengers to get what they want. On a buffet line, you can pick and choose items that appear to be low in fat and piece together a great meal.

Here are the cruise ship "how to's:"

As always, check with your travel agent or the customer services representative for the cruise line you are considering to ask for food service details. If you are really concerned about your meal options, or if you want to plan ahead, you may want to write to the cruise line and request sample menus and other meal information. Your travel agent may also be able to request this for you, or ask for it at the time you make your reservations.

The following information was available from various cruise lines at the time of writing:

CRUISE LINE: ROYAL CARIBBEAN

Vegetarian Options: Vegetarian lunch and dinner menus are being introduced aboard the nine-ship fleet. Currently, the "Monarch of the Seas" has separate vegetarian menus in place, and these will be gradually extended to the other ships. Meanwhile, menus on the other ships include meatless options, and several menu items are flagged as lowfat on each menu. The vegetarian options may include dairy and/or eggs, but many can be modified, and there are many other items that are totally free of animal ingredients.

Samples: *Regular menu, meatless luncheon* - melon cocktail, chilled strawberry bisque, chiffonade of iceberg lettuce mimosa, carpaccio of fresh vegetables, kernel corn, raspberry sherbet, beverages

Regular menu, meatless luncheon - peach nectar, clear vegetable soup, cauliflower garden salad, tropical fruit platter, string beans, orange sherbet, beverages

Regular menu, meatless luncheon - ambrosia fruit cocktail, chilled vichyssoise, health salad, tortellini calabrese, leaf spinach, cherry streusel pie, beverages

Vegetarian menu, luncheon - cheese tomato pizza, appetizer, chilled strawberry soup, chiffonade of iceberg lettuce mimosa, croissant sandwiches Hawaiian, apple custard pie, beverages

ROYAL CARIBBEAN continued...

Vegetarian menu, dinner - pineapple gondola, cream of asparagus soup, Boston lettuce mimosa with dressing, spaghetti Alfredo style with julienne of fresh vegetables and mushrooms, grilled plum tomatoes, steamed broccoli, assorted cheeses and fresh fruit, Key lime pie, beverages

Vegetarian menu, dinner - fruit cocktail with kiwi and lychee nuts, chilled cantaloupe soup, Suzy Wong salad, tempura fried broccoli and eggplant garnished with snow peas and Oriental noodles served with sweet and sour sauce, assorted cheeses and fresh fruit, Mandarin cheesecake, beverages

For more information: Travelers can call 1-800-852-3268 for more information or for sample menus. You may also FAX a request to 916/244-7037.

CRUISE LINE: CARNIVAL

Vegetarian Options: Two vegetarian entree options are noted on dinner menus but not for breakfast or lunch. Special dietary requests may be able to be accommodated, but requests must be made at least two weeks prior to departure. Travelers are also advised to talk with their waiter about special instructions for preparing menu items. Several lowfat menu items are flagged on each menu.

CARNIVAL continued...

Samples: *Regular menu, breakfast, meatless choice* - orange juice, baked apple, dry cereal with milk, beverage (other choices include eggs, pancakes, and French toast)

Regular menu, luncheon, meatless choice - apple juice, cream of tomato and coconut soup, mixed green salad and dressing, vegetable accompaniments, apple turnover with vanilla sauce, beverages. No meatless entree options listed - items would have to be modified.

Dinner menu, vegetarian choice - fruit cocktail, gazpacho Miami, tomato and cucumber salad, corn kernel creole, vegetable accompaniments, assorted cheeses, chocolate fudge cake, beverages

Dinner menu, vegetarian choice - pear nectar, cream of asparagus soup, sliced cucumber and Belgium endive in lemon dressing, vegetable brochette on pilaf rice, vegetable accompaniments, assorted cheeses, Napoleon, beverages

For more information: The address is Carnival Cruise Lines, Carnival Place, 3655 NW 87 Avenue, Miami, Florida 33178-2428.

CRUISE LINE: CUNARD

Vegetarian Options: No special menus for vegetarians, but ship can accommodate almost any special dietary request with at least thirty days notice prior to departure. Items that are low in fat, but not necessarily vegetarian, are noted on the Golden Door Spa menu.

Samples: *Queens Grill Luncheon, The Golden Door Suggestion* - chilled juice, spinach ravioli, Boston lettuce mimosa, fresh fruit salad, American glacé ice cream

Queens Grill Luncheon, The Golden Door Suggestion - plate of fresh melon, fresh herb omelette, spinach and watercress salad with feta cheese, American glacé ice cream

Queens Grill Dinner, meatless choice - pineapple juice, chilled apricot soup with coconut cookies, Mexican omelette with crisp vegetables, sour cream and cheese, apricot sorbet, (no meatless entrée), sautéed mixed vegetables, leeks with mushrooms, cucumber with yogurt and mint salad, creme caramel

For more information: Contact customer services at 1-800-223-0764.

CRUISE LINE: PRINCESS CRUISES

Vegetarian Options: No special menus for vegetarians, but special diets are accommodated. Travelers are urged to speak with the maitre d' about special requests.

Samples: *Regular menu, luncheon, meatless choice* - fruit and vegetable juices, spring vegetables vinaigrette, chilled zucchini bisque, salad of red beans, chick peas, and white beans on bed of shredded lettuce, white and green noodles with tomato sauce and basil, spinach omelette with French fries or vegetarian quesadilla with guacamole and pico de gallo sauce, banana bread with kirsch sauce, cheese and crackers, fresh fruit

Regular menu, dinner, meatless choice - broiled grapefruit with rum and raisins or celery branch stuffed with Stilton cheese mousse, chilled banana and papaya soup, spinach flan with cream sauce, assorted vegetables, strawberry tart with whipped cream, assorted cheeses and crackers, fresh fruit

Regular menu, dinner, meatless choice - mint flavored pineapple cup, mushroom and barley soup, mixed green salad with dressing, vegetable pojarsky (breaded, mixed vegetable patty) with cheese sauce, assorted vegetables, fruit and sherry trifle, assorted cheeses and crackers, fresh fruit

For more information: Contact Princess Cruises at 1-800-527-6200.

CRUISE LINE: CELEBRITY CRUISE LINES AND FANTASY CRUISES

Vegetarian Options: There is a vegetarian menu, which changes daily.

Samples: Sample entrees include vegetable strudel, vegetables tempura, vegetarian casserole in puff pastry with cheese sauce, and pasta with vegetables.

For more information: Contact the cruise line at 1-800-437-6111.

In general ....

Cruise ships are renowned (or notorious) for offering abundant meal service nearly round-the-clock. Vegetarians should have little trouble finding delicious, lowfat, and meatless options. The only problem may be resisting all of the *high fat* offerings.

Some ships offer separate vegetarian menus, and most of the menus change daily. Some items will be low in fat and others will be high in fat. Some items will be totally vegetarian and some will contain dairy and/or eggs. Therefore, even when a vegetarian menu is offered, some modifications may be needed to suit individual needs. Most cruise lines can accommodate special instructions.

Even ships that do not offer separate vegetarian menus can usually accommodate vegetarians wanting lowfat, meatless food. Make a special request when you book your reservation or discuss the options with a customer services representative. Modifications of regular menu items can usually be made, since the food is prepared aboard ship. Buffets can be convenient, too, because you can pick and choose from many items to put together your own lowfat meal.

HELPFUL HINTS

- Avoid locations where meals are being served if you are not hungry. Decide which meals you will attend and plan other activities such as swimming or playing shuffleboard, for times when additional meals are being served.

- Many meals on cruise ships are served buffet-style. Remember to survey the array of food on a buffet line and decide what you will take before walking through the line. See the section about cafeterias for other suggestions which may apply.

- Cruise ships are registered in various countries and may serve foods typical of their country of origin. Ships registered in Greece or Italy, for instance, may offer foods typical of those countries. Other cruise lines offer "continental" fare. So, suggestions given in earlier sections pertaining to ethnic restaurants and American cuisine may be helpful as well.

- On a cruise, some meals may be eaten off the ship at a restaurant at the port of call. Again, suggestions given earlier for restaurant dining may apply.

- Try a hot beverage, such as a cup of cappuccino or herb tea, in place of rich desserts.

HELPFUL HINTS

• Meals are sometimes served family-style, with a whole tray or bowl of food left on the table. In other cases, diners may order an entree from a menu. Then waiters come around to the tables and offer several side dishes and other parts of the meal to whomever wants them. Second helpings are sometimes available. In this case, ask for small servings of foods if you are unsure of what else will be offered. Take larger servings of lowfat items such as some salads, fresh fruit, and bread.

• In general, fill up on the fresh fruits and vegetables which are usually so plentiful on cruise ships. Experiment with some of the exotic produce available in some tropical climates. Watch out for rich sauces, dips, and spreads. Limit whipped cream, butter and margarine, salad dressings, and other fatty additions. Stay away from fried foods and rich entrees and desserts. Don't hesitate to ask if something can be modified to make it lower in fat.

Cruising with Brad Scott ----

"When cruising through the Caribbean, I found it easy to eat lowfat, vegetarian foods. I let my travel agent know I wanted the vegetarian menu when I booked the cruise with Carnival, and I verified that the kitchen received the request when I boarded the ship. At dinner, I chose my entree from the vegetarian menu and ordered appetizers, vegetables, salads, baked potatoes, and desserts from the standard menu. Breakfast included fresh fruit, hot or cold cereal, and bread. I usually ate lunch on one of the five islands we visited. I even found vegetarian cafes in St. Thomas and Barbados!"

 # Part II

Staying On Track At Home

Menu Magic

Are weekend breakfasts family-time for you? If so, maybe you find it difficult to avoid some of those old high fat family breakfast traditions - eggs, biscuits, French toast, and so on. Or maybe the toughest time for you is at the other end of the day - fixing an evening meal at home after a hectic day can be a special challenge. Unfortunately for many, what's quick may not always be healthiest.

Have a look at the meal conversions that follow. What simple changes can you make in your own family menus to cut the fat?

(Note: simple changes made to reduce fat are in bold.)

Breakfast:

#1 Before: After:

Orange juice   Orange juice
Cereal with whole milk   Cereal with *skim milk*
Toast with margarine and jelly   Toast with jelly *(no margarine)*
Coffee with cream and sugar   Coffee with *skim milk* and sugar

---

Breakfast Examples:

#2   Before: **After:**

Grapefruit juice   Grapefruit juice
Danish pastry   *Bagel with jelly*
Coffee with cream and sugar   Coffee with *skim milk* and sugar

---

#3   Before: **After:**

Orange juice   Orange juice
Cheese omelet   *Scrambled egg substitute (1/2 cup)*
                                            with salsa

Toast with margarine   Toast with *jelly*
Fried potatoes   *Baked potato wedges*
Coffee with cream and sugar   Coffee with *skim milk* and sugar

---

#4   Before: **After:**

Orange juice   Orange juice
Cheese-filled blintz topped   *Fruit-filled blintz with*
  with fruit and sour cream   *maple syrup*
Coffee with cream and sugar   Coffee with *skim milk* and sugar

Lunch Examples:

#1   **Before:**   **After:**

Cheese, lettuce, and tomato   *Tomato and pesto sandwich*
  sandwich with mayonnaise   *on rye bread*
Coleslaw   Coleslaw
Potato chips   *Bowl of lentil soup*
2 chocolate chip cookies   *1 chocolate chip cookie*
Glass of whole milk   *Sparkling water*

#2   **Before:**   **After:**

Grilled cheese sandwich   *Toasted cheese* sandwich *with*
                                     mustard and half the cheese

Tomato soup (made with   Tomato soup *(made with skim*
  whole milk)   *milk)*
Vegetable sticks with   Vegetable sticks *with salsa*
  sour cream dip
Water   Water

Lunch Examples:

#3   Before: **After:**

Macaroni and cheese   Macaroni *topped with fresh,*
                               chopped tomatoes and grated
                               Parmesan cheese

Bran muffin   Bran muffin
Salad with Italian dressing   Salad with *no-oil* dressing
Iced tea   Iced tea

#4   Before: **After:**

Bean burrito with sour   Bean burrito with *plain*
  cream and salsa   *nonfat yogurt* and salsa
Tossed salad with Ranch   Tossed salad with *lemon juice*
  dressing   *and pepper*
Soft drink   Soft drink *(or water!)*

Dinner Examples:

#1 Before: After:

Before:	After:
Vegetable lasagna	Vegetable lasagna *(made with skim milk ricotta cheese)*
Boiled potatoes with margarine	Boiled potatoes with *salt, pepper and parsley*
Steamed broccoli with margarine	Steamed broccoli with *lemon juice*
Roll with margarine	Roll *(no margarine)*
Water	Water

#2 Before: After:

Before:	After:
Cheese and nut loaf with peanut butter sauce	*Lentil loaf with catsup*
Baked potato with margarine	Baked potato with *salt and pepper (or catsup!)*
Three bean salad	Three bean salad *(made with no-oil vinaigrette)*
Whole grain yeast roll with margarine	Whole grain yeast roll *(plain)*
Apple juice	Apple juice

Dinner Examples:

#3 Before: **After:**

Before	After
Eggs rancheros	*Bean enchiladas*
Hash brown potatoes	*Oven-baked home fries*
Spinach salad with vinegar and oil	Spinach salad with *lemon juice and pepper*
Sparkling water	Sparkling water

#4 Before: **After:**

Before	After
Cauliflower-cheese pie	*Bowl of gazpacho*
Steamed vegetable medley with margarine over rice	Steamed vegetable medley over rice *(no margarine)*
Cornbread with margarine	Cornbread *(no margarine)*
Fruit punch	Fruit punch

Snack Examples:

#1 Before: **After:**

Before	After
Regular microwave popcorn	*Lowfat (or nonfat)* microwave popcorn
Soft drink	Soft drink

Snack Examples:

#2 <u>**Before:**</u>   <u>**After:**</u>

Peanut butter and crackers   Crackers *(half with peanut butter,*
                                 half with jelly)

Orange juice   Orange juice

#3 <u>**Before:**</u>   <u>**After:**</u>

Bagel and cream cheese   Bagel *with jam*
Sliced apple   Sliced apple

#4 <u>**Before:**</u>   <u>**After:**</u>

Nachos (chips, beans, cheese,   *Half as many* nachos
  and salsa)   *(without the cheese)*
                                 Vegetable sticks dipped in salsa
Beer   Beer *(or sparkling water)*

Dessert Examples:

#1 <u>**Before:**</u>   <u>**After:**</u>

Chocolate chip cookies   *Gingersnaps*
Whole milk   *Fruit juice*

#2 <u>**Before:**</u>   <u>**After:**</u>

Dish of ice cream with hot   *Fruit sorbet topped with*
  fudge topping   * fresh berries*

#3 <u>**Before:**</u>   <u>**After:**</u>

Chocolate cake   *Warm gingerbread with applesauce*

#4 <u>**Before:**</u>   <u>**After:**</u>

Pumpkin pie   Pumpkin *pudding (no crust)*

Grocery Store Strategies

Tips for Smart Shoppers

Are you a one-stop shopper, or do you hit two or three grocery stores before your trip can be a success? Maybe your style is a quick stop at the corner deli or the neighborhood natural foods store on your way home from work, preferably for something ready-to-eat. Peoples' lifestyles and needs vary, but certain habits are universally helpful for any shopper who cares about eating well. For instance:

• *It pays to shop with a list. Keep a slip of paper on your refrigerator or cupboard door and jot down items as you see you need them. Then take that list with you to the store. Having the list with you will keep you from forgetting the laundry soap again. More importantly, lists will also help you avoid impulse purchases, especially high fat snacks and sweets.*

• *Avoid grocery shopping when you are hungry. The grocery store can be a minefield when you are famished. Suddenly, everything looks good, and certain high fat items are more likely to find their way into your basket. Have a piece of fruit or a bagel before you go shopping, if necessary.*

• Read labels. If you are considering trying a new product, check the ingredient list and the nutrition labeling. How many grams of fat are in one serving? How many servings are you likely to eat at one sitting? What percentage of calories comes from fat?

• Take a few extra minutes in the summertime and early fall to drive past roadside fruit and vegetable stands to buy locally-grown produce when it's in season. (Keep a string bag in your car - they're handy and will remind you to stop.)

Some people shop weekly, biweekly, or monthly. Some even shop daily. Whatever your style, some measure of planning is sure to help you in meeting your diet goals. To help you construct your shopping list, and to aid in meal planning as well, the lists that follow provide ideas about grocery items you may want to have on hand. The lists include: items that are perishable and usually need to be purchased weekly; items that can be purchased monthly or less often; ideas for foods that can be fixed ahead of time and frozen for later or eaten during the week; and items that are quick and easy and can be picked up on the way home from work.

Specialty foods are also available and can be quick and convenient. However, they are frequently expensive and may be high in fat, as well. A list of specialty items that are relatively low in fat (under 30% of calories from fat) is included for those who like to have some of these on hand. A section on label reading is also included, incorporating 1993's new federal food labeling regulations.

Finally, 30 days' worth of quick meal ideas are provided, for those who need a little more help getting started.

An Inside Peek: *Shopping with Sue Havala* ----

"I eat fairly simply, and I don't use recipes to make my day-to-day foods. Instead of planning out a week's menu in advance, I tend to keep certain staples around the house, and at mealtime I fix whatever I feel like having based upon what I have available. I can be pretty creative when it comes to putting together a meal, but sometimes I just have a bowl of cereal and glass of juice for supper. When I shop, though, I usually do stick with a few good habits - I shop with a list, I skip the junk foods and rarely buy desserts, and I always buy several types of fresh fruits and fresh vegetables to have on hand at home."

An Inside Peek: *Shopping with Mary Clifford* ----

"You never hear of "impulse shopping" in relation to healthy foods. It's always done with foods like sugar-crusted frosty creme cakes or extra-salty double-fried fritter chips. The best way I know to avoid those kinds of impulse purchases is just to skip certain aisles completely! For instance, I steer clear of the candy aisle, cookies, and potato chip section altogether. "Out of sight, out of mind" really does work. If I need a special dessert or meal for company, I decide in advance what sort of foods I want. That way I don't wander around thinking everything looks good, and end up buying one of each!

Weekly Shopping Lists

Everyone has a different shopping style that suits his or her particular lifestyle and personality. Some people like to plan all of their meals a week ahead. Then, they draft a shopping list to correspond to their menus for the week. Others are comfortable having a variety of staples and other foods in the house, and they plan meals a day or an hour in advance, drawing ideas from whatever they have on hand.

Either approach can be fine, although planning ahead usually gives people a greater degree of control over meals. Especially for people who are actively learning new lowfat eating skills, it may be helpful, at least for a while, to plan meals and corresponding shopping lists a few days or a week ahead.

The first four weekly shopping lists that follow incorporate the meals and snacks illustrated in Menu Magic ... At Home - the modified, or lower fat versions. Try your hand at creating some additional menus from these weekly lists as well. A master grocery list follows, showing items that are typically purchased weekly due to their perishability.

Week 1

☐ Orange juice
☐ Whole grain cereal

- ☐ Rye bread
- ☐ Skim milk
- ☐ Fresh tomatoes
- ☐ Vinaigrette coleslaw from deli (or make your own with grated cabbage and no-oil vinaigrette dressing)
- ☐ Canned lentil soup (or make your own with a bag of dried lentils)
- ☐ A few chocolate chip cookies from bakery case (treat!)
- ☐ Mineral or sparkling water
- ☐ Frozen lowfat vegetable lasagna (or make your own using part-skim or nonfat ricotta cheese, lasagna noodles, and fresh vegetables, such as sliced carrots, broccoli, zucchini and yellow squash)
- ☐ Potatoes (such as red potatoes or new potatoes)
- ☐ Fresh or frozen broccoli
- ☐ Fresh lemon
- ☐ Lowfat or nonfat microwave popcorn
- ☐ Gingersnaps
- ☐ Soda (fruit juice mixed with seltzer or mineral water is better for you!)

Week 2

- ☐ Grapefruit juice
- ☐ Bagels
- ☐ Skim milk
- ☐ Whole grain bread
- ☐ Lowfat or nonfat cheese slices
- ☐ Canned tomato soup
- ☐ Fresh carrots
- ☐ Fresh green pepper
- ☐ Salsa
- ☐ Bag(s) of lentils

☐ Baking potato
☐ Cans of kidney beans, garbanzo beans, wax beans, and green beans (to make bean salad; have no-oil vinaigrette dressing on hand)
☐ Whole grain rolls
☐ Can of apple juice (frozen concentrate)
☐ Peanut butter
☐ Lowfat, whole grain crackers
☐ Fruit sorbet
☐ Fresh fruit (berries or any other seasonal fruit)

Week 3

☐ Orange juice
☐ Egg substitute (or make tofu scramblers)
☐ Whole grain bread
☐ Baking potatoes
☐ Skim milk
☐ Macaroni
☐ Fresh tomatoes
☐ Frozen bran muffins (or make your own from scratch)
☐ Salad ingredients - greens, cucumber, sprouts, radishes, whatever else you do not have on hand)
☐ No-oil vinaigrette dressing if not on hand
☐ Flour tortillas
☐ Canned pinto beans (or bag of dried beans)
☐ Sparkling water if none on hand
☐ Bagels
☐ Fresh fruit (apples or whatever is in season)
☐ Whole grain gingerbread mix
☐ Unsweetened applesauce (or make your own using fresh apples)

Week 4

- ☐ Orange juice
- ☐ Frozen fruit blintzes
- ☐ Skim milk
- ☐ Flour tortillas
- ☐ Canned pinto beans (or bag of dried beans). Try black beans as an alternative. For example, black bean burritos are a treat.
- ☐ Plain, nonfat yogurt
- ☐ Salad ingredients (greens, tomatoes, whatever you would like that is not on hand)
- ☐ Canned soup such as gazpacho
- ☐ Fresh broccoli, zucchini, yellow squash, and red pepper (or a similar mixture of frozen vegetables)
- ☐ Brown rice
- ☐ Whole grain cornbread mix (or buy cornmeal and make cornbread from scratch at home - it's easy!)
- ☐ Frozen juice concentrate
- ☐ Tortilla chips (try to find the nonfat variety)
- ☐ Green pepper, bag of celery, and/or carrots
- ☐ Flavored seltzer water
- ☐ Canned pumpkin (follow directions on can to make pumpkin pie filling, or modify to exclude milk or eggs)

Master Weekly Shopping List

(suggestions only - these are items likely to be purchased weekly because they are perishable)

- ☐ TOFU (fresh)

☐ FRESH VEGETABLES (especially those in season)
  Potatoes - white, red, sweet
  Carrots
  Celery
  Cucumbers
  Spinach
  Kale
  Collard greens
  Peppers - red, green
  Onions - green, yellow, red
  Garlic
  Broccoli
  Cauliflower
  Squash - acorn, zucchini, yellow, etc.
  Beets
  Asparagus
  Brussels sprouts
  Lettuce - Romaine, leaf, others
☐ FRESH FRUITS (especially those in season)
  Apples
  Pears
  Bananas
  Oranges
  Grapefruit
  Tangerines
  Lemons and limes
  Kiwi
  Melons
  Peaches, plums, nectarines
  Pineapple
  Strawberries
  Blueberries
☐ SOY OR NONFAT/LOWFAT:
  Cheese

Yogurt
Milk
Margarine
☐ BREADS
Whole wheat or multigrain
Rye
Rolls
Bagels
English muffins
Pita pockets
☐ FRESH DELI ITEMS such as salads, spreads, pizza

An Inside Peek: Shopping with Brad Scott ----

"Shopping for lowfat foods is easy ever since I learned to read labels. If I can't find the fat content, it usually means the food is not lowfat. I always remember to check the serving size, because some manufacturers make their products seem low in fat by using unrealistically small serving sizes."

"I try to fill my cart with mostly fresh produce, beans, and whole grains, which are naturally low in fat. Foods which are fresh and minimally-processed are usually the best-tasting and best for you."

Monthly Shopping List

(These items can be purchased less often, since they can keep longer in the cupboard or freezer.)

Cupboard Staples

☐ CANNED GOODS
   Canned tomatoes
   Tomato sauce and paste
   Spaghetti sauce
   Beans (canned or dry) - garbanzo, black, pinto, kidney, split
      peas, and lentils
   Canned soups - lentil, vegetable, vegetarian split pea,
      tomato
☐ DRY ITEMS
   Oatmeal
   Barley
   Rice - brown, white, basmati, wild
   Breakfast cereals - Shredded Wheat, NutriGrain, and other
      whole grain varieties
   Pasta
   Whole grain crackers and matzos
   Wheat germ
   Bulgur wheat
   Whole wheat flour

Whole grain pancake mix
- [ ] SOY MILK (aseptic packages or a mix)
- [ ] TOFU (in aseptic packages)
- [ ] CONDIMENTS
  Maple syrup
  Jams and jellies
  Salsa
  Blackstrap molasses
  Nonfat or reduced fat salad dressings
  Vinegar - red wine, cider, rice, etc.
  Mustard
  Catsup
  Chutney
- [ ] SPICES AND VEGETABLE BOUILLON
- [ ] MINERAL WATER AND CLUB SODA
- [ ] VEGETABLE OIL (small bottles of one or two)
  Corn
  Safflower
  Canola
  Olive
  Vegetable oil spray
- [ ] DRIED FRUIT
  Raisins and currants
  Apricots
  Mixtures
  Chopped dates
- [ ] NUTS AND SEEDS
  Peanut butter and almond butter
  Walnuts
  Almonds - slivered, whole, sliced
  Sunflower seeds
  Tahini
- [ ] SNACKS
  Nonfat tortilla chips

Pretzels
Plain popcorn
Lowfat cookies (gingersnaps and others)

Freezer Staples

☐ FROZEN, PLAIN VEGETABLES
Broccoli
Spinach
Corn
Green beans
Peas
Soup mix (mixtures of vegetables for soup; usually includes potato pieces, okra, green beans, peas, carrots, etc.)
Mixed vegetables (variety of combinations, such as broccoli-cauliflower-carrots, or French-cut green beans-onions-mushrooms)
Stir-fry mix
☐ FROZEN FRUIT
Blueberries
Strawberries
Raspberries
☐ FROZEN FRUIT BARS
☐ SORBET
☐ JUICE MIXES
Blends (pineapple-orange, orange-peach, etc.)
Lemonade
Orange juice
Grapefruit juice
☐ SPECIALTY FOODS
Tempeh
Veggie burger patties
Avocado dip
Frozen entrees (such as Legume, Healthy Choice, Life

Choice, etc. - see section on lowfat specialty foods)
- [ ] WAFFLES
- [ ] MUFFINS

An Inside Peek: Shopping with Reed Mangels ----

"*Most of the food I buy is lowfat. I prefer to prepare my own food most of the time instead of relying on processed foods, so I buy a lot of fresh fruits and vegetables, whole grains, pasta, and beans. I don't buy eggs or dairy products (or meat, fish, and poultry, for that matter).*"

"*I do use a soy margarine on bagels for breakfast. I use a brand which has less fat and fewer calories than regular margarine. When I do buy processed foods, like salad dressings or cookies, I read the label and try to find the ones which do not contain animal ingredients as well as the ones which are lower in fat. I use these foods on an occasional basis.*"

"*When I buy a mix, like instant refried beans or a veggie burger mix, I've found that I can reduce or eliminate the amount of oil called for in the directions. When I plan a meal that is higher in fat, such as stir-fried vegetables with a peanut butter sauce, I cook the vegetables in water or vegetable stock in place of oil and serve it with lots of rice.*"

Ideas for the Weekend Cook

For the week:

Fruit salads (use seasonal fruits)
  Chopped apples, pears, and figs
  Cantaloupe chunks with blueberries
  Mixed melon balls
  Strawberries and bananas
  Peaches and blueberries

Green salads
  Mixed greens
  Spinach

Coleslaw

Other vegetable salads
  Three-bean
  Carrot raisin
  Pasta and vegetable salad
  Marinated vegetable salad
  Tomato-cucumber salad

Whole grain muffins

Bean chili

Soups
  Lentil
  Split pea
  Vegetable
  Bean

Hummus

Tofu-stuffed shells

Vegetable lasagna

Rice/vegetable
  casseroles

Whole grain
  pancake batter

Brown rice (to have
  on hand, reheats
  quickly)

To freeze:

Soup

Chili

Leftover pancakes

Muffins

Casseroles

Tofu-stuffed shells

Vegetable lasagna

An Inside Peek: Cooking with Sue Havala ----

"I really like the weekend cook idea - it works very well for me. About once a week, especially right after I've gone grocery shopping, I take about an hour to fix a couple of things - usually salads, which I am not as likely to take the time to fix otherwise immediately before a meal. I like to make spinach or mixed green salads with lots of other fresh vegetables added, or I might make a bean salad or marinated fresh vegetable salad. Sometimes I make a pot of vegetable soup. I use Knorr tomato-basil soup mix and add mixed frozen vegetables and two or three cans of beans, such as dark red kidney beans, garbanzo beans, and pinto beans. I find that preparing a few items ahead of time helps to ensure that I'll eat well during the week."

"Quick Stop" Shopping List

☐ Hummus
   Combine it with pita bread, deli rye, a bagel, crackers, or
      vegetable sticks
☐ Bagels
☐ Ready-made tossed salads
☐ Ready-made fruit salads
☐ Chinese take-out
☐ Thai take-out
☐ Ready-made pizza with vegetable toppings (heat it up at
      home or buy a ready-made pizza crust and add your own
      toppings at home)
☐ Ready-made veggie sandwiches (lowfat fillings such as bean
      and vegetables, veggie pockets, etc.)
☐ Other ready-made or take-out items
   Stir-fried vegetables
   Soup
   Chili
   Rice and beans
   Bean burrito

What About Specialty Foods?

There are many convenient vegetarian specialty items on the market today. Many are found in natural foods stores or other "specialty" stores, but increasingly these products are finding their way into the supermarket, too.

Which products are the best? You may find that you need to evaluate some a little differently from others when you try to determine which to buy. When you think about the fat content of a particular product, give some consideration to how you might use it. For instance, a frozen veggie burger patty might contain 8 grams of fat, and by calories it may be 50% fat. However, when you add a bun, condiments, lettuce and tomato, and if you serve the burger with a lowfat side dish such as a fruit salad, then the overall fat content of the meal may be all right. On the other hand, if you are thinking about buying a frozen dinner that is essentially "all inclusive," a meal that contains 20 grams of fat may not be the best choice.

Some people who are watching their fat intake may simply choose to maintain a tally of how many grams of fat they eat per day. If your budget for the day allows you 30 grams of fat, then you might find that there is enough room for a couple of lowfat cookies containing 2 grams of fat each, or a frozen dinner that contains 10 grams of fat.

To get you started in the right direction, the list that follows will give you an idea of some of the specialty products available today. All of these are relatively low in fat. Again, depending upon your specific needs or requirements, you may find that some of these products fit into your diet better than others.

The products listed were found in specialty stores (natural foods stores) on the East and West coasts. Regular neighborhood grocery stores also carry mainstream brand name products (and, increasingly, some of the "natural foods" brands) that fit the criteria below. We limited our survey to specialty stores, but do check out your supermarket, too, and see what's available. Prices may be lower there than at many specialty stores.

Products are listed in various categories. Items within each category have been chosen to conform to the "fat criteria" set for that category. For instance, a limit of 15 grams of fat per serving was set for frozen entrees. So, all of the frozen entrees listed have no more than 15 grams of fat per serving, and many have less. Again, remember that there are other products not listed that may also work well in your diet, depending upon how they are eaten. Like the veggie burger example earlier, some higher fat specialty foods can be balanced out with other lower fat foods within a meal.

Behind the Scenes with Ann Truelove ----

Ann helped research products in stores in the Baltimore, MD area. After visiting several natural foods stores and looking specifically for lowfat food items, Ann observed:

*"To my surprise, many of the items in the health food stores I went to were high in fat. Personally, I thought that most of the products, since they were in "health" food stores, would be low in fat or at least **lower** in fat than the mainstream or brand name items. One bag of cheese-flavored tortilla chips was exactly the same as the Doritos chips that one can find at any corner store - just the packaging looked more "natural" and was more expensive. Another frustration was that so many packages had **NO** nutrition information on them."*

Breads and Muffins ($\leq$ 2 grams of fat per serving):

Cedarlane Fat Free Whole Wheat Tortillas
Fattorie & Pandea Wholewheat Breadsticks
Shiloh Farms
    Bread's For Life
    Sprouted 7-Grain
    Nature's Garden Bakery Rye
    Egyptian Wheat Kamut Bread
    Spelt
Lifestream Essene Sprouted Grain
Nature's Path Manna Bread
Rudy's Bakery Spelt Bagels
Health Valley:
    Fat-Free Muffins
    Fat-Free Oat Bran Muffins
    Fat-Free Muffins Twin Pack
Wendy Sue and Tobey's Lite Pineapple Oatbran Muffins
Garden of Eatin Bible Bagel - Onion
Food for Life:
    100% Flourless 7 Sprouted Grain
    Ezekiel 4.9 Sprouted Grain

Burgers ($\leq$ 6 grams of fat per patty):

Soy City Foods Veggie Burger (3 oz.)
Yves
Meat of Wheat
Amara's Burgers
Prima Veggie - Gardenburger
Kendrob's Veggie Burger
Light Life:
    Lemon Grill
    American Grill
    BarbaCue Grill
    Sun Party Bean Patties
Mandarin Garden
Morningstar Farms:
    Garden Vege-Patties
    Prime Patties

Cereals (≤ 2 grams of fat per serving):

New Morning:
- Fruit-e-o's
- Oatio's

Nature's Path:
- Millet Rice
- Heritage
- Corn Flakes
- Multigrain
- Fiber O's

Erewhon:
- Raisin Bran
- Aztec (Corn & Amaranth)
- Poppets
- Crispy Brown Rice
- Kamut Flakes
- Apple Stroodles

Breadshop:
- Puffs 'n Honey
- Triple Bran

Perky's:
- Nutty Rice
- Original
- Almond & Raisin

Golden Temple Fruit Muesli

Arrowhead Mills:
- Rice and Shine
- Seven Grain
- Bear Mush
- Instant Oatmeal
- Puffed Wheat
- Puffed Corn
- Puffed Millet

Health Valley:
- Fat-Free 10 Bran Cereal
- Fat-Free Granola
- Fat-Free Sprouts 7

Barbara's Raisin Bran

Trader Joe's Apple Cinnamon Granola

Cheese, dairy or non-dairy (≤ 3 grams of fat per ounce):

Lifetime Fat Free Monterey Jack

Zero - Fat Rella Cheese Alternative:
>   Jalapeno Jack
>   California Cheddar Style

Almond Cheeze:
>   Mozzarella
>   Cheddar
>   Garlic & Herbs

White Wave Soy A Melt Fat Free:
>   Cheddar Style
>   Mozzarella Style

Cookies (≤ 2 grams of fat per serving):

Frookie:
>   Lemon
>   Chocolate
>   Peanut Butter
>   Oatmeal Raisin
>   Ginger Spice
>   Chocolate Chip
>   Fig Fruitins
>   Apple Fruitins

Nature's Warehouse:
>   Fig Bars - Raisin
>   Fig Bars - Wheat Free
>   Fig & Oats - Wheat Free

Health Valley:
>   Fat-Free Fruit Centers Cookies
>   Fat-Free Cookies
>   Fat-Free Jumbos Cookies
>   Fat-Free Healthy Chips Cookies
>   Fat-Free Mini Fruit Centers Cookies
>   Healthy Granola Cookies
>   Fruit Chunks Cookies

Big Deal Bakery Oat Bran Raisin

Barbara's Oatmeal Raisin

Trolls:
> Honey Vanilla
> Troll Berry

Mitchelhill - Healthy Life:
> Muesli Cookies
> Honey Gram Cookies

Crackers (≤ 2 grams of fat per serving):

Barbara's All Natural

Wheatines:
> Original
> Sesame

Wasa Crispbread:
> Hearty Rye
> Light Rye

Nejaimes Lavache Crisp Wafer Bread:
> Onion & Poppy
> Dill & Garlic

Dar Vida Swiss Crackers Whole Wheat with Sesame Seeds

Ryvita Crisp Bread:
> Sesame Rye
> Tasty Light Rye

Lavosh Hawaii 10-Grain

Health Valley
> Fat-Free Organic Whole Wheat
> Sesame Stoned Wheat

Devonsheer Rye Melba Toast

Ak-Mak Original Sesame Crackers

Fantastic Foods Fiber Crisp

Kavli Muesli Crispbread

Edwards & Son Zesty Parmesan

Red Oval Farms Stoned Wheat Thins

Desserts (≤ 3 grams of fat per serving):

(Frozen Desserts)

Unbelievable Cheesecake

Stars Frozen Yogurt: Vanilla, Blueberry

Living Lightly: Raspberry, Carob Peppermint, Mint Carob Chip, Vanilla, and Espresso

Toffutti Better Than Yogurt: Passion Island Fruit, Strawberry Banana, Chocolate Fudge, Peach Mango, and Coffee Marshmallow Swirl

Sweet Nothings: Blueberry, Mango Raspberry, Raspberry, Vanilla, Black Tiger, Chocolate, Tigerstripe Espresso Fudge, and Chocolate Mandarin

Nouvelle Sorbet: Raspberry, Apricot, Lemon, Passion Fruit, and Strawberry

Tofutti Frutti: Apricot Mango, Three Berry, and Vanilla Apple Orchard

Stoneyfield Farm:
Dutch Chocolate Frozen Yogurt
Decaf. Coffee Frozen Yogurt

Stars Nonfat Frozen Yogurt: Almond Fudge

(Cakes)

Holland Honey Company:
Original
Double Spice Honey Cake

Salad Dressings ($\leq$ 2 grams of fat per teaspoon):

Pritikin:
Italian
Garlic & Herb
French Style
Sweet & Spicy

Anne's

Montserrati Lemon & Dill

Na Soya Russian Delight

Ayla's:
Italian
Creamy Dill
French
Lemon Mustard

Paula's No Oil Dressing Lemon and Dill

Walden Farms Fat Free Bleu Cheese Dressing

Entrees ($\leq$ 15 grams of fat per serving):

Colonel Sanchez Tamales

Suyada's Real Falafel

Tumaro's Tofu Enchilada Verde

Legume:
    Manicotti Florentine with Tofu and Sauce
    Mexican Enchiladas
    Classic Lasagna
Jaclyn's Grilled Tofu in Peanut Butter Sauce with Brown Rice, Carrots
      and Corn
Amy's:
    Vegetable Lasagna
    Mexican Tamale Pie
Putney Pasta:
    Tortelloni Mexicana
    Cheese Tortellini
    Agholotti

Pizza ($\leq$ 5 grams of fat per serving):

Pizsoy
Jaclyn's Fat-Free Pizza
Tombstone Light Vegetable Pizza

Snack Chips, etc. ($\leq$ 2 grams of fat per serving):

Bearitos:
    Tortilla Chips (no oil, no salt)
    Tortilla Chips (with salt)
    Blue Corn
Guiltless Gourmet No Oil Tortilla
Hain:
    Plain Mini Rice Cakes
    White Cheddar Mini Popcorn
Barbara's:
    Mini Pretzels
    9 Grain Pretzels
    Honeysweet Pretzels
Harry's:
    Whole Wheat Honey Pretzels
    Sourdough Pretzels
Childers Potato Chips
Health Valley Cheese Puffs
Soken Brown Rice Wheels
Treetop Apple Chips

Lundberg Rice Cakes
Health Valley:
> Fat-Free Caramel Corn Puffs
> Fat-Free Cheese Flavor Puffs

Pacific Grain No Fries Ranch O's

Soups (≤ 3 grams of fat per cup):

Nile Spice Lentil Curry
Health Valley:
> Fat-Free Soup
> Fat-Free Chili

Bearitos Chili
Taste Adventure:
> Red Bean Chili
> Split Pea
> Minestrone
> Navy Bean
> Black Bean
> Curry Lentil

Hain:
> Veggie Broth
> Vegetarian Split Pea
> Black Bean

Progresso Lentil
Tabatchnick Soups
Fantastic Foods Pinto Beans and Rice Mexican Lowfat Soup with
> Sauces in a Salsa Roja (All their soups are ≤ 3 grams fat except
> for the ones which have noodles. They have different packaging.)

Milk Substitutes (≤ 3 grams of fat per cup):

Edensoy Extra Vanilla (8.45 fl. oz.)
Westsoy:
> Lite
> Wholesome & Hearty

Health Valley Fat Free Soy Moo
Rice Dream:
> Original
> Vanilla Lite
> Carob Lite

Vegelicious White Almond Beverage
Amazake Original
Vitasoy Light:
>   Vanilla
>   Original
Soy Products (≤ 5 grams of fat per serving):
(Hot dogs)
Yves Veggie Wieners
Light Life:
>   Meatless Smart Dogs
>   Lean Links
(Burgers) See "Burgers" on page 204.
Yogurt, dairy and non-dairy (≤ 3 grams of fat per cup):
White Wave Dairyless Yogurt: Vanilla, Strawberry, Blueberry, Peach
>   Raspberry, and Apricot Mango

An Inside Peek: Cooking with Mary Clifford ----

"I hate preparing dinner every night. Not only because I don't have time, but who wants to do dishes before bed or wake up to them the next morning? Since my husband also likes to cook, we usually pick a quiet evening to prepare several batches of our favorites, then freeze them in small containers. That way, we always have something healthy to eat that requires nothing more than reheating. It's also easier because you can do all your food prep at one time and you wash pots and pans only once. If you're making a casserole and a stew, for example, you can chop and cook all the onions at once (another good reason to cook with a partner -- you can share the work!)"

30 Days of Quick Meals

Day 1:	Day 2:	Day 3:	Day 4:	Day 5:
Nonfat tofu hot dogs, vegetarian baked beans, & steamed greens	Lentil soup (canned), & toasted rye bread with tomato slices & pesto spread	Take-out Chinese lo mein & vegetables (request no oil)	Order out - vegetable pizza (cheeseless), & mixed green salad	Veggie burger mix (or frozen patty) on a whole wheat roll with lettuce, mustard, tomato, & catsup, & navy bean soup
Day 6:	**Day 7:**	**Day 8:**	**Day 9:**	**Day 10:**
Hummus on whole wheat toast, deli pasta salad, & sliced orange (go light on the hummus)	Scrambled tofu with green peppers & onions on a Kaiser roll, & fresh fruit	Microwave-baked potato with catsup or salsa, & vegetable soup	Peanut butter sandwich (thin layer of peanut butter) with sliced bananas, & apple with cinnamon	Whole wheat spaghetti topped with tomato sauce, & green beans
Day 11:	**Day 12:**	**Day 13:**	**Day 14:**	**Day 15:**
Deli take-out - vinaigrette coleslaw, fruit salad, & bagels	Whole wheat fettucine topped with steamed mixed vegetables & a sprinkling of grated Parmesan cheese	Ratatouille (canned or frozen), & English muffin	Split pea soup, whole wheat toast with tomato slices & spicy mustard or chutney	Large take-out garden salad with lowfat or nonfat vinaigrette dressing (or lemon juice & pepper)

Day 16:	Day 17:	Day 18:	Day 19:	Day 20:
Whole wheat macaroni tossed with small amount of olive oil, (or none at all), garlic, & cannelloni beans & steamed greens	Eggplant Parmesan (from frozen) on a hoagie roll (this item is usually higher in fat; use a small portion of eggplant Parmesan & balance out with lower fat choices the rest of the day)	Bean tacos, quick rice, & steamed broccoli	Instant couscous topped with steamed mixed vegetables	Vegetarian chili, whole grain crackers, & fresh fruit
Day 21:	Day 22:	Day 23:	Day 24:	Day 25:
Take out Chinese stir-fried vegetables (request no oil) & rice	Lentil-rice pilaf (box mix), steamed greens, & tomato Juice	Canned black beans (heated) topped with salsa, English muffin, & steamed broccoli	Vegetable lasagna (lowfat, frozen entree), & hard roll	Microwave-baked sweet potato with lemon juice & brown sugar, & small take-out green salad
Day 26:	Day 27:	Day 28:	Day 29:	Day 30:
Whole wheat pita pockets stuffed with chopped lettuce, carrots, sprouts, cucumbers, & tomatoes with no-oil vinaigrette dressing, & fresh fruit slices	2 bean burritos (from frozen; may be higher in fat than some other meals - get them without cheese, if possible), sliced whole tomato, & green pepper sticks	Vegetarian chili over quick rice, & steamed greens	Falafel (from mix) in pita pockets (a higher fat meal; balance out with lowfat foods the rest of the day), & fresh fruit	Instant black bean dip served with toasted pita wedges & salsa, & sliced orange

Making Sense of Food Labels

Why read food labels? If you haven't discovered it already, food labels are the best source of information about a particular product and can make comparison shopping a snap. Just as the saying goes .... "read the fine print" .... the detailed nutrition information provided on most food labels tells the real story about a product and may even clarify bold statements made on the front of the label.

Many of those "bold statements" on food packages, however, have misled and confused consumers. Remember the case of the brand-name cheesecake? It was labeled "light" - only for us to find out that the company was referring to the *texture* of its cheesecake, not the product's fat or calorie content. The current food labels have been criticized for many format and design problems, but sweeping changes are underway.

In 1989, the Food and Drug Administration (FDA) announced intentions to overhaul food labels, and it issued a set of proposals for doing so. At the time, FDA Commissioner David Kessler described label reform this way: "The goal is simple: a label the public can understand and count on -- that would bring them up-to-date with today's health concerns. It is a goal with three objectives: First, to clear up confusion; second, to help us make healthy choices; and third, to encourage product innovation, so that companies are more interested in tinkering with the food in the package, not the words on the label." The effort to improve the format and content of food labels also required the cooperation of the United States Department of Agriculture (USDA), since meat and poultry products come under USDA jurisdiction.

At about the same time that FDA issued its label reform proposals, the Nutrition Labeling and Education Act (NLEA) of 1990 became law. The NLEA specified that if FDA's proposals were not finalized by November 8, 1992, then the original proposals issued by the agency would become law with an effective date of May 8, 1993. Months passed, with input from industry, consumers, and health professionals. It appeared that USDA and FDA would not agree on a consistent format for labels and that, consequently, labels on meat and poultry, which are regulated by USDA, would be different from labels on foods regulated by FDA. In the end, however, a compromise was struck.

The key changes taking place in food labels are listed below. Anyone who is interested in reading the full details can request a copy of the new labeling regulations from the Government Printing Office Bookstore, 710 North Capitol Street, N.W., Washington, D.C. 20402 for $4.50, or call (202)512-0132. They are available on computer diskette as well.

KEY CHANGES IN FOOD LABELS UNDER NLEA LAW

• Nearly all foods will have nutrition labeling.

• Labels will include information on the amount per serving of saturated fat, cholesterol, dietary fiber, and other nutrients that are particularly related to today's health concerns.

• Labels will depict nutrient reference values to help label-readers see how foods fit into their diets.

• There will be clearly-defined meanings for words such as "light," "lowfat," and "high fiber," so that these words will mean the same on one product as they do on any other.

• In juice drinks, the total percentage of juice will be listed.

KEY CHANGES IN FOOD LABELS UNDER NLEA LAW (cont.)

• Claims about the relationship between a nutrient and specific diseases will be allowed, such as calcium and osteoporosis, or the link between dietary fat and cancer.

• Serving sizes will be standardized so that it will be easier to compare nutritional compositions of one product with another.

• There will be voluntary listing of nutrition information for many raw foods.

(Note: meat and poultry products are regulated by USDA and are not subject to the NLEA regulations. However, USDA's regulations will be similar to FDA's new rules.)

Manufacturers are required to have the new food labels in place by May, 1994. The regulations relating to health claims and certain parts of the labeling rule went into effect as of May, 1993. The new labels contain the following mandatory dietary information:

• total calories	• dietary fiber
• calories from fat	• sugars
• total fat	• protein
• saturated fat	• vitamin A
• cholesterol	• vitamin C
• sodium	• calcium
• total carbohydrate	• iron

There are many more specifics about how the new food labels will appear and what they will contain. The complete details can be found in the *Federal Register* or by writing the Government Printing Office for a copy of the regulations.

Here is a sample of the new food labeling format:

Nutrition Facts

Serving Size 1/2 cup (114 g)
Servings Per Container 1

Amount Per Serving

Calories 220   Calories from Fat 100

	% of Daily Value*
Total Fat 11 g	17%
Saturated Fat 5 g	25%
Cholesterol 15 mg	5%
Sodium 400 mg	17%
Total Carbohydrate 25 g	8%
Dietary Fiber 1 g	4%
Sugars 6 g	
Protein 5 g	

Vitamin A 6%   •   Vitamin C 15%   •   Calcium 4%   •   Iron 2%
* Percents (%) of a Daily Value are based on a 2,000 Calorie diet. Your Daily Values may vary higher or lower depending upon your calorie needs:

Nutrient		2,000 Calories	2,500 Calories
Total Fat	Less than	65 g	80 g
Sat. Fat	Less than	20 g	25g
Cholesterol	Less than	300 mg	300 mg
Sodium	Less than	2,400 mg	2,400 mg
Total Carbohydrate		300 g	375 g
Fiber		25 g	30 g

1 g Fat = 9 Calories
1 g Carbohydrate = 4 Calories
1 g Protein = 4 Calories

Vegans should note that as in the past vitamin B12 will not be required to be listed on food labels. However, if vitamin B12 has been added to a product, it may be listed in the ingredient listing. Since the amount will not be listed on the food label, though, anyone wanting this information will have to write the company and ask for it.

At the time of this writing, new food labels are already hitting the shelves. However, here is help for those who are interested in the old food labels:

NUTRITION INFORMATION PER SERVING

SERVING SIZE .... 7 3/4 OZ. (220 g) (A)
SERVINGS PER CONTAINER 2
CALORIES 170
PROTEIN (GRAMS) 11
CARBOHYDRATE (GRAMS) 40
FAT (GRAMS) ....1 (B)
SODIUM ....780 mg/serving

• Look carefully at the serving size (A). Food manufacturers have been known to say a serving is 1/2 of a candy bar or 1/4 cup of yogurt. If you normally eat more or less than the serving listed on the label, you will need to adjust for that when looking at the amount of fat in the product.

• Next, look at the number of grams of fat in the food (B) and adjust this for your usual serving size. Think about the amount of fat you'd like to have in your diet. How does this food fit in?

• Don't be misled by terms like "no cholesterol" or "light." "No cholesterol" often appears on labels of margarines and oils, foods that normally would not contain cholesterol anyway. Check the amount of fat in the food. Until the new label laws are implemented, "lite" or "light" on most labels can mean whatever the manufacturer wants it to mean. The product may be light in color or texture. Check the nutrition label for the amount of fat and compare it to similar foods.

Other Points to Consider When Assessing Food Labels:

- **Is the product a whole meal or just one part of the meal?** You may decide that a frozen dinner that contains 8 grams of fat is okay, considering that it's the whole meal. On the other hand, 8 grams of fat may be too much for a side-dish, for instance.

- **Will extra fat need to be added when I prepare this product?** If you plan to add margarine or oil to the food, take that extra fat into consideration when you assess the fat content of the product according to its label. For example, a bag of microwave popcorn may list its fat content as 4 grams of fat per serving. But if you know that you'll add some melted margarine to the popcorn, take that into consideration as well (can you do without the added fat?).

- **How does this item fit into my total diet (for the day or for the long haul)?** It may be okay to eat a higher fat treat once in awhile.

- **How many servings am I really likely to eat?** If a product seems high in fat, can you split it with a companion? For instance, a frozen eggplant Parmesan entree may contain too much fat if eaten "as is" as an entree. But if you split it with someone, and eat it on a roll as an eggplant Parmesan sandwich, then you may be able to work it into your diet.

If reading food labels isn't already a habit for you, begin by getting familiar with the food labels on products you already have at home. Look through your cupboards, refrigerator and freezer and read the labels.

Finally, take a few minutes the next time you go grocery shopping and read the labels on the products you typically buy or are thinking of buying. Pick up some of the new items that are on the market now and read the nutrition labels. Are they products you would like to try, given the label information you have read? Compare the labels and nutrition information on similar products. For example, pick up two different packages of processed cheese slices and compare the labels. You may be amazed at what you learn when you "read the fine print."

Part III

Lifestyle Tips

Do you have some specific questions about fats in the diet? Would you like to learn how to control your weight without counting calories? Part III of this book contains practical guidance to help you make dietary changes. There is even a section just for vegans, or those of you who already avoid all animal products.

Part III also features three special sections that will stimulate your imagination. Try your hand at "The Eaters' Challenge" - a quiz that rates the nutritional quality of your diet. The article, "What is Moderation?" reprinted from *Vegetarian Journal*, is a thought-provoking exploration of that old American platitude, "everything in moderation." You may recognize the names of some of those who responded to the question. Finally, Dr. Jerome Marcus offers a tongue-in-cheek solution to our nation's deficit problem.

 # About Fat

Everyone has told you to cut back on the fat in your diet - why?

Our Western-style diet centers around foods that are very high in fat. In the typical American diet, the greatest source of fat is meat and high fat dairy products. We also add a tremendous amount of fat by frying foods and adding other fats such as salad dressings, mayonnaise, margarine, and sour cream to our food.

The more fat people consume, the less fiber they tend to get from their diets. Fiber-rich foods, such as vegetables, fruits, legumes, and whole grains are typically low in fat and calories. High fat foods are concentrated in calories and have a tendency to "push out" or displace fiber-rich foods from the diet. Take a look at this example:

A person drinks three cups of lowfat milk one day - the number of servings of dairy foods currently recommended by the U.S. government for young women. Those three cups of milk provide about 400 calories, 15 grams of fat, and no fiber.

Think about how much food in the form of fruits, vegetables, or grains 400 calories could "buy," how much fiber, and how little fat would be gotten in exchange for those calories.

*400 calories **could** buy all of this:*

1 cup of broccoli	*1/2 cup of rice*
1 banana	*1/2 cup oatmeal*
1 orange	

The group of foods listed in this example contains 12 grams of fiber and only 3 grams of fat. These foods are nutrient-dense, too, providing 4 grams of iron and 259 mg. of calcium.

Diets that are high in fat and low in fiber are associated with many of the chronic diseases that afflict Western nations. These diseases, sometimes referred to as "diseases of affluence," include heart disease, some types of cancer, diabetes, high blood pressure, conditions such as obesity and diverticulosis, and others.

In past years, a lot of attention has been paid to the various forms of fat in the diet and their effect on cholesterol levels, low density lipoproteins, and other risk factors for disease. Saturated fats, for instance, which come mainly from animal products but are also present in tropical oils, stimulate the production of cholesterol. Nutritionists advise people to reduce their intake of saturated fats by cutting back on such foods as butter, cream, sour cream, high fat meats, and dairy foods.

On the other hand, polyunsaturated fats, which are present mostly in foods of plant origin, have a slight cholesterol-lowering effect. However, high intakes of polyunsaturated fats are associated with an increased risk of some types of cancer. Monounsaturated fats, such as olive oil and peanut oil, are more neutral in their effects on blood fats, although some studies have shown that populations with diets high in mono-unsaturated fats have less heart disease.

With all that in mind, remember that when we talk about nutrition and diet, there is a good deal of "gray area," or subjects for which there are not necessarily clear-cut recommendations. Sometimes recommendations can differ, depending upon an individual's circumstances. For instance, someone who is an athlete and who consumes several thousand calories a day may be able to fit more fat in his/her diet than someone who is not so active.

When we talk about keeping the fat content of the diet low, then, we have to acknowledge that there can be exceptions and it may be acceptable to eat a high fat food once in a while. It's also possible to balance one high fat food during a day with other lowfat foods the rest of the day. Generally speaking, when we cut back on fat in the diet, however, the goal is to keep the diet as nutritious as possible by replacing high fat foods with foods that provide plenty of fiber, vitamins, and minerals.

How can we put all of this information into practice?

A very practical approach to the issue of dietary fats is to focus your attention on the thing that is going to give you the biggest return for your efforts. Rather than worrying too much about the various forms of fat, it is more efficient to simply reduce your *total* intake of fat. If your fat intake is low enough, then other factors will fall into place.

For instance, if your fat intake is low enough, then your cholesterol intake will probably also be low, and your fiber intake will probably go up. If your fat intake is low enough, then you probably don't need to focus on where the small amount of fat in your diet comes from (although, if given the choice, polyunsaturated or monounsaturated fats are the best choices).

For more information about dietary fat, refer to the sections on weight control, label reading, and keeping a food diary. In general, women may want to strive for a fat intake of not more than about 30 to 35 grams of fat per day. Men may aim for 40 to 45 grams of fat per day.

Also note that throughout this book, "Menu Magic" sections have shown how typical high fat meals can be made into lower fat meals by making simple changes. In the nutrient analyses that follow, the calcium content of the modified menus decreased in some instances. This is because many of the menus contained cheese and other high fat dairy foods which were reduced or substituted out for lower fat menu items. One result was a reduction in the calcium content of the modified menu.

Less calcium in the diet is not necessarily a concern for vegetarians and people who moderate their protein intake (moderate protein is about 40-60 grams of protein per day for most people). People who eat less protein probably need far less calcium in their diets than people who eat a typical American protein-laden diet.

Questions and Answers

Q: I've heard that canola oil is better than corn oil for lowering my cholesterol level. Which is the best oil to use?

A: Polyunsaturated oils have a slight cholesterol-lowering effect. In theory, canola oil has more of this effect than safflower oil, safflower oil has more of this effect than corn oil, corn oil has more of this effect than soybean oil, and so forth. However, it isn't practical or advisable to increase your oil intake in order to lower your cholesterol level, because increasing your intake of fat significantly will probably result in weight gain and may increase your cancer risk. Practically-speaking, if your total intake of fat can be kept low, then the differences in cholesterol-lowering effects of the various kinds of oils is probably not significant. Buy the most economical oil you can find, whether it's canola oil, corn oil, safflower oil, or another vegetable oil.

Q: My weight is fine. What should be my goal for fat intake?

A: Even though your weight is where you want it, you are still best off following a high fiber, lowfat diet. People who eat this way usually lose weight if they have weight to lose. Those who are at their ideal body weights will maintain that weight if they eat according to their appetites. A high fiber, lowfat diet is generally health-supporting. Although it varies among individuals, women can generally be advised to hold their fat intake to about 30 to 35 grams of fat per day; men can aim for 40 to 45 grams of fat per day. Refer to the section on weight control for more information.

Q: I've heard that fish oil is high in omega-3 fatty acids and that these are good for lowering my cholesterol level. Are there any vegetarian sources of omega-3 fatty acids?

A: Some fish oils are high in omega-3 fatty acids, and some people have taken supplements of fish oil to lower their cholesterol levels. However, fish oil is not generally recommended. Due to its high calorie content in the amount that would need to be consumed to be effective (fat is a concentrated source of calories), taking fish oil could make some people gain weight. You are probably better off just focusing on reducing your total fat intake.

There are many foods of plant origin that contain linolenic acid, one of the omega-3 fatty acids. These foods include some cereal grains (such as rice and wheat bran, wheat and oat germ, and others), salad dressings, oils, and margarine, legumes (such as chickpeas and lentils), nuts and seeds, some vegetables (such as cauliflower, broccoli, and spinach) - even strawberries, raspberries, and avocados. The effect of these non-marine sources of omega-3 fatty acids on blood fat levels is being studied.

Some of these foods are healthful whether or not they contain omega-3 fatty acids. Whole grains, fresh fruits, and vegetables are full of fiber, vitamins and minerals. Once again, however, it doesn't make sense to focus on the omega-3 fatty acid content of these foods. The oils are too high in fat calories and would not be health-supporting in the quantities needed to lower cholesterol levels. The other plant foods noted are bulky - their cholesterol-lowering effect would more likely be due to their soluble fiber content than omega-3 fatty acids.

Q: If my total fat intake for the day is low, is it okay to eat some high fat foods? For example, could I put some cream cheese on my bagel?

A: Much of the fat that we get in our diets is a result of habit: using fatty salad dressings, adding margarine or sour cream to vegetables and breads, and eating fried foods. So, it's best to replace old high fat habits like these with new lowfat habits, like eating fruit purees on toast instead of margarine, or adding salsa to a baked potato instead of sour cream. With that said, it still may be practical to allow a few old high fat favorites to sneak into the diet occasionally, in limited amounts. For instance, it may be convenient to use a little peanut butter on a sandwich now and then, or to smear a small amount of cream cheese on a bagel. In the scheme of things, it's probably okay to add a little fat when the rest of the diet is made up of lowfat foods - the overall diet can still balance out to be low in fat.

Weight Control the Lowfat Way

Anyone who is overweight can attest to the day to day annoyances they have to endure - shopping for a flattering pair of slacks, trying to sit comfortably in a coach airline seat, or feeling guilty over enjoying a piece of birthday cake. But the psychosocial problems brought on by obesity are only the beginning. Obesity has far-reaching medical effects, including increased risk for high blood pressure, adult-onset diabetes, and heart disease. Conditions such as arthritis are also worsened by extra pounds. Adults aren't the only ones affected - obesity is a major public health problem for children, influencing their self-image today and setting the stage for health problems tomorrow.

The quest for weight control has supported an entire industry of dieting gimmicks, including a market for pills, books, diet plans, beverages, mechanical gadgets, and special outfits, all professing to be the key to effective weight loss. Diet plans have ranged from the low calorie variety to those attributing special weight loss properties to certain foods. Some diets have emphasized a particular nutrient, such as the high protein, low carbohydrate diets popular in the 1970s.

All of these approaches missed the boat, and almost none resulted in permanent weight control. The good news is that through all the trial and error, a very clear, effective approach to weight control has finally emerged and the concept is very simple.

For many years, weight loss plans focused on calorie counting. New research, however, has revealed that it isn't the calories that count. In a major study of relationships between diet and disease which was conducted in the People's Republic of China[1], researchers observed that **the Chinese eat several hundred calories per day more than Americans. Yet, overall, the Chinese are slimmer than their American counterparts. How can the Chinese eat more food and weigh so much less?** The answer may be due, in part, to more physical activity on the part of the Chinese. However, the biggest factor may be dietary fat - the Chinese get only 15-24% of their calories from fat as compared to the approximately 40% for Americans.

Fat is a concentrated form of energy. Gram for gram, fat provides over twice the number of calories provided by carbohydrate or protein. The human body is very efficient at storing dietary fat as body fat.

The typical Western-style diet is very high in fat. Meals which center around meat and which relegate the grains and vegetables to the side of the plate or leave them off entirely result in a diet that is low in fiber and too high in protein and fat. Liberal use of dairy products, such as milk and cheese, adds extra fat and protein and no fiber.

Old, traditional weight loss diets adhered to the concept of the Basic Four Food Groups, giving prominence to foods of animal origin - meats and dairy products. Calories were cut by reducing portion sizes but the basic composition of the meals was left the same. Meals were short on volume. An old stand-by tip to dieters was to serve food on small plates to make tiny portions less obvious. But the result was that dieters were left hungry and dissatisfied. Diets like these were low in fiber and

[1] Chen, J., Campbell, T.C., Li, J., and Peto, R.: Diet, Life- style and Mortality in China. A study of the characteristics of 65 counties. Oxford University Press, Cornell University Press, and the China People's Medical Publishing House, 1990.

caused constipation. No wonder most dieters fell off the wagon.

Lowfat vegetarian diets contain plenty of fresh fruits, vegetables, and whole grain breads and cereals. In contrast to the old-time diets, the ample lowfat vegetarian meals are filling and satisfying. The bulkiness of the diet helps to prevent constipation. Sometimes the high fiber content of vegetarian diets causes people to experience more flatulence, or gas, than before. However, the body gradually adapts to the increased fiber intake and the problem subsides. Since vegetarian diets are mostly (or entirely, if vegan) plant-based, protein and fat are present only in moderate amounts, while complex carbohydrate and fiber are plentiful. These characteristics of vegetarian diets are broadly health-supporting and make weight control much easier.

Getting Started

Have you ever heard the saying, "Worry about the dollars and not the pennies?" Think of dietary fat as the dollars. Focusing on how much fat your diet contains is the most efficient method of weight control for most people. The key is to know how much fat your diet contains and to have a goal or limit in mind. For most women, a limit of 35 grams of fat per day will result in weight loss. For most men, a limit of 45 grams of fat per day is a reasonable goal. However, individuals vary in their needs. Dietary goals can be tailored more accurately for individuals with some simple calculations.

The first step is to decide how much you would like to weigh. This can be determined a couple of ways. Some people know by experience at what weight they feel their best. If so, use that weight. Otherwise, refer to the 1983 Metropolitan Life Insurance Table[1] to estimate your best weight.

[1] Courtesy of Metropolitan Life Insurance Company.

METLIFE HEIGHT AND WEIGHT TABLES

MEN

Height Feet Inches	Small Frame	Medium Frame	Large Frame
5 2	128-134	131-141	138-150
5 3	130-136	133-143	140-153
5 4	132-138	135-145	142-156
5 5	134-140	137-148	144-160
5 6	136-142	139-151	146-164
5 7	138-145	142-154	149-168
5 8	140-148	145-157	152-172
5 9	142-151	148-160	155-176
5 10	144-154	151-163	158-180
5 11	146-157	154-166	161-184
6 0	149-160	157-170	164-188
6 1	152-164	160-174	168-192
6 2	155-168	164-178	172-197
6 3	158-172	167-182	176-202
6 4	162-176	171-187	181-207

WOMEN

Height Feet Inches	Small Frame	Medium Frame	Large Frame
4 10	102-111	109-121	118-131
4 11	103-113	111-123	120-134
5 0	104-115	113-126	122-137
5 1	106-118	115-129	125-140
5 2	108-121	118-132	128-143
5 3	111-124	121-135	131-147
5 4	114-127	124-138	134-151
5 5	117-130	127-141	137-155
5 6	120-133	130-144	140-159
5 7	123-136	133-147	143-163
5 8	126-139	136-150	146-167
5 9	129-142	139-153	149-170
5 10	132-145	142-156	152-173
5 11	135-148	145-159	155-176
6 0	138-151	148-162	158-179

Once you have determined your best weight, your level of physical activity needs to be considered. Follow along with the example provided in Figure A (see pg. 233). Estimate your level of physical activity - low, medium, or high. A **low activity level** means that you are mostly sedentary. Playing cards or golf, working at a desk job, and limited walking are examples of low level activities.

A **medium activity level** applies to someone who is physically active for 15-20 minutes about three times per week. Activities might include swimming, brisk walking, cycling, rowing, or playing tennis.

Someone who is more active than this - for more than 20 minutes continuously, at least three times per week - would be considered at a **high level** of physical activity. Multiply your ideal weight in pounds by the number of calories per pound that corresponds to your usual level of activity. The number that results is an estimate of the number of calories you need per day.

Next, not more than 30% of your daily calories should come from fat. Most adults would fare better by keeping their fat intake significantly lower. A figure such as 10-20% of calories from fat may be best. This number can even be adjusted as you go if need be. (Note that the Metlife Height and Weight Table used in this book does not apply to children. Nutritionists recommend that children's fat intakes remain a little higher than most adults, since children need the extra calories for growth. A fat intake of 25-30% of calories is reasonable for most children.)

Multiply your total daily calorie intake by your percent fat goal. Again, look at the example provided. For instance, if you want to hold your fat intake to 20% of your total day's calories, multiply your total calorie intake by 0.20. The result is the total number of calories per day that will come from dietary fat.

The last step is an easy one. Every gram of fat provides 9 calories. Divide the total fat calories by 9 calories per gram. The result is the number you've been waiting for - the number of grams of fat that will be your goal for the day. In other words, you will strive to keep your fat intake no higher than this number of grams of fat each day.

Figure A

Calculating Your Fat Gram Goal

Step One: Determine your best weight.

Example: 125 pounds

Step Two: Determine your activity level. Multiply the corresponding value by your best weight.

Low activity = 12 calories per pound
Medium activity = 13 calories per pound
High activity = 14 calories per pound

Example: If activity level is medium,
125 pounds x 13 calories per pound = 1625 calories

Step Three: Determine how many calories per day will come from fat.

Example: If your goal is 20% of calories from fat:
1625 calories x .20 = 325 calories from fat

Step Four: Determine how many grams of fat will be your limit for the day.

Example: Since there are 9 calories in a gram of fat:
325 calories divided by 9 calories per gram of fat =
36 grams of fat per day.

You will limit your fat intake to about 36 grams per day.

Again, the most efficient way to approach weight control is to focus on the fat content of the diet as opposed to counting calories. In fact, most people who have weight to lose can eat as much as they want, as long as they stay within their fat grams goal, and still lose weight. Lowfat foods are bulky and filling, and they are less calorie-dense than foods which are high in fat. Also, lowfat foods are not converted to body fat as easily as fatty foods. Most people who follow a fat-controlled diet will get full and stop eating before they consume so many calories that they can't lose weight.

There are cases where some people *do* consume such a great volume of food, even lowfat foods, that they cannot lose weight. However, this is the exception. In that case, a registered dietitian or a behaviorist may be able to help the person control food intake with additional counseling.

Although the focus is not on calories per se, estimating a target fat goal is easiest if you have a rough idea of how many calories you need. That is why the concept of calories is considered in the fat gram example above. Again, an alternative would simply be to choose a number of grams of fat to start with, without regard to calories, and to adjust from there after assessing the results over a period of time.

For instance, you may opt to simply hold your fat intake to 40 grams per day. After several weeks, if you find you are losing weight at a satisfactory rate, you can stay at that fat level. If you are losing too quickly, you can add more fat; if you still aren't losing weight, you can cut back a little more.

The following quick reference charts provide fat gram goals for diets that derive 10-30 percent of their calories from fat.

Quick Guide to Fat Gram Goals

For a 1,200 calorie diet:

Percent of Calories Desired From Fat	Fat Intake Per Day Should Not Exceed
30 percent	40 grams
25 percent	33 grams
20 percent	27 grams
15 percent	20 grams
10 percent	13 grams

For a 1,500 calorie diet:

Percent of Calories Desired From Fat	Fat Intake Per Day Should Not Exceed
30 percent	50 grams
25 percent	42 grams
20 percent	33 grams
15 percent	25 grams
10 percent	17 grams

For an 1,800 calorie diet:

Percent of Calories Desired From Fat	Fat Intake Per Day Should Not Exceed
30 percent	60 grams
25 percent	50 grams
20 percent	40 grams
15 percent	30 grams
10 percent	20 grams

For a 2,000 calorie diet:

Percent of Calories Desired From Fat	Fat Intake Per Day Should Not Exceed
30 percent	67 grams
25 percent	56 grams
20 percent	44 grams
15 percent	33 grams
10 percent	22 grams

For a 2,500 calorie diet:

Percent of Calories Desired From Fat	Fat Intake Per Day Should Not Exceed
30 percent	83 grams
25 percent	69 grams
20 percent	55 grams
15 percent	42 grams
10 percent	28 grams

Sometimes it helps to see how all of this translates into food. A good basic menu guide, developed by the Physicians Committee for Responsible Medicine[2], is printed below.

THE NEW FOUR FOOD GROUPS

Food Group	Number of Servings	Serving Size
Whole grains	5 or more	1/2 cup hot cereal 1 oz. dry cereal 1 slice bread
Vegetables	3 or more	1 cup raw 1/2 cup cooked
Legumes	2 to 3	1/2 cup cooked beans 4 oz. tofu or tempeh 8 oz. soy milk
Fruits	3 or more	1 medium piece of fruit 1/2 cup cooked fruit 1/2 cup fruit juice

Using the **New Four Food Groups** as a guide, a few sample menus are given below. When dairy products (except fat-free varieties) or fats such as margarine or oil are added to the basic meal plan outlined by the **New Four Food Groups**, the fat content of the menu increases.

[2]Physician's Committee for Responsible Medicine, P.O. Box 6322, Washington, D.C. 20015

Sample Menus:

#1   Breakfast:

2 oz. dry whole grain cereal
8 oz. soy milk (2% fat)
Fresh orange

#1   Morning Snack:

Bagel with jam
Apple

#1   Lunch:

2 bean burritos (no cheese) at Taco Bell
Water with lemon

#1   Dinner:

1 cup stir-fried vegetables over 1 cup cooked rice
6 oz. apple juice

Total fat for the day: 20 grams

Sample Menus:

#2   Breakfast:

1/2 cup oatmeal with brown sugar and cinnamon
4 oz. soy milk (2% fat)
1 slice whole wheat toast with 2 teaspoons peanut butter
8 oz. orange juice

#2   Lunch:

1 cup lentil soup
Tomato and mustard sandwich on rye bread
Small spinach salad with oil-free vinaigrette dressing
Water

#2   Dinner:

1-1/2 cups cooked pasta tossed with 2 teaspoons olive oil, steamed, mixed,
        chopped vegetables and fresh basil
Large piece of Italian bread, no butter
1/2 cup steamed broccoli with lemon juice
1/2 cup fresh fruit salad
Water

#2   Snack:

3 lowfat cookies
4 oz. soy milk

Total fat for the day: 25 grams

Sample Menus:

#3　Breakfast:

1 bagel with jam
1/2 cup applesauce
8 oz. soy milk (2% fat)

#3　Lunch:

Sandwich on whole wheat bread with 2 slices American cheese, tomato slices,
　　　lettuce, and mustard
1 cup vegetable soup
Green pepper slices
Water

#3　Dinner:

3 bean tacos
1/2 cup cooked rice
1/2 cup steamed broccoli with 1 teaspoon margarine
Watermelon wedge
Water

#3　Snack:

3 cups microwave popcorn (lowfat)

Total fat for the day:　35 grams

Sample Menus:

#4   Breakfast:

3 pancakes with maple syrup
6 oz. orange juice

#4   Lunch:

1 cup vegetarian chili
6 whole grain crackers
Large mixed green salad with 2 tablespoons Italian dressing
Water

#4   Dinner:

Veggie burger on a bun with mustard, catsup, and pickles
Oven-baked French fries with catsup
1/2 cup steamed green beans with 1 teaspoon margarine
1/2 cup cooked carrots with 1 teaspoon margarine
Water

#4   Snack:

1 pear

Total fat for the day: 45 grams

Staying on Track

A food record or food diary can be a very effective tool to help you watch your diet. By keeping a written record of foods eaten, you will be more aware of your diet in general. That awareness can help you make conscious decisions about eating, rather than unconscious or impulsive choices. Having more control over your eating behavior will, of course, make it easier for you to meet your goal. Anyone who has taken a course in time management or stress management may already be familiar with this concept, since it is a useful tool for many situations where behavior change is the goal.

Food diaries can monitor more than just what foods are eaten. They can also be a record of times that foods are eaten as well as other circumstances surrounding meals, such as where the food was eaten, what mood you were in, who else was present, and so forth. This information can be very helpful in targeting specific behavior intervention strategies.

For instance, individuals who find that they always eat high fat foods while watching television in the family room may make a pact to only eat at the kitchen table instead. Or people who find that they lose control and head straight for the refrigerator as soon as they get home after work may decide to have a piece of fruit before they leave the office, to keep themselves from being so hungry when they arrive home.

So, food diaries can help you maintain a high level of awareness about eating habits and to identify problem areas that need attention.

Refer to the section of this book about keeping a food diary (page 247) for instructions and a sample food diary.

There are many strategies that will help you stick to your lowfat diet. Some of these ideas are presented in the *Make New Habits Stick Chapter* (see pg. 247.) You should begin at your own pace. A reasonable schedule might look like this:

<u>Week 1</u>: Just begin by keeping a food diary for a week. Don't even worry about making any diet changes yet. Just get into the habit of keeping the diary. Become aware of some of the behaviors that may be problematic for you.

<u>Week 2</u>: Continue to keep the diary, and now begin to count the grams of fat you are eating each day. Refer to food labels and the references cited in the food diary section for help in figuring how much fat various foods contain. Tally the fat grams and total them for each day. Become aware of where the fat is coming from in your diet. Which foods contribute the most fat?

<u>Week 3</u>: Continue to keep the diary, but now begin to hold your fat intake to your goal. Keep a running total of your fat intake throughout the day. Adjust your food choices as appropriate throughout the day to stay within your fat budget.

<u>Week 4</u>: Now review some of the other behavioral strategies presented in the *Make New Habits Stick Chapter*. Choose one to focus on for the next couple of weeks. Then add another.

At this point, there may be trouble spots that you've identified yourself by keeping the food diary. You may opt to focus on solutions to these problems, giving yourself a couple of weeks for each change you want to make. Remember that you can proceed as slowly or as quickly as you want to with these changes. Some people opt to make changes overnight, and others are more comfortable with a more gradual approach.

What Are Your Expectations?

How much weight do you expect to lose, and how quickly do you plan to lose it? Most health professionals suggest that you try to lose no more than 1-2 pounds per week, which is considered a safe rate of weight loss. In practice, some people may lose a little more at first, then slow down, and some may lose weight more consistently. Individuals vary in their response to dietary changes.

Some people also find that they reach a plateau at some point. Weight loss slows down and then seems to stop. This can be frustrating if your goal weight has not been reached. There may be various reasons for this to happen. Some of the things you can consider or do if this should happen are:

- *See a registered dietitian for an evaluation of your diet at this point. Are you consuming too great a volume of food, even though it may be low in fat? If so, you may be taking in enough calories that you cannot lose the extra fat weight.*

- *Is your weight goal realistic? Could you already be at a weight that is healthy for you?*

- *This may be a point at which physical activity level will have to increase if further weight loss is going to occur. Evaluate your physical activity level. An exercise physiologist can help. Locate one by calling your local community gym or hospital outpatient services department.*

What If I'm At My Goal Weight?

Some people worry that once they reach their goal weight, they will continue to lose weight. What usually happens, though, is that people who are at their best weight will simply stay at that weight without any conscious effort (other than remaining on their healthy, lowfat diet). The key is to eat according to your appetite. If you are not eating enough to maintain your best weight, your body will let you know by signaling hunger. You will respond by eating more healthy, lowfat foods. That might mean taking second helpings at mealtime. People who eat lowfat diets eat a bigger volume of food than do people who eat the typical, high fat American diet. In fact, people who eat lowfat diets often snack between meals, too. That's okay. It's hard to go overboard if you are eating the right kinds of foods.

Additional Resources

Changing long-standing eating habits is a process that involves re-education in a variety of ways. This may include reading about diet and nutrition, "field experience" at the grocery store (and reading food labels), experimenting with new recipes, and perhaps spending a little more time planning meals at first. There are many good books and other teaching tools that you may find very helpful. Some of these are listed below:

COOKBOOKS

Laurel Robertson, Carol Flinders, and Brian Ruppenthal. *The New Laurel's Kitchen*. Berkeley, CA: Ten Speed Press, 1986.

Debra Wasserman and Charles Stahler. *Meatless Meals for Working People*. Baltimore, MD: The Vegetarian Resource Group, 1991.

Debra Wasserman and Reed Mangels. *Simply Vegan*. Baltimore, MD: The Vegetarian Resource Group, 1991.

Mary McDougall. *The McDougall Health-Supporting Cookbook, Volume I.* Clinton, NJ: New Win Publishing, Inc., 1985.

Mary McDougall. *The McDougall Health-Supporting Cookbook, Volume II.* Clinton, NJ: New Win Publishing, Inc., 1986.

Bobbie Hinman and Millie Snyder. *Lean and Luscious and Meatless.* Rocklin, CA: Prima Publishing, 1992.

OTHER BOOKS

Keith Akers. *A Vegetarian Sourcebook.* Denver, CO: Vegetarian Press, 1989.

Dean Ornish. *Dr. Dean Ornish's Program for Reversing Heart Disease.* New York, NY: Random House, 1990.

Dean Ornish. *Eat More, Weigh Less.* New York, NY: HarperCollins, 1993.

Neal Barnard. *The Power of Your Plate.* Summertown, TN: Book Publishing Company, 1990.

Make New Habits Stick -
Food Diaries and Tips for Maintaining a Lowfat Diet

Many people with good intentions find themselves slipping from their healthy eating habits when faced with certain situations, such as parties or dinners at friends' homes. Lapses are likely to occur, too, when life gets a little too hectic and planning meals takes a backseat to just getting through the day. There are strategies for dealing with situations like these that may help.

One powerful tool for aiding people in changing their eating habits is a food diary. A food diary is a record of what has been eaten over the course of the day. It can be simple or elaborate, depending upon its specific purpose. A simple food diary might include information about the time a food was eaten, what type of food it was, and the portion size. Some people find it helpful to record even more information, such as their degree of hunger at the time they ate, the place where they ate, or how they were feeling emotionally when they ate the meal. Information collected on food diaries helps people become more aware of what they eat, and it may give them clues about why they eat what they do. Moreover, food diaries can provide structure that some people find helpful when they are making a lifestyle change, and they can also be an effective teaching tool.

Below is an example of a simple food diary, developed to help keep track of fat. Food diaries can be kept on looseleaf paper, on file cards, in spiral notebooks, or even on scrap pieces of paper. In addition to the information noted on the sample below, you may want to add a column to note your *feelings* at the time you ate the snack or meal, as well as a column to note other *activities* that may have been going on while you were eating (TV, reading, etc.). Some people even like to note other people that were present while they were eating.

FOOD DIARY:

Date/Time	Food Consumed	Amount

Keep a record of how much fat you eat for a week or two. What foods are contributing the most fat to your diet? How does your fat intake compare to your daily goal? Are any changes necessary in your diet?

Keeping a food diary for a week or two can make you aware of habits you may not have previously noticed and can teach you some helpful things about yourself. For instance, is there a certain time of day during which willpower fades and you are more likely to experience a lapse? What can be done to prevent this from occurring? (e.g. eat an apple before you leave work, so you don't raid the refrigerator as soon as you get home).

Food diaries also come in handy during periods when routines are disrupted. Some people, for example, have difficulty maintaining their good eating habits during the holidays. By keeping a simple food diary for a week or two, they manage to retain more control by being more aware of what they are eating. This idea works well on vacations, when work schedules become frantic, and during periods of upheaval or other difficulty.

A few more points about food diaries:

- Keep your diary with you at all times, and record meals or snacks as soon as possible after eating them. When you wait until the end of the day to record your foods, you risk forgetting some of what you've eaten. More importantly, keeping tabs on your fat intake will do more good if you can make adjustments in your diet throughout the day. It's harder to adjust "after the fact."

    For example, let's say your goal is to limit your fat intake to 40 grams per day. If, by dinnertime, you've already consumed 35 grams of fat, you might opt for a lower fat meal than you might have if you didn't realize how much fat you had already eaten.

- Be specific when you record the type of food eaten. Was there margarine on the toast? What was the sandwich made of?

- Estimate amounts or serving sizes to the best of your ability. If you have no idea of what one tablespoon of salad dressing looks like, take a few minutes to experiment with some household measuring cups and spoons. Measure out a cup of cereal into a bowl, or see what 1/2 cup of rice looks like on a plate. You will feel more confident about your food record, and estimates of your fat intake will be more accurate.

- Food labels will provide information about the fat content of many of the foods you will record. However, when label information is unavailable, the fat content of other foods can be estimated with the help of a "fat counter," a small, quick reference book that can be purchased at most bookstores. Another good reference book that gives the complete nutrient content of foods is Bowes and Church's *Food Values of Portions Commonly Used, 15th Edition*, revised by Jean Pennington, Perennial Library, Harper & Row Publishers, New York, New York.

  Wondering how much fat you're getting in your favorite fast food fare? The Center for Science in the Public Interest has revised its excellent *Fast Food Guide*. This second edition of the guide, published by Workman Publishing, New York, 1991, is by Michael Jacobson and Sarah Fritschner.

- Food diaries can be used just like checkbooks. If you know that a special event is coming up this week, you might opt to "bank" a few grams of fat each day, saving them up to "spend" on a higher fat meal later in the week. This method helps some people retain more control over situations like parties, special meals, or while on vacation and helps them to budget for treats.

There are other strategies, too, that can help you stick to your healthful lowfat diet. Consider some of the ideas that follow. Can you think of others that would suit your lifestyle?

- **Eat at least three meals per day.** Some people actually prefer to eat more often than that - six small meals spread throughout the day works well for many people. People who eat a lowfat diet may find they get hungry between meals if they eat less frequently. Well-planned snacks can prevent the hungries, which can otherwise lead to impulsive eating and poor food choices.

- **Substitute lowfat alternatives to fatty condiments on foods like potatoes, rice, vegetables, and toast.** For instance, try using jam or jelly alone on toast, instead of spreading margarine or butter first. Catsup or salsa are good on potatoes. Try adding herbs or spices to rice and vegetables, instead of margarine and butter. Tomato sauce or salsa work well as toppings on these, too. Try some of the "no-oil" salad dressings on raw vegetables and salads, or use lemon juice and flavored vinegars. Mustard and chutney are good sandwich spreads to use in place of mayonnaise.

- **Social events may call for special strategies.** Try not to arrive at parties hungry. Eat your usual meal at home before leaving, or have a piece of fruit or other lowfat snack before you leave the house. At dinner parties, take only a small amount of the main dish if it seems creamy or fatty. Load up on vegetables, salad and bread instead (without adding extra fat). Take a half portion of dessert, and eat only half of *that* if it seems high in fat.

  Don't be shy about telling your host at the time a dinner invitation is extended that you are a vegetarian or that you are on a lowfat diet. Offer to bring a portion of the meal or to help with the cooking. It is also helpful to practice gracefully and diplomatically refusing fatty foods when someone is pressuring you to take them.

- **Avoid risky situations when you can.** Do you find you suddenly lose control of your car as you pass the donut shop and, incredibly, find yourself at the counter buying donuts "for the folks in the office ("not for me")" on your way to work in the morning? If that's the case, consider taking an alternate route to avoid traps like these.

- **The same rule applies to risky foods.** Avoid bringing certain foods into the house if you know they pose a problem for you. Let's say, for instance, that you really have a hankering for an ice cream cone. If you choose to have it, then go out to an ice cream store and get one, instead of bringing an entire half gallon of ice cream home from the grocery store.

- **Support is an important factor in the success of behavior changes.** Recruit support from family members and friends and encourage them to make the same healthful changes in their lifestyles if they seem receptive. If family members bring foods into the house that are a problem for you, discuss this with them. Is there a place where some of these foods can be stored where they are not readily visible (and, therefore, not as likely to "cue" you to eat them)? Sometimes it helps to store foods like chips or cookies in opaque containers (so you can't see what's inside) and to put them in the back of the cupboard or refrigerator where they take more effort to reach. Maybe family members would be agreeable to not bringing certain foods home if they know they are a problem for you.

- **Remember that eating well isn't "all or nothing."** It's what you do consistently, or over the long haul, that counts. Therefore, it may be acceptable for some people to splurge a little on special occasions and holidays. This may not be a good idea for everybody - some people are better off not making exceptions. Do what's right for you.

And For You Vegans Out There...

Vegetarian diets are usually lower in fat than nonvegetarian diets ... but not always. As you know by now, even vegetarians can get too much fat in their diets, particularly when they include high fat dairy products and eggs. On the other hand, vegan diets - vegetarian diets which exclude all eggs and dairy foods - are much less likely to be too high in fat. Vegan diets are characteristically bulky and lower in calories, since the vegetables, grains, legumes, and fruits that make up the diet are high in fiber and low in fat. For that reason, vegans tend to be slimmer than other vegetarians and non vegetarians.

There are, however, always exceptions ... and there are vegans who do indeed have diets that are high in fat. This section is for those who suspect they may be getting more fat in their diet than is desirable. It may also be good reinforcement for anyone - vegan or otherwise - who needs a reminder that excess fat comes from more than just dairy and eggs.

Excess fat sneaks into vegan diets mainly in two ways - either 1) foods that are naturally high in fat or are processed and contain lots of fat and 2) fat that is added to foods.

Look at the list of foods in the box that follows. All of these are included in vegan diets, but all of them are high in fat. Some are high in fat because they have been deep-fried in oil -

falafel and French fries, for instance. Others are high in fat because they are made with high fat ingredients such as tofu, or they have a relatively large amount of oil added in processing.

Some High Fat Vegan Foods

Many veggie burger patties	Most tofu hot dogs
French fries	Onion rings
Falafel	Hummus
Some ready-made salads	Most soy cheeses
such as tabouli	Peanut butter
or pasta salad	Puff pastry
Pastry-type pie crusts	Many brands of soy milk
(dessert pies and pot pies)	and soy yogurt
Many non-dairy frozen	Many cookies, cakes,
desserts (ice cream-type)	and other desserts

Many vegan foods become high in fat when extra fat is added to them, like dressings added to otherwise fat-free salads, or avocado layered onto sandwiches. Some of these sources of fat are listed in the box below:

Some High Fat Vegan Ingredients

Tahini (sesame butter)	Soy margarine
Vegetable oils	Avocado
Soy mayonnaise	Salad dressings
Peanut butter	Olives
and other nut butters	Coconut

Remember that any of the foods or ingredients listed in the preceding boxes may be worked into *some* people's diets. It all depends upon balance and individual needs. In other words, it may be okay for some people to eat French fries with their meal once in a while, especially if they keep the remainder of the meal low in fat, or if they otherwise keep their overall diet low in fat. Others may prefer to consistently avoid all high fat foods and ingredients. In the example that follows, one high fat vegan meal is converted into a lower fat vegan meal, but the modified menu still includes one high fat food:

Before:	**After:**
Veggie burger	Veggie burger
French fries with catsup	*Baked potato* with catsup
Mixed green salad with 2 T of Italian dressing	Mixed green salad with *lemon juice and pepper*
Fat content: 42 grams	Fat content: 14 grams

Menu Magic

The menu make-overs that follow demonstrate how fatty vegan meals can be made lower in fat - all by paying attention to balancing high fat foods with lower fat foods, substituting some high fat ingredients with lower fat ingredients, or cutting back on added fat.

Vegan Examples:

#1   Before: After:

Veggie pita sandwich (pita pocket,   Veggie pita sandwich
   chopped fresh vegetables and   *(no dressing)*
   mixed greens, vinaigrette dressing)   *Cup of gazpacho*
Plate of onion rings with catsup   Melon slices
Melon slices   Water
Water

Calories (Kcal):	726		Calories (Kcal):	252
Fat (grams):	45		Fat (grams):	5
Protein (grams):	9		Protein (grams):	13
Carbohydrate (grams):	76		Carbohydrate (grams):	42
Calcium (mg):	116		Calcium (mg):	112
Iron (mg):	4		Iron (mg):	3
Dietary fiber (grams):	3		Dietary fiber (grams):	3

Vegan Examples:

#2   Before:

Large salad from salad bar:
  mixed greens and fresh vegetables,
  4 olives, 4 T sunflower seeds,
  3 T French dressing
Hard roll
Water

Calories (Kcal):	625
Fat (grams):	42
Protein (grams):	17
Carbohydrate (grams):	54
Calcium (mg):	140
Iron (mg):	6
Dietary fiber (mg):	7

After:

Large salad from salad bar:
  mixed greens and fresh
  vegetables, 4 olives, *1 T*
  sunflower seeds, *flavored*
  vinegar and pepper
Hard roll
Water

Calories (Kcal):	270
Fat (grams):	10
Protein (grams):	11
Carbohydrate (grams):	41
Calcium (mg):	103
Iron (mg):	4
Dietary fiber (mg):	5

Vegan Examples:

#3   **Before:**   **After:**

2 handfuls tortilla chips   *1 handful* tortilla chips
  with salsa   with salsa
Bean burrito   Bean burrito
Chalupa (corn tortilla, beans,   Chalupa *(no guacamole;*
  lettuce, tomato, guacamole)   *add salsa)*
Water   Water

Calories (Kcal):	836		Calories (Kcal):	607
Fat (grams):	28		Fat (grams):	14
Protein (grams):	28		Protein (grams):	24
Carbohydrate (grams):	125		Carbohydrate (grams):	103
Calcium (mg):	276		Calcium (mg):	251
Iron (mg):	8		Iron (mg):	7
Dietary fiber (grams):	6		Dietary fiber (grams):	4

Vegan Examples:

#4 **Before:**

2 tofu hot dogs on buns with
   catsup and mustard
1/2 cup baked beans
Handful of potato chips
Soft drink

Calories (Kcal):	970
Fat (grams):	40
Protein (grams):	29
Carbohydrate (grams):	131
Calcium (mg):	143
Iron (mg):	6
Dietary fiber (grams):	10

After:

1 tofu hot dog on bun with
   catsup and mustard
1/2 cup baked beans
Large apple
Soft drink

Calories (Kcal):	660
Fat (grams):	16
Protein (grams):	17
Carbohydrate (grams):	120
Calcium (mg):	122
Iron (mg):	3
Dietary fiber (grams):	13

HELPFUL HINTS

- Vegans should limit the fatty foods and ingredients listed in the boxes printed on the preceding pages, or balance high fat foods with lowfat foods.

- Read labels of pre-packaged and convenience foods, since some are high in fat.

HELPFUL HINTS

- Vegans should eat at least 3 times per day. Consider adding lowfat snacks, too, if you find you get hungry between meals - this can help stave off impulsive high fat choices that may occur if you are over-hungry.

- Some good vegan cookbooks include:

  Debra Wasserman and Reed Mangels, Ph.D., R.D. *Simply Vegan*. Baltimore, MD: The Vegetarian Resource Group, 1991.

  Mary McDougall. *The McDougall Health-Supporting Cookbook II*. Piscataway, NJ: New Win Publishing, Inc., 1986.

  Joanne Stepaniak and Kathy Hecker. *Ecological Cooking*. Summertown, TN: The Book Publishing Company, 1991.

# Working With Recipes

Most everybody has a few recipes or meals that are favorites. Is Thursday pizza day at your house? Do you serve make-your-own burritos once a week? If you are like most people, you probably choose from about eight to twelve meal ideas that have become your favorites over time. Maybe you're tired of the same old things, or maybe you've realized that some of your favorites are high enough in fat that they need to be relegated to the "once in a while" category. Either way, it may be time to incorporate a few new ideas into your repertoire.

Bookstores are full of wonderful cookbooks for vegetarians. Natural foods stores may also carry a wide selection of cookbooks, including many that are not as easily found in mainstream stores. Vegetarian cookbooks often contain recipes which include generous amounts of cheese, eggs, and sometimes other high fat ingredients such as sour cream, oil, and butter. Mixed in with these recipes may be a few lowfat gems, however. Many people find that they only use one or two recipes from each of their cookbooks, but finding a new favorite or two can make the cost of the cookbook worth it. On the other hand, some vegetarian cookbooks do a good job of keeping the fat content of recipes low, so shop around, and try some of the cookbook suggestions listed at the end of this section.

Finding a few new recipes that are good enough to become regulars can mean some experimentation. Expect to find a few flops along the way, as well as some so-so dishes that won't quite make your list. Also expect to spend some *time* before you are finished - a little time invested up front, though, will be worth it in the end. However, recipes do not have to be complicated to be good. In fact, some of the most satisfying dishes may have as few as two or three ingredients, and these don't take much time to prepare.

There are many other sources of good recipes. Do you have a family favorite that happens to be high in fat? Consider testing it again with some modifications. Even traditional, old-time cookbooks can be sources of new ideas. Recipes can often be modified fairly simply and still turn out well. To reduce the amount of fat and cholesterol in recipes, try some of the substitutions that follow:

Whole Egg Replacers (Binders)

1 banana, mashed = 1 egg
2 Tablespoons cornstarch or arrowroot starch = 1 egg
Commercial egg replacer, available in natural foods stores or by mail order (such as Ener-G Egg Replacer)
1/4 cup tofu = 1 egg (blend tofu with liquid ingredients before they are added to dry ingredients)
2 egg whites = 1 whole egg
1 egg white + 2 teaspoons vegetable oil = 1 whole egg
Commercial egg substitute (such as EggBeaters)

Meat Substitutes (in stews, soups, etc.)

Tempeh (cultured soybeans, usually packaged in slabs)
Tofu (freezing then thawing leaves tofu with a chewy or meaty texture; it will turn yellowish)
Wheat gluten or seitan (this is made from wheat and has a meaty texture)
Bulgur wheat (cracked, rolled wheat. Adds texture to chili, casseroles)
Textured vegetable protein (TVP)

High Fat Dairy Substitutes

Cheese
Soy cheese (low in cholesterol and saturated fat, but may be high in
   polyunsaturated fat)
Nonfat or reduced fat dairy cheeses
"Yogurt cheese" (made by straining lowfat or nonfat yogurt through
   cheese cloth, leaving a cheese-like product)
Cream cheese substitute (made by blending 4 tablespoons of
   margarine with 1 cup dry lowfat cottage cheese, adding a small
   amount of skim milk if needed)

Milk
Soy milk (lowfat varieties)
Nut milks (blend nuts with water; these are still high in fat but
   lower in saturated fat and cholesterol than dairy milk)
Nonfat dairy milk

Sour Cream
Plain, nonfat, or lowfat yogurt
Soy yogurt (lower in saturated fat and cholesterol but may still be
   high in polyunsaturated fat)

Finally, the fat content of recipes can often be lowered
significantly just by changing some simple cooking techniques.
For example, vegetables can be sautéed in water rather than oil.
Use a pan with a nonstick surface, or spray a small amount of
vegetable oil spray onto the pan first. Then add enough water to
the pan to keep vegetables from sticking. Some people add a
few tablespoons of oil to the water when they cook pasta, to
prevent the pasta from sticking to itself or the pan. Reduce the
amount used, or try using no oil at all - the water may be
enough to prevent sticking. Think about the many ways that
you add extra fat to the foods that you prepare and consider
omitting that fat entirely.

Eater's Challenge

Think your diet is top notch? Not sure, and want to find out? Then try your hand at The Vegetarian Resource Group's **EATER'S CHALLENGE** and see how our experts rate your eating habits - vegetarian or not.

HERE'S HOW...

Circle the best answer to each of the questions that follow. Choose only one answer per question. Use your own judgment in choosing, and take the average of two answers, if appropriate. At the end of the quiz, you will add up the points corresponding to each answer to arrive at a final score.

PLEASE NOTE...

The quiz is designed to stimulate thought and interest about nutrition issues that affect most Americans and to help you evaluate your own eating habits in a general way. While the focus of the quiz is on such issues as fiber, fat, sugar, salt, and vitamin and mineral intake, it is not intended to cover everything or to give a precise measurement of your intake of these nutrients. Instead, use the results to help identify areas that need attention and to guide yourself in goal-setting and planning for a healthy eating style.

Quiz begins on next page. Have fun!

1. *How many servings of fruit do you eat most days? (A serving = 1/2 cup of juice or canned fruit, or 1 medium piece of fresh fruit.)*

(a) 4 or more   (b) 2-3   (c) 1   (d) 0
   +3   +2   0   -2

2. *How many servings of **fresh** fruit do you eat most days?*

(a) 3 or more   (b) 2   (c) 1   (d) 0
   +3   +2   +1   -2

3. *How many different kinds of fruit do you enjoy on a regular basis?*

(a) I eat only bananas (or apples)   (b) 3-4   (c) 5-6
          -2   -1   0

(d) 7-8   (e) 9-10   f) more than 10 (including <u>seasonal</u>
 +1   +2   favorites)....+3

4. *When you eat canned fruit or drink fruit juices, do they usually have sugar or other sweeteners added?*

(a) yes   (b) no   (c) eat only fresh fruit
 -2   +2   +3

5. *How many servings of vegetables do you eat most days? (one serving = 1/2 cup cooked, canned, frozen, or juice, or 1 cup raw; include potatoes, dried beans, and peas)*

(a) 0   (b) 1   (c) 2   (d) 3 or more
 -3   0   +1   +3

6. *How many servings of **fresh** vegetables, lightly steamed fresh, or steamed plain frozen vegetables do you eat most days?*

(a) 0	(b) 1	(c) 2	(d) 3 or more
-2	+1	+2	+3

7. How many different kinds of vegetables do you enjoy on a regular basis?

(a) don't eat vegetables   (b) eat only corn and green beans
       -3   -2

(c) 3-4   (d) 5-6   (e) 7-8   (f) 9-10   (g) more than 10 (including
   -1   0   +1   +2   seasonal favorites)....+3

8. When you prepare vegetables, do you add salt or salty condiments such as herb or garlic salts or soy sauce?

(a) usually	(b) sometimes	(c) rarely or never
-2	0	+2

9. When you prepare vegetables, do you add fats such as margarine, oil, animal fats, or cheese sauces?

(a) usually	(b) often	(c) sometimes	(d) infrequently	(e) rarely
-3	-2	-1	+1	or never....+3

10. How many servings of grain products do you eat most days? (such as rice, bread, dry cereal, oatmeal, pasta. One serving = 1/2 cup or one piece.)

(a) 0	(b) 1-2	(c) 3	(d) 4	(e) 5	(f) 6 or more
-3	-2	-1	+1	+2	+3

11. How many different varieties of grains do you enjoy on a regular basis? (for instance - rice, oatmeal, pasta, rye bread, bagels, whole wheat rolls, etc.)

(a) don't eat them   (b) 1-3   (c) 4-5   (d) 6-8   (e) 9-10
     -3   -2   0   +1   +2

            (f) more than 10
                +3

12. When you eat hot cereals, rice, or pasta, or eat toast or bagels, do you add margarine or other fats?

(a) usually   (b) often   (c) sometimes   (d) infrequently   (e) rarely
   -3   -2   -1   +1   or never...+3

13. Do you choose whole grain products, such as oatmeal, whole wheat bread, and dry cereals like Shredded Wheat or NutriGrain, instead of refined products, such as white bread or corn flakes cereal?

(a) usually   (b) often   (c) sometimes   (d) infrequently   (e) rarely
   +3   +2   0   -2   or never...-3

14. When you cook rice or pasta, do you add salt to the cooking water?

(a) usually   (b) often   (c) sometimes   (d) infrequently   (e) rarely
   -2   -1   0   +1   or never...+2

15a. If you are a vegetarian, how many servings of legumes such as beans or peas, lentils, tofu, or soymilk do you eat on a typical day? (one serving = 1/2 cup or 8 oz soymilk)

(a) 2 or more   (b) 1   (c) several per week
    +3   +2   +1

(d) less than several per week   (e) don't eat them
             -1   -2

15b. If you are a nonvegetarian, how many times per week do you eat a meatless (no meat, fish, poultry) lunch or supper meal? (Count meals with significant amounts of cheese or eggs, such as omelets, quiche, manicotti, or macaroni and cheese the same as you would a meat-centered meal).

(a) 9 or more	(b) 7-8	(c) 5-6	(d) 3-4	(e) 1-2	(f) 0
+3	+2	+1	0	-1	-2

16a. If you drink cow's milk or eat yogurt, what type do you usually eat?

(a) nonfat (skim) or 1/2%	(b) 1%	(c) 2%	(d) whole
+3	0	-1	-3

16b. If you do not use dairy products, how often do you eat green leafy vegetables such as spinach, kale, and broccoli, or eat other calcium-rich foods such as sesame seeds, sunflower seeds, tofu prepared with calcium, or dried figs?

(a) daily	(b) several times per week	(c) few times per week
+3	+1	-1

(d) 2 or fewer times per week....-2	(e) don't eat them -3	(f) take a calcium supplement...+1

16c. If you are a vegan, how often do you consume vitamin B12-fortified foods such as some breakfast cereals (check labels)?

(a) a few times per week	(b) periodically	(c) seldom	(d) never
+1	0	-1	-3

17. Regarding cheese, what type, if any, do you eat?

(a) only nonfat varieties	(b) reduced fat varieties such as part-skim mozzarella or lowfat cottage cheese...0
+2	

(c) mixed: some lowfat/
some regular...-2

(d) regular cheddar, provolone,
mozzarella, etc....-3

(e) don't eat cheese...+2

*18. How often do you eat cheese, including soy cheese?
(sandwiches, pizza, snacks, on pasta dishes, salads, etc.)*

(a) do not eat cheese or only in
small amounts, as a condiment...+2

(b) once a day
-3

(c) 5-6 times
per week...-2

(d) 3-4 times
per week...-1

(e) 1-2 times
per week...0

*19. How often do you eat unprocessed red meats each week? (such
as pork or lamb chops, hamburgers, steaks)*

(a) do not eat red meat   (b) 7 or more (c) 5-6 (d) 3-4 (e) 1-2
+3   -3   -2   -1   0

*20. How often do you eat processed red meats? (such as bacon, cold
cuts, sausage, hot dogs)*

(a) never   (b) rarely   (c) sometimes   (d) 1-2 times per week
+3   +2   0   -1

(e) 3-4 times per week   (f) more than 4 times per week
-2   -3

21. How large are your portions of meat after cooking?

(a) don't eat meat   (b) tiny - only use it as flavoring   (c) 1-2 oz.
+3   +3   +2

(d) 3-4 oz.   (e) 5-6 oz.   (f) 7 oz. or more
0   -2   -3

22. How are your meats usually prepared?

(a) fried   (b) baked, broiled, or boiled   (c) don't eat meat
    -3   +2   +3

(d) mixed: fried sometimes, fat-removing methods other times..0

23. How often do you use reduced fat or nonfat products such as nonstick vegetable spray, nonfat or reduced fat salad dressings, butter-flavored sprinkles, etc?

(a) usually (b) often (c) sometimes (d) don't add fat (e) rarely
   +3   +2   +1   to foods...+3   or never...-1

24. What would you most likely spread on sandwiches?

(a) mayonnaise, butter,or margarine (b) reduced fat mayonnaise
            -3   -1

(c) mustard   (d) chutney, salsa, or nothing
   +1   +2

25. What would you most likely add to a salad?

(a) creamy, mayonnaise-based   (b) reduced fat dressing
    dressing...-3   -1

(c) nonfat or "no-oil" dressing   (d) oil-based dressing
       +2   -2

(e) vinegar, lemon juice, or salsa (f) nothing (g) don't eat salads
       +2   +2   -1

26. What type of frozen dessert do you typically choose?

(a) ice cream   (b) ice milk, sherbet, or   (c) nondairy
     -3   frozen yogurt...-2   -1

(d) fruit ice, nonfat sorbet or frozen yogurt,   (f) don't eat them
     or other nonfat, nondairy type...+2   +2

27. *What type of cookie do you most often choose?*

(a) gingersnaps, any with less   (b) homemade with whole grains
     than 1 gram of fat per cookie...+1   and reduced fat...+2

(c) chocolate chip, butter cookies, regular commercial...-3

(d) don't eat them...+3

28. *What type of cake or pastry do you most often choose?*

(a) cheesecake, Danish   (b) frosted or creme-   (c) plain cakes
     pastry, or donuts...-3   filled layer cakes...-3   -2

(d) angelfood   (e) homemade plain cakes with   (f) don't eat them
     cake...+1   whole grains and reduced fat..+2   +3

29. *How often do you eat desserts such as cakes, cookies, ice cream, pies, or pastries?*

(a) daily   (b) 3-6 times per   (c) twice a week   (d) once a week
     -3   week....-2   -1   0

(e) couple of times a month   (f) rarely or never
     +1   +3

30. *Which of the following snack foods would you be most likely to choose?*

(a) snack chips, salty "mixes,"
caramel corn, or nuts...-3

(b) salted pretzels
-1

(c) buttered or salted popcorn
-1

(d) unsalted pretzels
+1

(e) unsalted, unbuttered
popcorn...+3

(f) don't eat salty snacks
+3

31. How often do you eat candies such as chocolate or candy bars?

(a) rarely or never   (b) infrequently   (c) sometimes
+3   +2   -1

(d) often   (e) daily
-2   -3

32. Which would you most likely choose as a snack?

(a) cake, pie, pastry, cookies, candy, or ice cream...-3

(b) only lowfat sweets like gingersnaps or hard candy...-1

(c) fruit...+3   (d) snack chips, nuts, or salty or greasy mixes...-3

(e) bagels, unbuttered popcorn,   (f) don't eat high fat snacks
whole grain cereal...+3   +3

33. What do you usually drink with meals?

(a) water (b) soft drinks (diet and regular) (c) milk (d) nothing
+3   -3   0   0

(e) tea or coffee (f) fruit juice (g) herbal tea (h) decaffeinated
-3   +1   0   tea or coffee...-1

34. How much water (including mineral or seltzer waters) do you
drink each day?

(a) several glasses   (b) 1-2 glasses   (c) none
        +3   0   -3

35. *How much tea, coffee, and cola do you drink?*

(a) none   (b) 1-2 cups   (c) 3-4 cups   (d) 5 or more cups
   +3   per day...-1   per day...-2   per day...-3

(e) only drink herbal   (f) only drink decaffeinated tea or coffee,
        tea...0   1 or more cups per day...-1

36. *How often do you choose alcoholic beverages (including beer and wine)?*

(a) never or rarely   (b) occasionally   (c) once a day
        +3   +2   0

    (d) twice a day   (e) more than twice a day
          -1   -3

DETERMINING YOUR SCORE

✍ Number of (+) points _____

✍ Number of (-) points _____

✍ Total (+) and (-)
    added together   _____

HOW DID YOU DO?

+62 to +102 = EXCELLENT. You know that food that is good for you can taste great, too. You have developed some good habits. Keep up the good work.

+22 to +61 = GOOD. You are striving to get the benefits of a diet rich in fiber and other nutrients yet moderate enough not to be excessive in fat and protein. Now consistency is the key. Determine which areas still need attention, then continue to let your good eating habits evolve.

-18 to +21 = FAIR. You know what needs to be done: more fiber, more fresh fruits, vegetables, whole grains, and less fat and protein, sugar, salt, caffeine ... The problem is putting it into practice. Try planning ahead more. Put your goals in writing, and shop with a list. Become a "weekend cook," try some new recipes, and check out some of the additional resources listed in this book. Above all, **KEEP WORKING ON IT!**

-102 to -19 = **BACK TO THE DRAWING BOARD.** It's not that you aren't trying, it's just that you need that extra **PUSH!!!** Start small. Pick one or two changes you would like to make this month, then add another each month. At the end of the year, take this quiz again. You may be pleasantly surprised to see that "cleaning up your act" doesn't have to be as hard as you may think!

*This article by Suzanne Havala appeared in **Vegetarian Journal** (Volume X., No. 6, November/December, 1991.)*

Deciphering Those Dietary Recommendations -

How Do You Define Moderation?

"Use sugars only in moderation."
"Moderate the use of egg yolks and organ meats."
"Use salt and sodium only in moderation."
"If you drink alcoholic beverages, do so in moderation."

The third edition, 1990, of the U.S. Department of Agriculture's Dietary Guidelines for Americans clearly advocates moderate consumption of certain foods and substances that are frequently consumed in excess in the U.S. Other similar sets of recommendations, issued by a variety of health promotion organizations, also call for moderation. But what do these recommendations really mean? How do **you** define the term "moderation?"

According to the Dietary Guidelines for Americans, moderation means "avoiding extremes in diet." Webster's Dictionary agrees - to moderate means to "lessen the intensity or extremeness" of something. But exactly how does this translate for me and you? Moderation is a relative term. How much is too much? How much is too little?

Health professionals and consumers alike have struggled with this question:

"Moderation means many things to many people. It can mean quantity; it can mean variety; it can mean balance; it can mean caution...We try to be palatable for the average consumer but do not make it clear enough to be understood. We, then, fall back on research and terms that are too technical and calculations that are too precise. Having been trained in preciseness, we forget the real world doesn't know what 6 grams of sugar means - even when we go to 'moderation of sugars,' like the Dietary Guidelines, we confuse the public **and** ourselves."

Kay Ach, M.P.H., R.D.
Breastfeeding Promotion Coordinator
Office of WIC Services, Department of Health
Olympia, Washington

"**I** typically am indicating a frequency of once (sometimes twice) per week for the 'in moderation' behavior in question. Of course, it always depends on what we're talking about....For instance, for the patient with diabetes it may range from a 'treat' once per week to that of a 'treat' only on special occasions (e.g., birthdays). For most of the behavior changes I work with, one time a week seems to be the 'moderation' definition."

Linda Gallagher, R.D.
Quality Improvement/Education Coordinator
Children's Hospital
Boston, Massachusetts

"**M**oderation, in eating or other aspects of life, is indeed a term that many use yet few examine the true definition. This term is not unlike 'common sense'... Moderation in a person's eating habits can mean many different things. It could propose the consumption of a small amount of a certain food, i.e. red meat. The term moderation is sometimes associated or confused with 'balanced.' Moderation often carries a connotation of unhealthy or fattening foods... Moderation is the taking of the knowledge of correct nutrition and applying it."

Chris Robertson
18 year old student
Chapel Hill, North Carolina

Most would agree that when we do try to describe what we mean by "moderation," definitions are vague at best. Even when an attempt is made to clarify the term, we still end up with generalities:

"**M**oderation in food choices means avoiding extremes in the diet - eating too much or too little of a particular nutrient or just concentrating on one or two food groups. It's important to recognize serving sizes and know the number of servings that should be eaten each day. There's a big difference between 6 ounces of lean meat and 12 ounces, or between 8 ounces of yogurt and 16! Keep in mind, too, that moderation does not mean deprivation. We can make trade-offs. It's all right to have a serving of a higher-fat or higher-calorie food if lower-fat, lower-calorie foods are eaten at other times of the day."

From the 1991 National Live Stock
and Meat Board's publication,
"Exploring Meat and Health"

"**T**here are no good foods or bad foods...there are only inappropriate amounts. The key to a healthy diet is to eat as many different foods as possible and to eat them in moderation. Moderation means the avoidance of extremes and there are hints in our day to day language as to what that means for specific foods. A cup of coffee ...not a gallon. A slice of toast...not a loaf. A piece of chocolate...not a box. The smallest self-contained unit for each food is usually a moderate amount."

Burt Wolf, TV Food Reporter
New York, New York

"**T**o me, eating in moderation is eating within reasonable limits, not excessive or extreme. Eating in moderation is eating a snack and three meals a day and eating until you are comfortable. Stopping when you are full, but you should fill yourself up and not go hungry. Also, it's not eating constantly and it's also not going around hungry. Eating in moderation is eating all kinds of foods. It's not just eating all healthy foods or bad foods. It is having a wide variety of foods in your diet."

Meredith Lester, 16 years old
Charlotte, North Carolina

In nutrition circles, use of the term "moderation" is often followed by the dictate that "there are no good foods or bad foods." The idea is that a balance between the two will produce moderation. Marian Burros, food writer for the *New York Times*, has an interesting perspective on the topic:

"**A**fter you have consumed the nutrients you need in a given day, if you have any calories left over, you can eat anything you want to eat. You don't have to go overboard and say 'never.'"

Regarding "good foods/bad foods": "There <u>are</u> some foods that are better than others. If you don't want to use the term 'bad foods' - there are foods and there are good foods. The good foods you can eat anytime and the foods you can eat occasionally."

Similarly: "Simply put, to me eating in moderation means not treating any food as a mortal enemy - anything can be okay now and again as long as one's typical daily fare is low in fat and high in fiber. By necessity, this means eating foods close to the earth - fruits, vegetables, grains, beans - as the basis of one's meals, and using animal protein, if at all, as a complement to vegetable protein and with only occasional splurges on high-fat fare."

Jane Brody
New York Times Science Writer
Brooklyn, New York

Generalized dietary recommendations leave many people unsure about just what foods and how much of them they should eat. Why are these recommendations so vague? Are they of any use?

One problem that nutritionists encounter when they deliver dietary advice is that advice given to individuals may be different from advice given to groups of people, or populations.

Recommendations made to an individual can be very specific, tailored to the needs of that person. Individuals' needs can vary a great deal from one person to the next. For instance, a person with high blood pressure and diabetes may be given advice that is markedly different from advice given to a healthy marathon runner.

SIMPLE, LOWFAT & VEGETARIAN

"**I** am careful to use examples of specific situations. If an individual and I are talking about cholesterol, we consider food items that need to be reduced. If we are discussing high sugar foods and weight loss is a goal, we discuss how to moderate the food choices."

> Sandra Facinoli
> Coordinator, Food & Nutrition Information Center,
> United States Department of Agriculture
> Beltsville, Maryland

"**M**oderation means 'within limits.' But according to Maharishi Ayurveda, the oldest natural system of medicine known to man, there are no universal limits that apply to every individual, and therefore there can be no standard recommendations of moderation. Each person is unique and exhibits biologic individuality, according to Ayurveda. Therefore, before any prevention or treatment recommendations can even be suggested, individual body type must be determined. This will determine dietary, lifestyle and behavioral routines for that specific individual...."

> Arthur Cohen, M.D.
> Pathologist & Certified Ayurvedic Physician
> Charlotte, North Carolina

Groups of people are made up of many individuals who may have varying needs. Therefore, dietary advice given to populations must be general enough to be able to be applied to most individuals and to meet the range of individual needs. In doing so, the recommendations inevitably become more vague.

"**M**ostly, it is a softening, CYA approach to be helpful, yet ambiguous."

> Kay Ach, M.P.H., R.D.
> Olympia, Washington

There is another reason that dietary recommendations for the public are ambiguous. Pressure from certain industry groups has also influenced the wording of dietary guidelines and resulted in "watered down" advice that shies away from specifics about recommended frequency and portion sizes of selected food products. These groups stand to lose if people eat less of their products.

"I never use the term [moderation] because it's so vague and the food industry uses it as a smokescreen to make people think whatever they're eating is okay."

> Bonnie Liebman, Director of Nutrition
> Center for Science in the Public Interest
> Washington, D.C.

A related case in point is the recent controversy over the U.S. Department of Agriculture's proposed "Eating Right Pyramid" which graphically deemphasized the role of meat and dairy products in a healthful diet. A story in the *Washingon Post* (April 17, 1991) describes how the Agriculture Department "yielded to pressure from the meat and dairy industries and abandoned its plans to turn the symbol of good nutrition from the 'food wheel' showing the 'Basic Food Groups' to an 'Eating Right Pyramid'..." According to the *Washington Post*, "representatives of the dairy and meat industries complained that the pyramid was misleading and 'stigmatized' their products." A representative of the National Cattlemen's Association said that the group "felt consumers would interpret the pyramid to mean they should drastically cut down on their meat consumption." The story goes on to describe how pressure from industry has influenced government dietary guidelines for many years.

Does this mean that nutrition advice doesn't mean anything? Maybe calling attention to the general kinds of dietary changes people should make will spur people to examine their own lifestyles more closely and motivate them to take steps in the right direction. On the other hand, some people think that the "moderate" approach as we know it needs to be replaced with more sure-footed, pointed recommendations:

"I do not use the term 'moderation' in relation to nutrition advising, except in an ironic sense to indicate that I know my listeners have no idea what it means. The basic principles of healthy nutrition are very clear: base the diet on a wide variety of fruits, vegetables, and grains, and, if you eat meat and dairy foods, choose those that are low in fat. When these principles are followed, moderation rarely needs to be an issue."

Marion Nestle, Ph.D., M.P.H.
Professor & Chair, New York University School of
Education, Health, & Arts Professions
Department of Nutrition, Food & Hotel Management
New York, New York

"**I** never use the word - it really is not useful, subject to incredible variation in interpretation, and, therefore, adds confusion to teaching nutrition. I think to tell someone to use or choose a food or drink in moderation when that person has a problem of over-consumption of that food is especially useless....Moderation can mean anything a person wants it to mean if the person is involved in some good old self-deception....The biggest joke is the direction of the new Dietary Guidelines for Americans which instructs to use sugars, salt, and sodium only in moderation when in our American diet even to moderate use would still result in great overuse. They have to find a better way to teach when working with such extremes as we have in many Americans' diets."

Kathleen Babich, R.N.
Public Health Nurse
Oakland County Health Department
Southfield, Michigan

Robert Pritikin, of Santa Monica, California is the Director of the Pritikin Longevity Centers. He concurs with the idea that, within the context of our American culture, terms such as "moderation" can be problematic:

"**M**oderation is a meaningless term. In this country, we're dying of moderation. It is an absurd concept. It refers to the norm of society rather than what's physiologic. At the Pritikin Longevity Centers we ask, 'What is the healthiest way to eat?' Moderation is a deceptive term; it reflects cultural norms."

In terms of the Pritikin plan: "if a person is raised on an ideal diet, a moderate program would be a continuation of what is healthy - of what you usually do, within the parameters of the individual's norm. The trick is to set up healthy parameters. Tastes are very cultural - not innate (with the exception of sugar) - trained. Tastes can be trained to different diets. Personally, my goal is 10% fat. I am primarily a vegetarian, using flesh only as a condiment."

The meaning of dietary moderation means many things to many people. Some find the term useful; others find it frustrating or outright misleading. Contrast the very different ways in which the following people understand the concept of moderation:

"The following is what I mean by "moderation" as it relates to diet:

1). Red meat 1-3 times per month
2). Most meats being chicken, fish, turkey
3). Dietary cholesterol intake <300 mg/day
4). Fat up to 25-35 gm/day
5). High fiber
6). Alcohol one (or less) per day
7). Avoid 'simple sugars,' i.e. candy bars, soft drinks, etc.

I tend not to go into saturated/unsaturated fats...if I can get patients to just lower fat grams I'm happy. I tell people high fiber helps elimination... binds cholesterol, reduces risk of diverticular disease, and may help prevent colon cancer. In terms of cholesterol I tell people, 'if it's a plant, it's safe.'"

Al Hudson, M.D.,Internist
Charlotte, North Carolina

"I wish to place my response in a broader context. Eating is a great <u>pleasure,</u> or should be, ideally serves an important social function in families, among friends, and in professional, political and recreational contexts, and, of course, is essential for health. Enjoyment of food clearly plays a very important role in my list of priorities for living. 'Moderation,' therefore, needs to be defined in terms of its influence on the enjoyment of eating. Under most circumstances, individuals should eat what they like in the amounts that they wish.

But, of course, there are constraints, based primarily on adverse effects of eating patterns on health. Thus, <u>gluttony</u> leads to obesity, can be antisocial, and is associated with a variety of chronic diseases. On the opposite tack, <u>anorexic behavior</u> can be nutritionally damaging and certainly belies the pleasure principle of eating. Needless to say, food intake practices that are nutritionally unsound, such as certain dieting regimens and bizarre diets, are excluded from any definition of moderation.

Finally, so much confusing hype exists about food and its relation to chronic diseases, much of it overstated or distorted, that many people, at least in the U.S., seem to be developing a <u>fear</u> of eating. Fear and pleasure are incompatible. While I enjoy eating carrot sticks for their crispness and texture and color and delicate taste, people who gnaw disconsolately on a plate of them for <u>fear</u> of eating more enjoyable foods would not be considered as eating 'in moderation,' according to my definition."

James A. Olson, Ph.D.
Distinguished Professor of Biochemistry
Iowa State University,
Ames, Iowa

When you hear or make recommendations advising people to use moderation in their eating habits, what do you think or mean? The responses given to this question by those who were surveyed shows how very differently people perceive the issue of moderation. In the two examples above, for instance, a physician responded with a very objective definition of moderation. A nutritional biochemist, on the other hand, related to the question in a much more subjective way.

People interpret the meaning and usefulness of dietary moderation in many different ways. Health professionals and the general public alike struggle with the definition of a "moderate" diet. Some are comfortable with a degree of ambiguity; others strive to pin it down to a specific set of criteria. Still others reject the popular use of the term altogether, pointing out ways in which the term is abused or otherwise confuses or complicates progress toward a more healthful American diet.

Does advocating the concept of dietary moderation make sense for our society right now? In the August 18, 1991 issue of *Parade Magazine*, Marilyn vos Savant answered the following question in her column, "Ask Marilyn:"

Q: Can you make a case for "balance in all things?"

A: I can, but I certainly wouldn't recommend it to everyone. Moderation may be fine for parents and politicians, but science, literature and art need the bold.

Are our current dietary guidelines for Americans bold enough? Is there a case for eating "in moderation?" What do **you** think?

*This article, previously published in **Vegetarian Journal**, (Volume XI., No. 4, July/August, 1992), was written by Suzanne Havala, M.S.,R.D.*

NOTE FROM THE EDITORS OF THE VEGETARIAN JOURNAL:

When we assigned this story to Sue Havala, we hoped to decipher and help readers understand exactly what moderation is. Our intention was to give the public specific knowledge on how to apply the term "moderation" to their eating habits.

After several months of investigation, what can we tell you? Views of moderation seem to fall into one of three totally different categories.

1) There are no good or bad foods. As long as you are not obese, anorexic, or have particular health problems, you can pretty much eat what you want.

2) Moderation has no meaning because the recommendations are so diluted due to the influence of politics and economics.

3) Moderation justifies the type of diet the particular person or organization wants to promote. For example, to the meat industry, moderation may mean there is a big difference between 6 ounces and 12 ounces of red meat a day. To a nutrition advocacy group, moderation may mean red meat one or two times a week, or in some cases no meat at all.

The common ground between these disparate views is that **eating in moderation involves thinking on the part of the individual.** When you see the word *moderation*, it should be a prod to look at your diet and your own concerns. Gather information, talk to your health provider if you have special needs, and then make decisions for yourself, without becoming overly obsessive about what you eat. For those of you who read *Vegetarian Journal*, you have probably decided to eat "moderately" within a framework of recommendations by authorities such as the American Cancer Society, The American Heart Association, and the United States Surgeon General, and thus focus your diet around fruits, vegetables, and grains. As humans acquire more nutrition knowledge, we will continue to define and redefine what *moderation* really means for your diet.

The Fat Tax:

An Idea Whose Time Has Come?

By Jerome Marcus, M.D.

There is abundant information which suggests that the population of the United States would benefit from reduced fat consumption. Heart disease, cancer, and stroke, the three most common causes of death, can at least in part be linked to excessive fat in the diet. Coincident with this is a desire on the part of our Federal Government to increase tax revenues. Is it possible that financial incentives could be set up which would link these two seemingly unrelated facts so that society might benefit?

Tax credits or tax reductions are frequently given to encourage that things be done or consumed by individuals or industry. Increased taxation frequently reduces the probability that something is going to occur. Since the consumption of fat is something which is overdone, maybe it is time to consider taxation as a means of fat control.

The best available data suggest that 37% of the calories in the average adult American's diet comes from fat. American Heart Association guidelines place the maximum acceptable intake at 30%. The 30% figure seems to have been arrived at rather arbitrarily. The thinking was that people could reduce fat consumption to this level without undue pain. Unfortunately, this thinking has given people a false sense of security. In reality, fat consumption should probably be no more than 22 or 24% of calories for prevention of heart disease. Authors from Pritikin to Ornish have demonstrated that fat consumption of perhaps 10% may lead to reversal of preexisting coronary artery disease. I have chosen 24% of the calories from fat as a compromise which may be consistent with prevention of coronary artery disease.

Perhaps a "fat tax" does make sense. How would it work? What would it do? The average woman consumes 1,640 total calories per day including about 67 grams of fat and the average man consumes 2,500 total calories including about 103 grams of fat. Reducing fats to 24% of calories would require fat reduction of 23 grams per day for women and 36 grams per day for men (Table 1).

TABLE 1		
	FEMALE	MALE
Total average calories per day	1,640	2,500
37% of calories from fat	67 grams	103 grams
24% of calories from fat	44 grams	67 grams
Difference	23 grams	36 grams

Reducing fat consumption by this amount would require some dietary changes, but nothing very painful. Butter or margarine in stick form typically has 11 grams of fat per tablespoon. Reducing fats from 37% to 24% of calories requires elimination of the equivalent of about two or three tablespoons of margarine or butter per day for the average woman or man respectively. That is something that could be done. Many salad dressings contain eight or more grams of fat per tablespoon. Many cheeseburgers served in fast food outlets have thirty or more grams of fat.

What should we do? Let's look at a fairly extreme model: suppose we put a tax of five cents on each gram of fat in a given food product. If people did nothing and the average American continued to consume 31,000 grams of fat per year, the typical person would pay $1,550 per year in fat taxes. This is an interesting number, because it represents approximately one half of the average cost of health care per person in the United States, or approximately $390 billion for the entire population. With an extra $390 billion dollars "contributed" to our government, our deficit problems would seemingly disappear.

However, if this wildest of sin taxes were instituted, we would hope to see other effects. That high-fat cheeseburger with 30 grams of fat would have a tax of $1.50. Look at Table 2 (next page) to see what would happen to some common products in the supermarket.

Fleischmann's margarine, which for all intents is pure fat, would increase in price by more than eighteen times. People would either stop buying butters, margarines, oils, and fats, or would use them very sparingly. Food manufacturers would have to search for lower fat alternatives. Breyer's Light Ice cream would cost approximately one third less than their regular ice cream, but would still be a luxury item. Pretzels would be a far more economical snack food than fried high-fat potato chips.

TABLE 2

PRODUCT	TOTAL GRAMS FAT	CURRENT-SUPERMARKET PRICE	FAT TAX	NEW PRICE
Fleischmann's Margarine (16 oz.)	352	$0.99	$17.60	$18.59
Breyer's Natural Vanilla, Chocolate & Strawberry Ice cream (half gallon)	128	$3.49	$6.40	$9.89
Breyer's Light Vanilla, Chocolate & Strawberry Ice cream (half gallon)	64	$3.49	$3.20	$6.69
Dannon Blueberry Yogurt (8 oz.)	3	$0.75	$0.15	$0.90
Dannon Blueberry Light Yogurt (8 oz.)	none	$0.78	none	$0.78
Wise Potato Chips (6 oz.)	60	$1.32	$3.00	$4.32
Snyder's Hard Pretzels (15.5 oz)	none	$1.98	none	$1.98

Fat consumption would change dramatically because it would save money. Lower fat and fat-free foods would abound. Society would benefit. Once at the 24% fat level, people would be leaner, healthier, and more productive. Institution of this fat tax in conjunction with public education would cause dramatic changes to take place quickly. Is it possible that, in this case, increased taxation could lead to a better society?

Beyond Fat

Afterword

At the time of this writing, "fat is where it's at." The connection between a high fat diet and degenerative disease has become widely understood by the general public. Dieters are counting their fat grams, shoppers are eyeing food labels for fat content, and food companies are creating new lowfat products and reformulating old ones. Even meat producers are calling attention to their efforts to raise leaner animals and lower fat meats. Skim milk, lowfat and non-fat cheeses, and other lowfat dairy foods are widely available, when only several years ago consumers wouldn't touch them.

Ten years ago, the culprit was dietary cholesterol. Today, fat is the primary target. Tomorrow? Tomorrow the focus is likely to be on animal protein. Research is showing that animal protein is associated with higher rates of cancer, heart disease, and other degenerative illnesses. So, unless meat and dairy producers can find a way to re-move the fat *and* the protein from their products, they can probably expect the demand for them to continue to decline.

At the same time, other nutrients are being touted for their beneficial effects. Interest in vitamin and mineral supplements is enjoying a revival, with beta carotene being the newest addition to the scene. White bread aficionados can even get their fiber from wafers, tablets, and powders.

What is noteworthy about the way that nutrition scientists have examined and viewed nutrition over at least the past fifteen years is that the emphasis has been on individual dietary components - the nutrient of the moment - rather than on the diet as a whole. What's more, current dietary guidelines emphasize the positive message of "eat more whole grains, fruits, and vegetables" while downplaying any negative message. The recommendation to consume less fat, saturated fat, and cholesterol is shrouded in ambiguity. Never do the guidelines come right out and say, "this means eat less meat and dairy foods." In the words of the nutrition community, "there are no good foods or bad foods. Any food can fit into a balanced diet."

What's wrong with this picture? Focusing on isolated dietary components (such as fat) instead of the big picture (the overall diet) can distract us from making more comprehensive changes which could yield much bigger benefits.

Think about this current-day example: people are cutting down on the fat in their diets, and more often than not they do this by making substitutions such as skim milk for whole milk, lean meats for fattier meats, lowfat cheeses for full-fat cheeses, etc. Most of the excess fat in the Western diet comes from animal products. So, in trying to reduce their fat intake, people exchange one kind of animal product for another. The relative balance of animal to plant foods in the diet, however, is essentially unchanged.

What's wrong with that? People who simply replace high fat animal products with lowfat animal products may have taken a step in the right direction, but they haven't gone far enough to bring about truly significant health benefits. In the example above, the fiber content of the diet is probably still too low and the protein content too high, for starters. There must be a major shift in the ratio of animal to plant foods in the diet if significant health benefits are to result.

T. Colin Campbell, Ph.D., professor of nutritional biochemistry at Cornell University, explains the concept well. Rather than saying, for instance, that too much fat in the diet causes disease, he suggests that "an improper balance of animal to plant foods is the chief cause." He bases this hypothesis on the "overwhelmingly compelling observations which suggest that the nutritional characteristics of foods of animal origin enhance degenerative diseases while the nutritional characteristics of foods of plant origin inhibit the development of these diseases."

According to Campbell, focusing on the question, "How much fat should our diet contain?" misses the mark because it doesn't consider the effects of the total diet. Instead, a more appropriate question would be "How rich in plant foods should a diet be to prevent degenerative diseases, while simultaneously optimizing overall health?" Focusing on one characteristic of the diet, such as fat, is diversionary - it distracts us from more comprehensive changes that need to be made in order to produce significant health benefits.

What's the bottom line here? The fat content of your diet is important, but don't lose sight of the big picture. Fat isn't the only characteristic that needs attention. A health-supporting, lowfat, vegetarian diet isn't going to look anything like the typical American diet - the ratio of animal products to plant products in the diet will have to change too drastically to permit that. Ultimately, we will all have to change our mindset about what our meals should look like. Once we do that, a whole new world of food options will open up - the variety is in the plant world.

Maybe the emphasis today on dietary fat is like any other transitional step in a process of change. At one time, the Basic Four Food Groups seemed like a good idea. But with time, that model evolved to meet the public's changing needs. The Center for Science in the Public Interest introduced its "New American Eating Guide," which addressed current health concerns by differentiating foods that were too high in fat and sodium from those that were lower in fat and higher in fiber. Eventually, the United States Department of Agriculture retired the old Basic Four in favor of the Eating Right Pyramid, which visually shows that foods of plant origin should make up the bulk of the diet (even though animal products are still emphasized by the number of daily servings suggested).

At about the same time that the Eating Right Pyramid was un-veiled, the Physicians Committee for Responsible Medicine introduced a more progressive replacement for the old Basic Four. The "New Four Food Groups" very accurately depicts plant matter as being "basic" to the human diet, with animal products only an optional addition to the diet - to be limited and not encouraged. All of these steps in the evolution of food guides for the public may be leading to the inevit-able endpoint of only two food groups - foods of animal origin and foods of plant origin - and the ratio of one to the other.

So, fat may be "where it's at" right now. But don't let your atten-tion remain there for very long. Set your sights on the next step. There's a bigger picture coming into view.

Suzanne Havala, M.S., R.D.

Part IV
Recipes -
Cooking With Mary

Side Dishes:

Main Dishes:

Desserts:

Introducing the Daily Reference Value

Daily Reference Value is a figure which will be used on new food labels. It compares the grams of fat in a food to a total maximum amount of grams that you should be consuming during a day. (Note that this "maximum" amount is a compromise acceptable to the general population. You may want to aim lower.)

Daily Reference Value was conceived as a simple way to give the person who knows little or nothing about grams of fat an idea as to whether a food is high or low in fat. There are actually two reference values on the new food labels: One for a person who eats **2,000** calories, and one for a person who eats **2,500** calories daily.

For the person who eats 2,000 calories a day, the DRV for fat is **65g**. For someone who eats 2,500 calories a day, the DRV is **80g**. How do these numbers translate into percentages?

Take our recipe for Spinach Salad with Sherried Raisins as an example. It has 2g of fat. Based on a 2,000 calorie/65g fat DRV, it fulfills 3% of the DRV for fat (2 divided by 65 = 3%).

For you to keep track of your fat grams using the DRV percentages, you would want to keep your total fat intake to 100% or less, if you want to eat less than 65g of fat each day.

For example, let's say you ate the following recipes in one day:

Italian Vegetable Stew	3%	*Fruited Couscous*	8%
Ginger-Roasted Vegetables	3%	*Paella*	8%
Black And Gold Salad	3%		

Since we based our percentages on how much of the 65g DRV they fulfill, just add up the numbers. You get 25%, meaning you've eaten 25% of your 65g limit.

Again, keep in mind that if you want to eat less fat than that, you need to eat less than 100%. Aiming for 75% of the DRV for fat would have you limiting yourself to about 50g of fat a day; aiming for 50% of the DRV would give you about 35g of fat.

So, while keeping track of grams of fat is probably the best way to watch your fat intake, the Daily Reference Value can be helpful in determining if a food is high or low in fat.

❖ Note: For this book, we have analyzed the recipes based on the 65 gram/2,000 calorie figure. You may want to eat less fat than that, particularly if you eat fewer calories.

Recipe Makeovers

From Fat to Fabulous

If you're like most people, you have a "favorite recipes" file bulging with high-fat dishes Don't throw out your recipe box just yet.

The same way there are basic tricks to cut down on fat when eating out, there are also some simple tips you can use to reduce the fat when cooking at home. We'll outline those tips, then show you some "befores" and "afters" to get you started on revising your own recipes.

First, steer clear of boring vegetable oils. Since you're cooking with less fat, you want the fat you do use to really count in terms of taste. So, buy oils infused with other flavors, such as sesame oil or hot chili oil. You'll get a lot of impact from a very small amount, while keeping a lid on the fat and calories.

Next, a quality vegetable broth is essential. Often, you can "sauté" in broth instead of oil, so the taste will really matter. Make up a big batch of your grandma's homemade-simmer-all-day variety and freeze it for future use. You can also use a vegetable bouillon cube or powder, or any spice mixture you're happy with, both in terms of flavor and sodium content.

You'll want to invest in quality nonstick cookware, if you don't have some already. Nonstick pots and pans are invaluable when sautéing, since you can add just a drop of oil and still brown foods.

Keep a set of measuring spoons and cups handy, and measure the fat and oil you add to your food or cook with. A "dab" of margarine or a "few drops" of oil can add up if you've always measured by eye.

Finally, be prepared to experiment, and expect a few failures as well as successes. While most main dishes can be easily altered, some foods, such as baked goods, can be a little trickier to play with. Unless you try, though, you'll never know if you can turn those old family favorites into healthy family favorites. Following are examples of how to turn dishes into lower fat recipes.

CREAM OF BROCCOLI SOUP

Start with a rich-tasting broth for the base and you won't need any other spices for this satisfying soup. Do keep in mind that it's best served immediately; it will thicken excessively and the flavors will wilt if allowed to sit overnight. Margarine and soy milk contribute 7 grams of fat in a mere 1/2 cup of this soup. Our next recipe shows how to make a tasty cream of broccoli soup that's suitable for even the lowest fat diet.

MAKES 6 HALF-CUP SERVINGS

1/4 cup (1/2 stick) soy margarine
3 cups cooked, chopped broccoli
2 tablespoons sliced green onion
1/4 cup unsifted whole wheat flour
1 cup soy milk
1 cup vegetable broth
3 tablespoons white wine
   or non-alcoholic white wine (optional)
Broccoli florets for garnish (optional)

1. In saucepan, melt margarine over medium heat. Add broccoli and onion. Cook, stirring until onion is bright green (do not let onion brown).
2. Whisk flour into onion mixture to form a thick paste (in French cooking, this is called a roux). Immediately whisk in soy milk and vegetable broth. Heat soup to boiling, stirring constantly. Add wine, if desired.
3. Pour soup into food processor or blender. Process until broccoli is pureed. If necessary, reheat soup before serving. Garnish with broccoli florets, if desired.

Calories per serving: 98   Total fat as % of daily value: 11%
Pro: 3g   Fat: 7g   Carb: 7g   Calcium: 29mg   Iron: 1mg
Sodium: 111mg   Fiber: 2g

LOW-FAT CREAM OF BROCCOLI SOUP

Frying takes the "bite" out of onions, so they're far less pungent than raw. Here, the onion is simply simmered in broth, so we've halved the amount to avoid overwhelming the other flavors. Also, the soup is thickened with cornmeal. This provides for a grainier texture, but it adds a hint of corn flavor.

MAKES 6 HALF-CUP SERVINGS

3 cups cooked, chopped broccoli
1 tablespoon sliced green onion
1 cup vegetable broth
1 cup 1% fat soy milk
3 tablespoons white wine or
    non-alcoholic white wine (optional)
3 tablespoons cornmeal
Broccoli florets for garnish (optional)

1. In saucepan, combine broccoli, onion, and broth. Heat to boiling.
2. Stir soy milk and wine, if desired, into broth. Reheat to boiling. Slowly whisk cornmeal into boiling soup, stirring until thickened and hot.
3. Pour soup into food processor or blender. Process until broccoli is pureed. If necessary, reheat soup before serving. Garnish with broccoli florets, if desired.

Calories per serving: 48   Total Fat as % of daily value: <1%
Pro: 2g Fat: <1g Carb: 8g Calcium: 22mg Iron: 1mg
Sodium: 27mg Fiber: 2g

HUMMUS

A rich, creamy version of the classic vegetarian dish, perfect for stuffed tomatoes during summer, or hearty sandwiches in a winter lunchbox.

MAKES 4 HALF-CUP SERVINGS

2-1/2 cups chick peas
1/4 cup chopped parsley
3 tablespoons tahini
2 tablespoons lemon juice
1/4 teaspoon garlic powder

In food processor or with potato masher in large bowl, process or mash all ingredients until smooth.

Calories per serving: 240   Total Fat as % of daily value: 14%
Pro: 11g   Fat: 9g   Carb: 31g   Calcium: 72mg   Iron: 4mg
Sodium: 14mg   Fiber: 8g

LOW-FAT HUMMUS

Not as creamy as the old-fashioned version, but every bit as savory, thanks to a few drops of sesame oil. The secret here is to make sure the hummus is as smooth as possible--no large pieces of chick peas, please! A food processor is invaluable. If you don't have a food processor, at the very least have a patient person with strong arms handle the potato masher.

MAKES 4 HALF-CUP SERVINGS

2-1/2 cups chick peas
1/4 cup chopped parsley
1 teaspoon sesame oil
2 tablespoons vegetable broth
1 tablespoon lemon juice
1/4 teaspoon garlic powder
1 teaspoon tahini for added creaminess (optional)

Process or mash all ingredients in food processor or with potato masher in large bowl until smooth.

Calories per serving: 182   Total Fat as % of daily value: 6%
Pro: 9g   Fat: 4g   Carb: 29g   Calcium: 56mg   Iron: 3mg
Sodium: 10mg   Fiber: 7g

CURRIED TOFU SALAD

Both versions of this warmly-spiced salad are best made the day before to allow the curry flavors to develop and blend, and the onion to soften. It can be served cold, but is especially good warm as a sandwich filling, or over grains or toast points.

MAKES 4 ONE-CUP SERVINGS

4 teaspoons dried minced onion
1/2 cup eggless mayonnaise
2-3 tablespoons curry powder
1/2 teaspoon paprika
1 pound firm tofu, mashed lightly or cut into cubes or
    slivers
2 cups chopped vegetables (such as carrots, radishes,
    peas, celery)

In large bowl, combine all ingredients. Cover and refrigerate several hours or overnight.

Calories per serving: 344   Total Fat as % of daily value: 46%
Pro: 11g   Fat: 30g   Carb: 10g   Calcium: 141mg   Iron: 7mg
Sodium: 130mg   Fiber: 5g

(Nutrient values will vary slightly depending on vegetables used.)

LOWER-FAT CURRIED TOFU SALAD

A simple mock mayonnaise made with silken tofu and lemon juice substitutes for egg-based mayo here (eggless or not, mayonnaise is pure fat).

MAKES 4 ONE-CUP SERVINGS

5 ounces silken tofu
1 teaspoon lemon juice
4 teaspoons dried minced onion
2-3 tablespoons curry powder
1/2 teaspoon paprika
1 pound firm tofu, mashed lightly or cut into cubes or
   slivers
2 cups chopped vegetables (such as carrots, radishes,
   peas, celery)

1. In food processor or blender, combine silken tofu and lemon juice. Process until smooth.
2. In large bowl, combine all ingredients. Cover and refrigerate several hours or overnight.

Calories per serving: 151   Total Fat as % of daily value: 11%
Pro: 14g   Fat: 7g   Carb: 10g   Calcium: 178mg   Iron: 9mg
Sodium: 132mg   Fiber: 5g

(Nutrient values will vary slightly depending on vegetables used.)

NUTTY BREADED VEGETABLES

Thanks to a bit of dry mustard, this tangy side dish will liven any dinner plate.

MAKES 6 SERVINGS

1 medium red onion, sliced into rings
1 clove garlic
1 teaspoon ground cumin
1/2 teaspoon dry mustard
1/4 cup oil
2 cups sliced raw vegetables (such as broccoli, carrots,
    zucchini, eggplant)
1/4 cup dry bread crumbs
1 tablespoon sesame seeds

1. In skillet, combine onion, garlic, cumin, mustard, and oil.
Cook over medium heat, stirring until onion is translucent.
2. Add vegetables to skillet. Cook over medium heat, stirring
until vegetables are crisp-tender and onion is browned. Toss
with bread crumbs and sesame seeds until vegetables are coated.
Serve immediately.

Calories per serving: 138   Total Fat as % of daily value: 15%
Pro: 3g   Fat: 10g   Carb: 10g   Calcium: 27mg   Iron: 0mg
Sodium: 113mg   Fiber: 3g

(Nutrient values will vary slightly depending on vegetables used.)

LOW-FAT BREADED VEGETABLES

Closer to poached than stir-fried, this rendering is nonetheless flavorful. Be sure to switch to prepared mustard, not dried.

MAKES 6 SERVINGS

1 teaspoon flavorful oil (such as sesame or chili oil)
1 medium red onion, sliced into rings
1 clove garlic
1 teaspoon ground cumin
1/4 cup vegetable broth
4 teaspoons prepared mustard
2 cups sliced raw vegetables (such as broccoli, carrots, zucchini, eggplant)
1/4 cup dry bread crumbs
1 tablespoon sesame seeds

1. In nonstick skillet, combine oil, onion, garlic, and cumin. Cook over medium heat, stirring until onion is translucent.
2. Add broth, mustard, and vegetables. Cover and cook until vegetables are crisp-tender. Uncover and cook, stirring, until any remaining liquid evaporates. Toss with bread crumbs and sesame seeds. Serve immediately.

Calories per serving: 67   Total Fat as % of daily value: 3%
Pro: 3g   Fat: 2g   Carb: 10g   Calcium: 30mg   Iron: 0mg
Sodium: 156mg   Fiber: 3g

(Nutrient values will vary slightly depending on vegetables used.)

STUFFED MUSHROOMS

Another classic dish, perfect for parties or as appetizers to a special meal. These can be made up ahead of time and refrigerated until ready to broil and serve.

MAKES 4 SERVINGS

12 large mushrooms (about 8 ounces)
2 tablespoons oil
1 teaspoon soy margarine (optional)
1/4 cup chopped green onion
1/2 cup fresh spinach, chopped
1/2 teaspoon basil
1/2 teaspoon crumbled rosemary
2 tablespoons nutritional yeast
1 slice stale whole wheat bread, cut into cubes
    (about 3/4 cup)

1. Remove stems from mushrooms. Place mushroom caps on heatproof serving platter. Slice off and discard any woody ends from stems. Finely chop remaining stems and set aside.
2. In skillet, combine oil, margarine, if desired, and onion. Cook, stirring, until onion is bright green. Add chopped mushroom stems, spinach, basil, rosemary, and yeast. Cook, stirring, until spinach is tender and mushrooms are browned. Remove from heat. Stir in bread cubes.
3. Heat broiler. Divide mixture into mushroom caps. Broil mushrooms about 5 minutes, or until golden. Serve immediately.

Calories per serving: 101   Total Fat as % of daily value: 12%
Pro: 2g   Fat: 8g   Carb: 7g   Calcium: 18mg   Iron: 1mg
Sodium: 65mg   Fiber: 2g

LOW-FAT STUFFED MUSHROOMS

Just as good, but this time, completely free of added fat.

MAKES 4 SERVINGS

12 large mushrooms (about 8 ounces)
1/4 cup vegetable broth
1/4 cup finely chopped onion
1/2 cup fresh spinach, chopped
1/2 teaspoon basil
1/2 teaspoon crumbled rosemary
2 tablespoons nutritional yeast
1 slice stale whole wheat bread, cut into cubes
   (about 3/4 cup)

1. Remove stems from mushrooms. Place mushroom caps on heatproof serving platter. Slice off and discard any woody ends from stems. Finely chop remaining stems.
2. In skillet, combine stems, broth, onion, spinach, basil, rosemary, and yeast. Cover and cook over medium heat, stirring occasionally, until onion is translucent and spinach is tender. Uncover and cook, stirring until any remaining liquid has evaporated. Remove from heat. Stir in bread cubes.
3. Heat broiler. Divide mixture into mushroom caps. Broil mushrooms about 5 minutes, or until golden. Serve immediately.

Calories per serving: 41   Total Fat as % of daily value: <1%
Pro: 2g Fat: 1g   Carb: 7g Calcium: 18mg Iron: 1mg
Sodium: 65mg   Fiber: 2g

 # Figuring Fat

Most health organizations recommend that you get no more than 30% of your *daily caloric intake* from fat. For many people, that advice is more confusing than helpful.

For example, can you eat a dish that gets 60% of its calories from fat? What about foods like oil, that get 100% of their calories from fat?

Yes, it is possible to eat the above dishes. The "30% or less of your daily from fat" guidelines doesn't mean **individual** foods; it means **total** calories for the day. You **can** eat foods that get a high percentage of their calories from fat, and still eat a diet that is low in fat overall.

The best way to keep track of your fat intake is by counting grams of fat in a food, not the percentage of fat. During the course of a day, add up the total grams of fat you eat. Even if some foods you eat are high in fat, if the total number of grams for the day is low, you are doing okay.

If you had the choice of a food which had 50% of its calories from fat, but only one gram of fat; or only 5% of calories of fat, but 20 grams of fat, which food would cause you to consume more fat: The food with 20 grams of fat would be fattier.

	Percentage of Calories from Fat	Grams of Fat
Food A	50%	1
Food B	5%	20

Percentage of fat can also be confusing because it can be given either in relationship to calories or in relationship to the weight of a product. The resulting numbers are very different and consumers can end up trying to compare "apples to oranges."

Take 2% milk as an example. It sounds like a lowfat product, but that 2% figure is based on how many grams of fat there are in relation to the weight of a serving. If you figure out how many grams of fat there are in relation to calories, 2% milk is really 35% fat!

 # Soups

HERBED PEA SOUP

Unlike traditional pea soups, this one isn't thick and murky. Rather, it's a flavorful broth full of toothsome split peas. Add fresh bread for a complete winter meal.

MAKES 4 SERVINGS

1/4 teaspoon sesame oil
1 green onion, sliced
4 cups vegetable broth
1-1/4 cups dried split green peas
1/2 teaspoon fines herbs (mixed herbs)
1/8 teaspoon turmeric (optional, for color)
1/4 cup sherry, white wine, or nonalcoholic wine
Julienne carrots for garnish (optional)

1. In heavy saucepan, heat oil over medium heat. Add green onion and sauté until bright green.
2. Add remaining ingredients except sherry and carrots. Heat to boiling, cover, and simmer about 45 minutes or until peas are tender but have not lost their shape.
3. Stir in sherry. Reheat to boiling. Serve immediately. Garnish with carrots for color, if desired.

Calories per serving: 230   Total Fat as % of daily value: <1%
Pro: 15g   Fat: 1g   Carb: 38g   Calcium: 36mg   Iron: 3mg
Sodium: 11mg   Fiber: 9g

MINESTRONE

This recipe comes from registered dietitian Janice Stixrud, R.D.

MAKES 4 SERVINGS

1 tablespoon olive oil
2 cloves garlic, finely chopped
1 large onion, finely chopped
2 - 3 carrots, sliced
1 - 2 large all-purpose potatoes, scrubbed and cut into
  chunks
2 - 3 stalks celery, finely chopped
1 cup tomato sauce
1-1/2 cups water
1 one-pound can kidney beans, rinsed
2 tablespoons tomato paste
2 teaspoons oregano
2 ounces uncooked spaghetti or macaroni (cooked
  according to package directions, omitting fat and salt)
3/4 cup peas

1. In large saucepan, heat oil over low heat. Add garlic, onion, carrots, potato, and celery. Cover and cook, stirring occasionally, about 20 minutes.
2. Add remaining ingredients, except spaghetti and peas, to sautéed vegetables. Raise heat to medium and cook, stirring occasionally, until potatoes and carrots are tender.
3. Stir spaghetti and peas into soup. Cook until hot throughout.

Calories per serving: 258   Total Fat as % of daily value: 5%
Pro: 10g   Fat: 3g   Carb: 50g   Calcium: 55mg   Iron: 4mg
Sodium: 299mg   Fiber: 10g

ITALIAN VEGETABLE STEW

A very quick soup to make. It can be a meal by itself with breadsticks or whole-grain crackers.

MAKES 4 SERVINGS

1 teaspoon oil
1 large onion, chopped
2 stalks celery, sliced
4 carrots, sliced
2 cups chopped turnips
3 cups vegetable broth
1/4 cup tomato paste
1 14-1/2 ounce can chopped tomatoes
2 teaspoons Italian seasoning
1 bunch broccoli rabe, chopped
1 cup chopped spinach
1/2 small cabbage, shredded

1. In large nonstick saucepan, heat oil over medium heat. Add onion and sauté until translucent.
2. Add remaining ingredients except broccoli rabe, spinach, and cabbage. Cover and cook, stirring occasionally, until turnips are tender.
3. Add broccoli rabe, spinach, and cabbage to stew. Cook, stirring until broccoli rabe is just tender. Serve immediately.

Calories per serving: 120   Total Fat as % of daily value: 3%
Pro: 5g   Fat: 2g   Carb: 24g   Calcium: 124mg   Iron: 2mg
Sodium: 273mg   Fiber: 8g

Sauces and Dips

ONION DIP

This quick dip is much creamier than versions made with nonfat yogurt. (Try this recipe with a package of vegetable soup mix for a heartier dip that can also be used as a spread.)

MAKES ABOUT 1-3/4 CUPS

1 one-pound package soft or silken tofu
1 envelope onion soup mix

In blender or food processor, process tofu and soup mix until well combined. Refrigerate until chilled.

Calories per tablespoon: 13   Total Fat as % of daily value: <1%
Pro: 1g   Fat: <1g   Carb: <1g   Calcium: 17mg   Iron: <1mg
Sodium: 23mg   Fiber: 0g

QUICK MAYONNAISE SUBSTITUTE

Most store-bought eggless mayonnaise is similar in fat content to regular egg mayonnaise. This homemade version can be whipped up in a jiffy and is lower in fat than both.

MAKES ABOUT 1-1/3 CUPS

One 10.25-ounce package soft or silken tofu
1/4 cup lemon juice
1/8 teaspoon garlic powder (optional)

In blender or food processor, process all ingredients until well combined. Refrigerate until chilled.

Calories per 2 tablespoons: 23   Total Fat as % of daily value: <1%
Pro: 2g   Fat: 1g   Carb: 1g   Calcium: 31mg   Iron: 2mg
Sodium: 3mg   Fiber: 0g

SAGE-ONION GRAVY

Massive amounts of caramelized onions add substance to this condiment, making it a cross between a relish and a gravy. It's best made just before serving, although you can sauté the onions the day before. This gravy can be served over your favorite burger, cutlet, or loaf.

MAKES ABOUT 2 CUPS

1 teaspoon oil
1 large onion, sliced thinly into rings
1 bay leaf
1/8 teaspoon rubbed sage
1-1/3 cups chilled vegetable broth
1 tablespoon red wine vinegar
1 teaspoon soy sauce
3 tablespoons flour

1. In large nonstick skillet, heat oil over medium-high heat. Add onion, bay leaf, and sage. Sauté, stirring occasionally, until onions are well browned.
2. In cup or small bowl, whisk together broth, vinegar, soy sauce, and flour. (Be sure broth is cooled to prevent flour from lumping.)
3. Stir broth mixture into onions and heat to boiling, stirring constantly until mixture is thickened and bubbly. Remove bay leaf and serve immediately.

Calories per 1/4 cup: 25   Total Fat as % of daily value: <1%
Pro: <1g   Fat: <1g   Carb: 5g   Calcium: 8mg   Iron: <1mg
Sodium: 44mg   Fiber: <1g

CREAMY MUSHROOM BASIL SAUCE

For a change of pace from tomato sauce, try this delicate topping over hearty pasta such as radiatore or rotelle.

MAKES ABOUT 1-1/4 CUPS

2 cloves garlic, chopped
8 ounces sliced fresh mushrooms
One 10.25-ounce container soft tofu
1 teaspoon vegetarian Worcestershire sauce
1 teaspoon lemon juice
1/2 cup packed fresh basil leaves

1. Coat a large nonstick skillet with vegetable cooking spray. Add garlic and mushrooms. Cover and cook over medium heat, stirring occasionally, until mushrooms collapse and give up their liquid.
2. Remove to food processor or blender. Add remaining ingredients. Process until smooth. Reheat if necessary.

Calories per 1/4 cup serving: 53   Total Fat as % of daily value: 5%
Pro: 5g   Fat: 3g   Carb: 4g   Calcium: 64mg   Iron: 4mg
Sodium: 8mg   Fiber: 2g

 # Side Dishes

SAUTÉED MUSHROOMS

Choose the smallest mushrooms you can find for this recipe. If you must use larger mushrooms, slice off any woody parts of the stem.

MAKES 8 APPETIZER SERVINGS

2-1/2 pounds small cremini mushrooms (do not slice)
1 tablespoon olive oil
1 tablespoon lemon juice
1/2 cup chopped fresh parsley
1 teaspoon oregano

1. In large nonstick skillet, heat oil over medium heat. Add mushrooms and sauté until golden and mushrooms have collapsed and given up their liquid.
2. Add remaining ingredients and cook until liquid evaporates. Let cool slightly to serve at room temperature.

Calories per serving: 52   Total Fat as % of daily value: 3%
Pro: 3g   Fat: 2g   Carb: 7g   Calcium: 12mg   Iron: 2mg
Sodium: 8mg   Fiber: 3g

SPINACH SALAD WITH SHERRIED RAISINS

Walnut oil adds a nutty flavor, but your favorite brand of olive oil will do nicely, too.

MAKES 8 SERVINGS

1-1/2 cups dark seedless raisins
1/2 cup golden sherry
2 tablespoons cider vinegar
1 tablespoon walnut oil
1/2 teaspoon thyme
1/4 teaspoon oregano
2 pounds fresh spinach, washed
1 small red onion, thinly sliced into rings

1. In small ceramic or glass cup or bowl, combine raisins and sherry. Let soak at least 1 hour.
2. Prepare dressing: Whisk vinegar, oil, thyme, and oregano, into sherry and raisins.
3. Combine spinach and onion slices; toss with dressing. Serve immediately.

Calories per serving: 152   Total Fat as % of daily value: 3%
Pro: 4g   Fat: 2g   Carb: 29g   Calcium: 130mg   Iron: 4mg
Sodium: 94mg   Fiber: 6g

GINGER-ROASTED VEGETABLES

The vegetables used here are merely a suggestion. Use your favorites, but keep in mind that heartier vegetables, such as eggplant, carrots, or winter squash, will hold up better under intense heat. Tomatoes will get mushy, but add lovely color and flavor. Mushrooms will shrivel and look perfectly awful, but add a marvelous, rich flavor, especially if you use an exotic species like shiitake or cremini. Whatever you use, cut the pieces rather large so they hold their shape and won't overcook.

MAKES 4 SERVINGS

2 teaspoons maple syrup (See note under *Fruited Couscous*.)
1 teaspoon sesame oil
1/2 teaspoon freshly grated ginger root
Dash hot red pepper sauce
1/2 pound eggplant, cut into slices or chunks
1 medium onion, quartered
1 medium tomato, quartered
1/4 pound mushrooms
1 large carrot, cut into thick diagonal slices

1. In large bowl, stir together maple syrup, sesame oil, ginger root, and red pepper sauce.
2. Heat oven to 400 degrees F. Toss vegetables with ginger mixture, making sure to coat evenly. Arrange vegetables on greased baking pan, pouring any remaining marinade over vegetables.
3. Bake vegetables 15-20 minutes, or until browned and tender. You may wish to sear them briefly under the broiler to intensify their color. Serve immediately.

Calories per serving: 67   Total Fat as % of daily value: 3%
Pro: 2g   Fat: 2g   Carb: 13g   Calcium: 44mg   Iron: 1mg
Sodium: 14mg   Fiber: 4g

ANTIPASTO PLATTER

Serve this lightly marinated medley in place of the usual crudite. Any vegetables will do here; cauliflower, broccoli, sweet pepper strips, carrots, cherry tomatoes, and zucchini are some examples. A few olives will also add a pretty shape and color.

MAKES 4 SERVINGS

3/4 pound raw or blanched vegetables
1 tablespoon cider, red wine, or balsamic vinegar
1-1/2 teaspoons olive oil
1/2 teaspoon basil
1/2 teaspoon oregano
1/4 teaspoon garlic powder

Toss vegetables with marinade ingredients. Let sit at least 3 hours or overnight. To serve, drain and arrange on platter. May be served chilled or at room temperature.

❖ Note: Whenever marinating vegetables, do not add broccoli until just before serving or it will turn an unsightly olive green.

Calories per serving: 34   Total Fat as % of daily value: 3%
Pro: 2g   Fat: 2g   Carb: 4g   Calcium: 26mg   Iron: <1mg
Sodium: 13mg   Fiber: 2g

(Nutrient values will vary slightly depending on vegetables used.)

BLACK AND GOLD SALAD

For more intense color, contrast the black and gold by serving it on red leaf or radicchio lettuce.

MAKES 6 SERVINGS

2 cups cooked black beans
1 cup whole kernel corn, cooked
1/2 cup chopped, seeded tomato
1/4 cup chopped fresh cilantro
2 teaspoons lime juice
2 teaspoons olive oil
1 teaspoon maple syrup
1 green onion, sliced
1/2 teaspoon ground cumin
Pinch of chili powder
Radicchio or red leaf lettuce for garnish (optional)

1. In large bowl, combine all ingredients except lettuce. Let sit several hours or overnight.
2. To serve, let salad come to room temperature. Arrange in lettuce cups or on beds of shredded lettuce.

Calories per serving: 126   Total Fat as % of daily value: 3%
Pro: 6g   Fat: 2g   Carb: 22g   Calcium: 22mg   Iron: 2mg
Sodium: 7mg   Fiber: 7g

PUFFED SWEET POTATOES

Vitamin-rich sweet potatoes are mashed, then baked until they form a golden crust outside while staying smooth and creamy inside. Maybe you should make extras!

MAKES 4 SERVINGS

1 pound sweet potatoes, peeled and cut into chunks
1/2 cup lowfat soy milk
Pinch of nutmeg

1. In large saucepan, cover sweet potatoes with water. Heat to boiling over high heat, then reduce heat to low and simmer until sweet potatoes are very tender, about 20 minutes. Drain well.
2. With potato masher or wooden spoon, combine remaining ingredients with sweet potatoes. Mash until smooth and well combined.
3. Heat oven to 400 degrees F. Grease a 1-quart baking dish. Place potatoes in baking dish and bake 25-30 minutes, or until golden. Serve immediately.

Calories per serving: 129   Total Fat as % of daily value: <1%
Pro: 3g   Fat: <1g   Carb: 29g   Calcium: 32mg   Iron: <1g
Sodium: 23mg   Fiber: 3g

HERBED GREEN BEANS

A very easy way to make plain old green beans special.

MAKES 4 SERVINGS

2 teaspoons margarine
1 pound green beans, trimmed and blanched (or frozen
    green beans, thawed)
1/4 teaspoon marjoram
Pinch of nutmeg

In large nonstick skillet, combine ingredients. Cook, stirring
until margarine is melted and green beans are coated. Serve
immediately.

Calories per serving: 52   % calories from fat: 3%
Pro: 2g   Fat: 2g   Carb: 8g   Calcium: 42mg   Iron: 1mg
Sodium: 32mg   Fiber: 3g

❖ Note: To blanch vegetables, drop in vigorously boiling water.
Let cook 1 - 2 minutes. Drain and rinse in cold or icy water to
stop them from cooking any further.

BAKED FRENCH FRIES

Oven-baked potato wedges are a tasty change from mashed or boiled.

MAKES 8 SERVINGS

3 pounds medium-size all-purpose potatoes
1 tablespoon vegetable oil or melted margarine
1 to 2 teaspoons chili powder

1. Heat oven to 425 degrees F. Coat a large, rimmed baking pan with vegetable cooking spray. Cut each potato in half, then cut each half into quarters lengthwise.
2. In large bowl, toss together potatoes and remaining ingredients until well coated.
3. Spread potatoes on greased pan. Bake about 20 minutes or until browned.

Calories per serving: 200   Total Fat as % of daily value: 3%
Pro: 4g   Fat: 2g   Carb: 43g   Calcium: 18mg   Iron: 3mg
Sodium: 17mg   Fiber: 4g

PEPPERED CABBAGE

Cabbage doesn't have to be mushy and bland. This version has a light glaze with a bite, thanks to extra spices. To avoid "cabbage smell" as well as a mouthful of mush, don't overcook this hearty vegetable.

MAKES 4 SERVINGS

1 teaspoon margarine
1/2 small onion, chopped
3/4 pound finely shredded cabbage
1/2 cup vegetable broth
1/4 teaspoon crushed red pepper
1/4 teaspoon black pepper
1/4 teaspoon paprika
1 tablespoon flour dissolved in 2 tablespoons cold water

1. In large nonstick skillet, melt margarine over medium heat. Add onion and sauté until translucent.
2. Add cabbage, broth, and spices. Cover and simmer about 5 minutes, stirring occasionally until tender.
3. Stir flour mixture into cabbage in skillet and reheat to boiling. Serve immediately.

Calories per serving: 34   Total Fat as % of daily value: <1%
Pro: 1g   Fat: <1g   Carb: 6g   Calcium: 40mg   Iron: <1mg
Sodium: 27mg   Fiber: 2g

BAKED PUMPKIN

An unusual side dish, this recipe comes from Carol Tracy, author of
Vegetarian Masterpieces.

MAKES 6 SERVINGS

3 cups raw pumpkin, peeled and cut into 1-inch cubes
3 cups potato, peeled and cut into 1-inch cubes
1-1/2 cups coarsely chopped onion
1 tablespoon vegetable oil

1. Heat oven to 350 degrees F. Spray a 9 x 13-inch baking pan
with vegetable cooking spray. Add vegetables and toss with oil.
2. Bake mixture about 45 minutes or until vegetables are
tender, stirring occasionally.

Calories per serving: 156   Total Fat as % of daily value: 5%
Pro: 3g   Fat: 3g   Carb: 31g   Calcium: 29mg   Iron: 2mg
Sodium: 10mg   Fiber: 4g

DILLED BARLEY AND CORN SALAD

Fresh dill works best in this mild, crunchy dish.

MAKES 4 SERVINGS

4 cups cooked, chilled barley
2 cups whole-kernel corn
1 cup sliced radishes
2/3 cup seeded, coarsely chopped cucumbers
2 medium-size sweet red peppers, cut into thin strips
6 tablespoons chopped fresh dill
1/4 cup finely chopped shallots

Dressing:
4 teaspoons olive oil
2 tablespoons distilled white vinegar
4 teaspoons Dijon-style prepared mustard

1. In large bowl, combine salad ingredients.
2. In cup or small bowl, stir together dressing ingredients. Toss with salad just before serving.

Calories per serving: 300   Total Fat as % of daily value: 8%
Pro: 8g   Fat: 5g   Carb: 62g   Calcium: 40mg   Iron: 2mg
Sodium: 73mg   Fiber: 8g

 **Main Dishes**

MEDITERRANEAN LENTIL SALAD

A flavorful olive oil would work very well with the mild lentils and salty olives. Serve on a bed of mixed green and red shredded lettuce, and add bread and soup for a complete meal.

MAKES 4 SERVINGS

2-1/2 cups cooked, chilled lentils
2 large seedless oranges, peeled and sectioned
2/3 cup finely chopped sweet red pepper
1/4 cup sliced black olives
1/2 cup chopped watercress

Dressing:
2 tablespoons red-wine vinegar
2 teaspoons olive oil
1 clove garlic, finely chopped

1. In large bowl, combine salad ingredients.
2. In cup or small bowl, stir together dressing ingredients. Toss with salad just before serving. Garnish with a few additional olives, if desired.

Calories per serving: 215   Total Fat as % of daily value: 6%
Pro: 12g   Fat: 4g   Carb: 35g   Calcium: 67mg   Iron: 5mg
Sodium: 60mg   Fiber: 9g

FRUITED COUSCOUS

Couscous is fine-grained semolina (which is also used to make pasta) and is commonly found in Middle Eastern markets, health food stores, and many larger supermarkets.

MAKES 4 SERVINGS

3 cups cooked, chilled couscous
2/3 cup chopped red apple
1/2 cup shredded carrot
1/3 cup finely chopped sweet green pepper
1/3 cup pineapple chunks, drained
2 green onions, sliced

Dressing:
2 tablespoons orange juice
2 tablespoons lime juice
1 tablespoon vegetable oil
1 tablespoon maple syrup*
1/8 teaspoon ground cardamom

2 tablespoons dark seedless raisins
1 tablespoon slivered almonds

1. In large bowl, combine salad ingredients.
2. In cup or small bowl, stir together dressing ingredients. Toss with salad just before serving. Garnish with raisins and slivered almonds.

Calories per serving: 245   Total Fat as % of daily value: 8%
Pro: 6g   Fat: 5g   Carb: 45g   Calcium: 40mg   Iron: 2mg
Sodium: 9mg   Fiber: 4g

* (Note: *Some* maple syrups use *lard* to prevent foaming when being boiled down to condense. Ask the company to be sure.)

RED-BEAN AND RICE SALAD

MAKES 4 SERVINGS

2 cups cooked kidney beans
2 cups thinly sliced zucchini
2/3 cup coarsely chopped sweet yellow pepper
1/2 cup cooked, chilled brown rice
1/2 cup chopped, fresh parsley
2 green onions, sliced

Dressing:
2 tablespoons red-wine vinegar
1 tablespoon olive oil
1 tablespoon stone-ground mustard

Additional parsley for garnish (optional)

1. In large bowl, combine salad ingredients.
2. In cup or small bowl, stir together dressing ingredients. Toss with salad just before serving. Garnish with additional parsley, if desired.

Calories per serving: 183   Total Fat as % of daily value: 6%
Pro: 9g   Fat: 4g   Carb: 30g   Calcium: 65mg   Iron: 3mg
Sodium: 54mg   Fiber: 12g

MACARONI WITH KIDNEY BEANS

Adapted from "The Unity Inn Vegetarian Cookbook" published in 1924, this may well have been a favorite of the busy vegetarian homemaker during the roaring twenties, since it takes only minutes to prepare.

MAKES 6 SERVINGS

2 tablespoons margarine
1 medium-size onion, coarsely chopped
6 tablespoons flour
1/4 teaspoon black pepper
2 cups vegetable broth
1 large ripe tomato, seeded and coarsely chopped
4 cups hot, cooked macaroni
1 one-pound can kidney beans, drained

1. In 3-quart saucepan, melt margarine over medium heat. Add onion and sauté until browned.
2. Whisk flour and pepper into sautéed onion until well combined and lightly browned.
3. Slowly whisk vegetable broth into onion mixture. Add tomato and continue cooking, stirring constantly until mixture is thickened. Fold in macaroni and kidney beans and cook until hot.

Calories per serving: 393   Total Fat as % of daily value: 6%
Pro: 20g   Fat: 4g   Carb: 71g   Calcium: 104mg   Iron: 7mg
Sodium: 65mg   Fiber: 16g

PAELLA

A traditional Spanish dish, paella is a colorful, flavorful casserole. Just add bread and some fresh fruit for dessert.

MAKES 8 SERVINGS

4 cups vegetable broth
1/2 teaspoon saffron threads
1/4 teaspoon cumin
1/4 teaspoon turmeric
1/4 cup olive oil
1 pound onions, coarsely chopped
3 cloves garlic, finely chopped
1 large sweet red pepper, cut into 1-inch chunks
1 large sweet green pepper, cut into 1-inch chunks
1 pound eggplant, cubed
2 cups short grain white or brown rice
1 pound sweet potatoes, peeled and cubed
1-1/2 pounds ripe tomatoes, seeded and coarsely chopped
1/2 cup fresh or frozen peas

1. Heat oven to 400 degrees F. In 3-quart saucepan, heat broth to boiling. Remove from heat. Stir in saffron, cumin, and turmeric. Set aside.
2. In very large, heavy oven-proof skillet with tight-fitting lid, heat oil over medium heat. Add onions and garlic; sauté until golden. Add peppers and eggplant. Cover and cook, stirring occasionally, about 5 minutes, or until peppers are brightly colored.
3. Pour hot saffron broth into vegetable mixture in skillet. Reheat to boiling; remove from heat.
4. Stir rice into vegetable mixture. Top with sweet potatoes and chopped tomatoes. Cover and place on rimmed baking sheet to catch any spills.
5. Bake paella about 20 minutes. Sprinkle with peas, then bake about 10 minutes longer or until rice is tender. Serve immediately.

***Paella** is continued on the next page.*

Paella (cont.): Calories per serving: 261   Total Fat as % of daily value: 8%
Pro: 6g   Fat: 5g   Carb: 50g   Calcium: 61mg   Iron: 2mg
Sodium: 15mg   Fiber: 7g

BROCCOLI STIR FRY WITH TOFU

MAKES 4 SERVINGS

1 teaspoon sesame oil
1/2 cup broccoli florets
1/2 cup diagonally-sliced carrots
3 cloves garlic, finely chopped
1/2 teaspoon ground ginger
3/4 cup unsweetened apple juice
1/2 cup water
3 tablespoons reduced-sodium soy sauce
2 tablespoons cider vinegar
2 tablespoons light brown sugar
4 teaspoons cornstarch
1 pound extra firm tofu, cut into 1-inch cubes
2 cups cooked, hot rice

1. In medium-size skillet, heat oil over medium heat. Add broccoli, carrots, garlic, and ginger. Cook, stirring until garlic is browned.
2. In cup or small bowl, stir together apple juice, water, soy sauce, vinegar, brown sugar, and cornstarch. Pour into skillet and heat to boiling, stirring constantly.
3. Add tofu to sauce mixture and cook 1 minute longer, or until hot through. Serve immediately over rice.

Calories per serving: 288   Total Fat as % of daily value: 11%
Pro: 13g   Fat: 7g   Carb: 46g   Calcium: 155mg   Iron: 8mg
Sodium: 415mg   Fiber: 4g

SCRAMBLED TOFU WITH CABBAGE AND MUSHROOMS

Soft tofu has the consistency of scrambled eggs, so you can serve this colorful dish for brunch or breakfast, or in pita pockets or over rice for lunch.

MAKES 2 SERVINGS

1 teaspoon margarine
1-1/2 cups sliced mushrooms
3/4 cup finely shredded green cabbage
1/4 cup sliced green onions
2 teaspoons curry powder
1/2 pound soft tofu, crumbled

1. In medium-size nonstick skillet, melt margarine over medium heat. Add mushrooms, cabbage, onions, and curry powder. Cover and cook about 10 minutes, or until mushrooms collapse and give up their liquid.
2. Add tofu to mushroom mixture. Cook, stirring gently, until liquid evaporates.

Calories per serving: 127   Total Fat as % of daily value: 11%
Pro: 11g   Fat: 7g   Carb: 8g   Calcium: 152mg Iron: 8mg
Sodium: 40mg   Fiber: 4g

TOFU ENCHILADAS

A crispy, flaky wrapping surrounds a rich, tomato-ey filling.

MAKES 4 SERVINGS

1 cup coarsely chopped onion
1 medium-size sweet green pepper, chopped
1-1/4 cups prepared tomato sauce
2/3 cup whole-kernel corn
2 tablespoons sliced black olives
1/2 teaspoon chili powder
1/2 teaspoon oregano
1/2 teaspoon basil
1/2 pound firm or extra-firm tofu, crumbled
8 flour tortillas

1. Coat large, nonstick skillet with vegetable cooking spray. Add onion and green pepper. Cook, stirring, until onion is golden.
2. Reserve 1/2 cup tomato sauce. Stir in remaining ingredients except tortillas. Cook, stirring until mixture comes to a boil. Remove from heat.
3. Heat oven to 350 degrees F. Spray a 13- by 9-inch baking pan with vegetable cooking spray.
4. Place one tortilla on cutting board or kitchen towel. Spread 1/2 cup filling mixture in center of tortilla. Roll tortilla over filling and fold in ends. Place seam-side down in greased baking pan. Repeat until all tortillas are rolled.
5. Bake enchiladas uncovered about 15 minutes or until tortillas are crisped. Serve immediately with heated reserved tomato sauce.

Calories per serving: 326   Total Fat as % of daily value: 14%
Pro: 12g   Fat: 9g   Carb: 56g   Calcium: 137mg   Iron: 6mg
Sodium: 913mg Fiber: 6g

PASTA PRIMAVERA

MAKES 6 SERVINGS

Dressing:
2 tablespoons chopped red onion
2 tablespoons chopped, fresh basil
1 clove garlic, finely chopped
2 tablespoons olive oil
2 tablespoons red-wine vinegar
1 tablespoon Dijon-style prepared mustard

Pasta:
12 ounces uncooked fettucine
1 cup broccoli florets
1/2 cup green peas
1 cup chopped fresh greens (kale, spinach, etc.)
1 green pepper, thinly sliced
1 cup cherry tomatoes, cut into quarters

1. In cup or small bowl, stir together dressing ingredients. Set aside.
2. Prepare fettucine according to package directions, omitting salt and fat. Add broccoli and peas to water just before draining, to blanch.
3. Drain pasta and stir in remaining ingredients. Toss with dressing. Serve immediately.

(Nutrient values will vary slightly depending on greens used.)

Calories per serving: 283   Total Fat as % of daily value: 9%
Pro: 9g   Fat: 6g   Carb: 50g   Calcium: 44mg   Iron: 3mg
Sodium: 57mg   Fiber: 5g

SESAME VEGETABLES WITH BULGUR

What a perfectly dreadful-sounding word "bulgur" is. But really, bulgur (cracked wheat) is very good, and adds a nutty flavor to recipes. Use bulgur wherever you would ordinarily use rice. As for the mushrooms, try shiitake if they're available.

MAKES 4 SERVINGS

1 tablespoon sesame oil
1 cup coarsely chopped red onion
1 cup uncooked bulgur
1 teaspoon sesame seeds
3 cups vegetable broth
1 carrot, thinly sliced diagonally
2 cups sliced mushrooms
1/2 cup cauliflower florets
1/2 cup broccoli florets
1 cup thinly sliced zucchini
1 tablespoon cornstarch
1 teaspoon dried thyme
1/2 teaspoon dried rosemary, crumbled

1. In large nonstick skillet, heat oil over medium heat. Add onions and cook, stirring occasionally, until lightly browned. Stir in bulgur and sesame seeds and cook about 2 minutes or until bulgur is lightly toasted.
2. Stir 2 cups of the vegetable broth into skillet and heat to boiling. Reduce heat to low, cover, and simmer about 15 minutes or until water is absorbed and bulgur is tender. Set aside and keep warm.
3. Pour 1/2 cup of the remaining broth into a large skillet. Add carrots, mushrooms, cauliflower, broccoli, and zucchini. Cover and cook over medium heat, stirring occasionally, until vegetables are tender.
4. In cup or small bowl, combine remaining ingredients with remaining 1/2 cup vegetable broth. Pour into vegetable mixture in skillet and cook, stirring until mixture comes to a boil. Remove from heat. Serve immediately over bulgur. *(Continued on the next page)*

Sesame Vegetables (cont.): Calories per serving: 244
Total Fat as % of daily value: 8%   Pro: 6g   Fat: 5g   Carb: 45g
Calcium: 46mg   Iron: 2mg   Sodium: 18mg   Fiber: 5g

GARLICKY BLACK BEANS AND SQUASH

Serve this over rice or, if you feel like a change, cracked wheat or couscous.

MAKES 4 SERVINGS

2-1/2 cups cubed winter squash, peeled (about 2
    pounds)
1 tablespoon olive oil
2 cups coarsely chopped onion
4 cloves garlic, finely chopped
2 carrots, thinly sliced
2 tablespoons chopped, fresh cilantro
2 teaspoons ground cumin
4 cups cooked black beans
1/2 cup vegetable broth

1. In large saucepan, cover squash with water. Heat to boiling.
Reduce heat, cover, and simmer about 15 minutes or until
tender. Drain and set aside.
2. In large nonstick skillet, heat oil over medium heat. Add
onion and garlic. Cover and cook, stirring occasionally until
onions are lightly browned.
3. Add cooked squash and remaining ingredients to skillet.
Cook, stirring until hot through.

Calories per serving: 356   Total Fat as % of daily value: 8%
Pro: 18g   Fat: 5g   Carb: 64g   Calcium: 110mg   Iron: 5mg
Sodium: 20mg   Fiber: 22g

MULTI-GRAIN CROQUETTES

These savory croquettes can easily be made ahead of time and reheated before serving, but be sure to form them into thick patties so they remain moist and aromatic when reheated.

MAKES 4 SERVINGS

1 teaspoon olive oil
1/4 cup finely chopped onion
1/4 cup finely chopped carrot
1/4 cup finely chopped celery
2 cups well-cooked brown rice
1 cup old-fashioned rolled oats, raw
1/2 teaspoon garlic powder
1/2 teaspoon cumin powder
1 cup vegetable broth
1 tablespoon vegetarian Worcestershire sauce
1 cup firm tofu, crumbled

1. In a large nonstick skillet, heat oil over medium heat. Sauté onion, carrot, and celery until vegetables are well browned.
2. Stir in remaining ingredients, except tofu. Simmer over low heat until broth is absorbed but mixture is still moist. Put into large mixing bowl and let cool. Do not wash skillet.
3. With potato masher or clean hands, add tofu to cooled grain mixture. Mash until well combined. Form into 8 patties.
4. Coat skillet with vegetable cooking spray, or brush **lightly** with pastry brush dipped in oil to help prevent sticking. Fry croquettes, turning once, until lightly browned. Repeat until all are fried, adding additional coats of oil or spray to prevent sticking. Serve immediately.

❖ Note: These may also be baked, but will not get as crispy or brown outside. To bake, place on greased pan in an oven heated to 400 degrees F for 20-25 minutes, turning once.

Calories per serving: 260   Total Fat as % of daily value: 9%
Pro: 11g   Fat: 6g   Carb: 42g   Calcium: 95mg   Iron: 5mg
Sodium: 14mg   Fiber: 5g

ROSEMARY-SCENTED POLENTA

Fried cornmeal mush hardly sounds appetizing, but that's exactly what trendy restaurants are serving when you see "polenta" on the menu. This simple, colorful, dish is filling and flavorful, making it one of the best "company" dishes there is. Be sure to serve it with a fragrant tomato sauce and plenty of garlic bread.

MAKES 4 SERVINGS

3 cups water
3 cups vegetable broth
1/2 teaspoon rosemary, crumbled
2 cups yellow cornmeal
1/2 cup chopped black olives
1/2 cup chopped sweet red pepper
1 teaspoon margarine, melted
Homemade or prepared tomato sauce

1. Coat a 9-inch by 13-inch rimmed baking pan with vegetable cooking spray. Set aside.
2. In a large saucepan, combine water, broth, and rosemary. Heat to boiling. Slowly whisk in cornmeal and cook over low heat, stirring constantly until thickened and bubbly. Stir in olives and red pepper.
3. Pour mixture into greased baking pan. Let cool several hours or overnight.
4. Heat oven to 400 degrees F. Cut cooled polenta into 8 pieces. Leave in baking pan. Brush with half of melted margarine. Bake 25 to 30 minutes, turning once and brushing with remaining margarine until golden. Serve with heated tomato sauce.

Calories per serving without tomato sauce: 264
Total Fat as % of daily value: 3%   Pro: 6g   Fat: 2g   Carb: 55g
Calcium: 12mg   Iron: 3mg   Sodium: 179mg   Fiber: 6g

ORZO-STUFFED PEPPERS

Orzo is rice-shaped pasta, and can be found in most markets. (For children, substitute alphabet or other fun shapes.) To blanch the peppers without putting on an additional pot of water to boil, use tongs to dip them in the boiling water the pasta is cooking in; remove when their color brightens and they are slightly tender - about 5 minutes.

MAKES 4 SERVINGS

4 large peppers, sliced in half lengthwise, seeds removed, and blanched
8 ounces orzo (about 2 cups cooked)
1 tablespoon margarine
1 cup chopped mushrooms
1 small onion, finely chopped
1 teaspoon Italian seasoning
Homemade or prepared spaghetti sauce

1. Prepare orzo according to package directions, omitting fat and salt. (If desired, substitute vegetable broth for some of the water to add extra flavor.)
2. Heat oven to 400 degrees F. In large skillet, melt margarine over medium heat. Add mushrooms and onion. Cover and cook, stirring occasionally until onions are translucent and mushrooms collapse and give up their liquid. Stir in orzo and Italian seasoning. Remove from heat.
3. Divide filling into peppers and top with about 2 tablespoons sauce. Bake 10 minutes or until hot throughout. Serve with additional heated sauce.

Calories per serving without sauce: 140   Total Fat as % of daily value: 5%
Pro: 4g   Fat: 3g   Carb: 25g   Calcium: 15mg   Iron: 2mg
Sodium: 39mg   Fiber: 3g

LASAGNA

Lasagna can be such a chore to make because you have to boil the noodles first, and then try not to tear them while assembling the dish. In this version, however, you don't cook the noodles before you bake it. You just assemble the lasagna, throw it in the oven, and forget it until it's done. Very easy.

MAKES 8 SERVINGS

1 one-pound box lasagna noodles
5 cups tomato sauce
1 one-pound bag frozen vegetable mixture (try some of the "exotic" mixtures, like Chinese or garden blend, which includes chickpeas and kidney beans)
1 cup crumbled tofu

1. Grease a 9 x 13-inch baking pan. Heat oven to 400 degrees F.
2. Layer bottom of pan with several noodles. Top with some of the sauce, then some of the vegetables. Repeat with another layer of noodles, then some of the tomato sauce, then some of the tofu. Repeat until all ingredients are used, ending with tomato sauce.
3. Cover lasagna tightly with foil. Bake about 65 minutes or until noodles are tender. Serve immediately. (If served the next day, you will need additional sauce, since the noodles will continue to absorb the liquid.)

Calories per serving: 327   Total Fat as % of daily value: 5%
Pro: 14g   Fat: 3g   Carb: 64g   Calcium: 83mg   Iron: 6mg
Sodium: 945mg   Fiber: 8g

(Nutrient values will vary slightly depending on vegetables used.)

KEBABS

A taste of the outdoors without all the fat and cholesterol of traditional grilled meals. This recipe comes from Carol Tracy, author of Vegetarian Masterpieces.

MAKES 6 SERVINGS

Marinade:
1/2 cup catsup
1 tablespoon olive oil
1 tablespoon molasses
1 tablespoon vinegar
1 teaspoon garlic powder
1/2 cup unsweetened pineapple juice
1 teaspoon prepared mustard

Vegetables:
1 pound firm tofu, cut into 1-inch pieces
1 cup onions, cut into chunks
1-1/2 cups small button mushrooms
3 tomatoes, cut into chunks
2 green peppers, cut into 1-inch squares
1 cup summer squash, cut into chunks

1. In large ceramic or glass bowl, combine marinade ingredients. Add tofu and onions and marinate overnight in refrigerator.
2. About an hour before serving, remove marinade from refrigerator. Alternate vegetables and marinated tofu and onions on skewers.
3. Grill or bake in oven at 400 degrees F for about 8 minutes. Turn, brush with remaining marinade, and return to grill or oven. Cook about 8 minutes longer, or until vegetables are just tender.

Calories per serving: 154   Total Fat as % of daily value: 9%
Pro: 9g   Fat: 6g   Carb: 19g   Calcium: 110mg   Iron: 5mg
Sodium: 426mg   Fiber: 4g

VEGETABLE-STUFFED PIZZA

Use any green vegetable here - Swiss chard, kale and other greens would work and pack lots of nutrition.

MAKES 6 SERVINGS

1 tablespoon olive oil
1 pound red onions, peeled and thinly sliced into rings
1 teaspoon ground oregano
1/2 teaspoon cracked black pepper
2 tablespoons balsamic vinegar
1 one-pound loaf frozen bread dough, thawed
3 tablespoons tomato paste
1/2 pound ripe tomatoes, sliced
1-1/2 cups chopped broccoli, Swiss chard, or spinach
1/2 cup sliced ripe olives

1. In large nonstick skillet, heat 1 teaspoon oil over medium heat. Add onions; sauté until very well browned. Stir in oregano, pepper, and vinegar.
2. Heat oven to 400 degrees F. Coat a baking sheet with vegetable cooking spray. Divide bread dough in half. Roll or stretch out half of dough to about a 10-inch circle. Place on pan.
3. Spread tomato paste over dough. Fan tomato slices over dough, then top with onion mixture. Sprinkle with broccoli and olives.
4. Roll or stretch out remaining dough. Place over vegetable filling. Moisten edges and pinch to seal. Brush pie with remaining oil.
5. Bake pizza about 20 minutes, or until crust is browned.

Calories per serving: 286   Total Fat as % of daily value: 11%
Pro: 9g   Fat: 7g   Carb: 48g   Calcium: 142mg   Iron: 3mg
Sodium: 467mg   Fiber: 5g

(Nutrient values will vary slightly depending on vegetables used.)

 # Desserts

DREAMY ORANGE TAPIOCA

Anyone who enjoyed orange-cream pops as a child will appreciate this refreshing treat.

MAKES 6 SERVINGS

1/4 cup quick-cooking tapioca
1/4 cup firmly-packed brown sugar
3 cups orange juice
2 tablespoons vanilla extract
Orange sections (optional)
Mint leaves (optional)

1. In medium-size saucepan combine tapioca, sugar, and orange juice. Let stand 5 minutes.
2. Heat mixture to boiling, stirring often. Remove from heat; stir in vanilla.
3. Let cool, then refrigerate until chilled. To serve, garnish with orange sections and mint leaves, if desired.

Calories per serving: 110   Total Fat as % of daily value: <1%
Pro: 1g   Fat: 0g   Carb: 27g   Calcium: 21mg   Iron: 0mg
Sodium: 5mg   Fiber: 0g

"CHEESE" CAKE

If you have a real sweet tooth, add a few tablespoons sweetener to the tofu mixture. Otherwise, your favorite fruit spread can be warmed and poured over this elegant dessert. Don't expect it to have the same texture as a cheesecake made with sour cream and cream cheese; however, it is flavorful and should satisfy most dessert fans. Try to make it a day ahead of time so it has a chance to chill thoroughly before serving.

MAKES 8 SERVINGS

1 cup wheat and barley cereal (such as Grape Nuts)
1 three-ounce pack unflavored Kosher gelatin (Beware: All Kosher gelatin may not be vegetarian.)
1 six-ounce container frozen orange juice
1/3 cup flour
1/2 cup chopped dates
1 pound firm tofu
1 tablespoon vanilla extract
No-sugar-added fruit spread or fresh fruit

1. Grease an 8-inch round baking pan. Sprinkle cereal into pan, shaking to cover bottom evenly. Set pan aside. Heat oven to 350 degrees F.
2. In small saucepan, combine gelatin and orange juice. Heat to boiling, stirring constantly.
3. Pour orange juice mixture into blender or food processor. Add remaining ingredients except fruit spread and process until smooth. Pour into prepared pan and bake 20-25 minutes or until golden.
4. Chill thoroughly before serving, preferably overnight. Serve with warmed fruit spread or fresh fruit.

Calories per serving without topping: 213   Total Fat as % of daily value: 5%
Pro: 16g   Fat: 3g   Carb: 33g   Calcium: 73mg   Iron: 4mg
Sodium: 114mg   Fiber: 5g

FRUIT BAKE

Serve this filling dessert hot or warm, right out of the oven. Since no sugar is added, top with a spoonful of maple syrup for a touch of sweetness.

MAKES 6 SERVINGS

2 cups sliced peaches
2 cups blueberries
2 tablespoons cornstarch
1 tablespoon lemon juice
1 cup whole wheat flour
1 teaspoon baking powder
1 tablespoon margarine
1 cup lowfat soy milk
Maple syrup for topping (See note under *Fruited Couscous.*)

1. Grease a 2-quart casserole. Heat oven to 425 degrees F.
2. In large bowl, combine peaches, blueberries, cornstarch, and lemon juice. Pour into greased casserole.
3. In same bowl, combine remaining ingredients except maple syrup. Pour over fruit mixture.
4. Bake 50-55 minutes, or until browned and fruit is bubbly.
Serve immediately with maple syrup or other sweet topping.

Calories per serving without maple syrup: 153
Total Fat as % of daily value: 5%   Pro: 4g   Fat: 3g   Carb: 30g
Calcium: 55mg   Iron: 1mg   Sodium: 81mg   Fiber: 5g

OLD-FASHIONED RICE PUDDING

Studded with sweet dried fruit, this pudding is good served warm or chilled.

MAKES 6 SERVINGS

1 cup cooked brown rice
1 cup unsweetened applesauce
1 cup lowfat soy milk
1 cup chopped, mixed dried fruit such as apricots, dates, raisins
1 tablespoon tahini
1 tablespoon vanilla extract
Apple wedges (for garnish, optional)

1. In heavy 3-quart saucepan, combine all ingredients except vanilla and apple wedges. Heat to boiling over medium heat.
2. Reduce heat to low. Cover and simmer, stirring occasionally until rice is very tender. (This depends on how tender it was cooked originally; it may take up to 30 minutes.)
3. Remove from heat and stir in vanilla. Let cool slightly and serve warm, or refrigerate to serve chilled. Garnish with apple wedges, if desired.

Calories per serving: 110   Total Fat as % of daily value: 3%
Pro: 2g   Fat: 2g   Carb: 22g   Calcium: 14mg   Iron: <1mg
Sodium: 7mg   Fiber: 2g

(Nutrient values will vary slightly depending on fruits used.)

NUTS AND BOLTS CEREAL SNACK

Registered Dietitian Gwinn Firing shared this recipe for a low-fat sweet-tooth satisfier. Most breakfast cereals are low in fat. They have added sugar, but you can find many that are only slightly sweetened. This fun, no-bake mixture is the perfect compromise for kids who want something sweet but whose parents don't want to give them pure sugar-flavored fat.

MAKES 10 SERVINGS

8 cups various breakfast cereals
2 cups dark seedless raisins

Combine all ingredients. Store in airtight container.

❖ Note: Some examples of sweetened cereals Gwinn uses: Apple Cinnamon Cheerios, strawberry or raisin-filled squares, Life, Graham Chex, Double Chex, and Quaker Oat Squares. (For potato chip lovers, Gwinn suggests Corn Chex, Shredded Wheat Squares, Kix, and Crispix.)

Calories per serving: 194   Total Fat as % of daily value: <1%
Pro: 4g   Fat: <1g   Carb: 46g   Calcium: 51mg   Iron: 5mg
Sodium: 228mg   Fiber: 3g

(Nutrient values will vary slightly depending on cereals used.)

FOR MORE INFORMATION

COOKBOOKS

Edyth Young Cottrell. *Oats, Peas, Beans & Barley Cookbook.* Santa Barbara, CA: Woodbridge Press, 1989

Bobbie Hinman and Millie Snyder. *Lean and Luscious and Meatless.* Rocklin, CA: Prima Publishing, 1992.

Mary McDougall. *The McDougall Health-Supporting Cookbook,* Volume I. Clinton, NJ: New Win Publishing, Inc., 1985.

Mary McDougall. *The McDougall Health-Supporting Cookbook,* Volume II. Clinton, NJ: New Win Publishing, Inc., 1986.

Jennifer Raymond. *The Peaceful Palate.* Palo Alto, CA: Jennifer Raymond, 1992.

Laurel Robertson, Carol Flinders, and Brian Ruppenthal. *The New Laurel's Kitchen.* Berkeley, CA: Ten Speed Press, 1986.

Lorna Sass. *Recipes from an Ecological Kitchen.* New York City, New York: William Morrow and Company, Inc., 1992.

Joanne Stepaniak and Kathy Hecker. *Ecological Cooking.* Summertown, TN: The Book Publishing Company, 1991.

Steve Victor. *The Lighthearted Vegetarian Gourmet.* Boise, ID: Pacific Press Publishing Association, 1988.

Lindsay Wagner & Ariane Spade. *The High Road to Health, A Vegetarian Cookbook.* New York City, New York: Prentice Hall Press, 1990.

Debra Wasserman. *The Lowfat Jewish Vegetarian Cookbook -- Healthy Traditions From Around The World.* Baltimore, MD: The Vegetarian Resource Group, 1994.

Debra Wasserman and Charles Stahler. *Meatless Meals for Working People*. Baltimore, MD: The Vegetarian Resource Group, 1991.

Debra Wasserman and Charles Stahler. *No-Cholesterol Passover Recipes*. Baltimore, MD: The Vegetarian Resource Group, 1986.

Debra Wasserman and Reed Mangels. *Simply Vegan*. Baltimore, MD: The Vegetarian Resource Group, 1991.

Debra Wasserman, editor. *Vegetarian Journal's Guide to Natural Foods Restaurants in the United States and Canada*. Garden City Park, NY: Avery Publishing Group, Inc., 1993.

OTHER BOOKS

Keith Akers. *A Vegetarian Sourcebook*. Denver, CO: Vegetarian Press, 1993.

Neal Barnard. *A Physician's Slimming Guide*. Summertown, TN: The Book Publishing Company, 1992.

Neal Barnard. *The Power of Your Plate*. Summertown, TN: The Book Publishing Company, 1990.

Georgia Hodgkin, M.S., R.D., Editor. *Diet Manual Including A Vegetarian Meal Plan*. Loma Linda, CA: The Seventh Day Adventist Dietetic Association, 1990.

Michael Jacobson and Sarah Fritschner. *Fast Food Guide*, 2nd Edition. New York, NY: Workman Publishing, 1991.

Dean Ornish. *Dr. Dean Ornish's Program for Reversing Heart Disease*. New York, NY: Random House, 1990.

Dean Ornish. *Eat More, Weigh Less*. New York, NY: HarperCollins, 1993.

Jean Pennington. *Bowes and Church's Food Values of Portions Commonly Used*, 15th Ed. New York, NY: HarperPerennial, 1989.

ORGANIZATIONS

Center for Science in the Public Interest, 1875 Connecticut Avenue, N.W., Suite 300, Washington, D.C. 20009-5728. (202) 332-9110.

Physicians Committee for Responsible Medicine, P.O. Box 6322, Washington, D.C. 20015. (202) 686-2210.

Vegetarian Nutrition Dietetic Practice Group, c/o The American Dietetic Association, Suite 800, 216 West Jackson Blvd., Chicago, IL 60606-6995.

The Vegetarian Resource Group, Vegetarian Journal, P.O. Box 1463, Baltimore, MD 21203. (410) 366-8343.

VEGETARIAN MAGAZINES

Vegetarian Gourmet, P.O. Box 7641, Riverton, NJ 08077.

Vegetarian Journal, P.O. Box 1463, Baltimore, MD 21203.

Vegetarian Times, P.O. Box 446, Mount Morris, IL 61054.

Veggie Life, P.O. Box 57159, Boulder, CO 80323.

Other Books Available From The Vegetarian Resource Group

If you are interested in purchasing any of the following VRG titles, please send a check or money order made out to *The Vegetarian Resource Group,* (Maryland residents must add 5% sales tax) and mail it along with your order to: *The Vegetarian Resource Group, P.O. Box 1463, Baltimore, MD 21203.* Make sure you include your shipping address. Or call (410) 366-VEGE to order with a credit card. Price given includes postage in the United States.

MEATLESS MEALS FOR WORKING PEOPLE
Quick and Easy Vegetarian Recipes
Debra Wasserman & Charles Stahler

Vegetarian cooking can be simple or complicated. *The Vegetarian Resource Group* recommends using whole grains and fresh vegetables whenever possible. However, for the busy working person, this isn't always possible. **Meatless Meals For Working People** contains over 100 delicious fast and easy recipes, plus ideas which teach you how to be a vegetarian within your hectic schedule using common convenient vegetarian foods. This handy guide also contains a spice chart, party ideas, information on fast food chains, and much, much more.

TRADE PAPERBACK, $6.00

SIMPLY VEGAN

Quick Vegetarian Meals
Debra Wasserman
Reed Mangels, Ph.D., R.D.

Simply Vegan is an easy-to-use vegetarian guide that contains over 160 kitchen-tested vegan recipes (no meat, fish, fowl, dairy, or eggs). Each recipe is accompanied by a nutritional analysis.

Reed Mangels, Ph.D., R.D., has included an extensive vegan nutrition section on topics such as Protein, Fat, Calcium, Iron, Vitamin B12, Pregnancy and the Vegan Diet, Feeding Vegan Children, and Calories, Weight Gain, and Weight Loss. A Nutrition Glossary is provided, along with sample menus, meal plans, and a list of the top recipes for iron, calcium, and Vitamin C.

Also featured are food definitions and origins, and a comprehensive list of mail-order companies that specialize in selling vegan food, natural clothing, cruelty-free cosmetics, and ecologically-based household products.

TRADE PAPERBACK $12.00

NO CHOLESTEROL PASSOVER RECIPES

100 Vegetarian Passover Recipes
**Debra Wasserman &
Charles Stahler**

For many, low-calorie Passover recipes are quite a challenge. Here is a wonderful collection of Passover dishes that are non-dairy, no-cholesterol, eggless, and vegetarian. It includes recipes for eggless blintzes, dairyless carrot cream soup, festive macaroons, apple latkes, sweet and sour cabbage, knishes, broccoli with almond sauce, mock "chopped liver," no oil lemon dressing, eggless matzo meal pancakes, and much more.

PAPERBACK $5.00

THE LOWFAT JEWISH VEGETARIAN COOKBOOK

Healthy Traditions From Around The World
BY DEBRA WASSERMAN

Features over 150 lowfat Jewish vegetarian recipes with an international flavor. Recipes do not contain dairy or eggs. Nutritional analysis given for each recipe. Mouth watering dishes include Polish Apple Blintzes, Eggless Challah, Lebanese Green Bean Salad, Armenian Tomato Soup, Ruth's Eggless Kneidlich, Czechoslavakian Noodles With Poppy Seeds, Moroccan Couscous & Pumpkin Dish, Passover Vegetarian Kishke, Russian Noodles With Cherries, Ukrainian Kasha Varnishkes, Broccoli & Lemon Sauce, Romanian Apricot Dumplings, "Egg" Cream Soda, & much more...

TRADE PAPERBACK AVAILABLE SPRING 1994 $15.00

VEGETARIAN QUANTITY RECIPES
From The Vegetarian Resource Group

Here is a helpful kit for people who must cook for large groups and institutional settings. It contains 28 vegetarian recipes including main dishes, burgers, sandwich spreads, side dishes, soups, salads, desserts, and breakfast. Each recipe provides a serving for 25 and 50 people, and a nutritional analysis. The kit also contains a listing of companies offering vegetarian food items in institutional sizes and "Tips for Introducing Vegetarian Food Into Institutions."

PACKET $15, $5 Low income

VEGETARIAN JOURNAL'S FOOD SERVICE UPDATE NEWSLETTER
Edited by Mary Clifford, R.D.

This three times a year newsletter is for food service personnel and others working for healthier food in schools, restaurants, hospitals, and other institutions. Vegetarian Journal's Food Service Update offers advice, shares quantity recipes, and spotlights leaders in the industry who are providing the healthy options being looked for by consumers.

Newsletter
$20 for non-members
$5 for current Vegetarian Resource Group Members or Subscribers ($25 includes both *Vegetarian Journal* and *Vegetarian Journal's FoodService Update*)

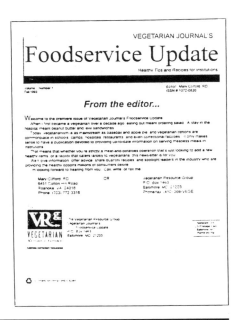

Vegetarian Journal's Guide To Natural Foods Restaurants
In The United States And Canada

**OVER 2,000 LISTINGS OF
RESTAURANTS & VACATION SPOTS**

For the health-conscious traveler, this is the perfect traveling companion to insure a great meal -- or the ideal lodgings -- when away from home. And for those who are looking for a nearby place to eat, this unique guide offers a host of new and interesting dining possibilities.

As people have become more health conscious, there has been a delightful proliferation of restaurants designed to meet the growing demand for healthier meals. To help locate these places, there is now a single source for information on over 2,000 restaurants, vacation resorts, and more.

The Vegetarian Journal's Guide to Natural Foods Restaurants (Avery Publishing Group, Inc.) is a helpful guide listing eateries state by state and province by province. Each entry not only describes the house specialties, varieties of cuisine, and special dietary menus, but also includes information on ambiance, attire, and reservations. It even tells you whether or not you can pay by credit card. And there's more. Included in this guide are listings of vegetarian inns, spas, camps, tours, travel agencies, and vacations spots.

Paperback $13

THE VEGETARIAN GAME

This computer software educational game contains 750 questions. Learn while having fun. Categories include health/nutrition, how food choices affect the environment, animals and ethical choices, vegetarian foods, famous vegetarians, and potluck.

Three age levels: 5-9; 10 or older /adults new to vegetarianism; and individuals with advanced knowledge of vegetarianism or anyone looking for a challenge.

IBM PC compatible with CGA or better or Hercules graphics MS DOS 2.0 or higher

SOFTWARE $19.95
When ordering, indicate 3.5" or 5.25" disk.

THE VEGETARIAN GAME

Learn while having fun! Test your knowledge with 750 questions:
  Health and Nutrition; Famous Vegetarians
  How Food Choices Affect the Environment
  Animals and Ethical Choices
  Vegetarian Foods; Pot Luck

<u>Three levels</u>: Children ages 5 to 9; Ages 10 to Adult new to vegetarianism;
Anyone with advanced knowledge of vegetarianism or individuals looking for a challenge

IBM PC and 100% compatibles with CGA or better or Hercules graphics	ISBN 0-931411-11-4
MS Dos 2.0 or higher	$19.95
☐ 3.5" disk	The Vegetarian Resource Group
☑ 5.25" disk	PO Box 1463
	Baltimore, MD 21203

VEGETARIAN JOURNAL REPORTS

This 112 page book consists of the best articles from previous *Vegetarian Journals*. Included are a 28 Day Meal Plan, a Vegetarian Weight Loss Guide, Tips for Changing Your Diet, a Vegetarian Guide for Athletes, Information for Diabetic Diets, plus Indian Recipes, Eggless Dishes, and many more vegetarian resources.

PAPERBACK $12

What is The Vegetarian Resource Group?

Our health professionals, activists, and educators work with businesses and individuals to bring about healthy changes in your school, workplace, and community. Registered dietitians and physicians aid in the development of practical nutrition related publications and answer member or media questions about the vegetarian diet.

Vegetarian Journal **is one of the benefits members enjoy.** Readers receive practical tips for vegetarian meal planning, articles relevant to vegetarian nutrition, recipes, natural food product reviews, and an opportunity to share ideas with others. All nutrition articles are reviewed by a registered dietitian or medical doctor.

The Vegetarian Resource Group also publishes books and special interest newsletters such as *Vegetarian Journal's Food Service Update* and *Tips for Vegetarian Activists.*

The Vegetarian Resource Group is a non-profit organization. Financial support comes primarily from memberships, contributions and book sales. **Membership includes the bimonthly *Vegetarian Journal.***

To join, send $20 to The Vegetarian Resource Group, P.O. Box 1463, Baltimore, Maryland 21203.

Notes

INDEX

SUBSCRIBE TO
VEGETARIAN JOURNAL

The practical magazine for those interested in health, ecology, and ethics.

Each issue features:

- **Nutrition Hotline** -- answers your questions about vegetarian diets.
- **Low-fat Vegetarian Recipes** --- quick and easy dishes, international cuisine, and gourmet meals.
- **Natural Food Product Reviews**
- **Scientific Updates** -- a look at recent scientific papers relating to vegetarianism.
- **Vegetarian Action** -- projects by individuals and groups.

VEGETARIAN Journal ISSN 0885-7636 is published bi-monthly by the independent Vegetarian Resource Group.

To receive a one year subscription, send a check for $20.00 to The Vegetarian Resource Group, PO Box 1463, Baltimore, MD 21203. Canadian and Mexican subscriptions are $30.00 per year and other foreign country subscriptions are $40 per year. All non USA subscriptions must be paid in U.S. funds by postal order or Mastercard/Visa credit card.

Name: _____

Address: _____

_____ Zip: _____

Additional Copies of

Simple, Lowfat & Vegetarian

may be purchased by sending $14.95
(Maryland residents add 5% sales tax) to:

The Vegetarian Resource Group
P.O. Box 1463, Baltimore, MD 21203.

Inquire about orders in quantity

To Join

The Vegetarian Resource Group

and Receive the Bimonthly

Vegetarian Journal

for One Year
Send $20.00 to the Address Above